BLACK TALK, BLUE THOUGHTS,
and walking the color line

Erin Aubry Kaplan

BLACK TALK,
BLUE THOUGHTS,
and walking the
COLOR LINE

DISPATCHES FROM A BLACK JOURNALISTA

With a Foreword by Michael Eric Dyson

NORTHEASTERN UNIVERSITY PRESS Boston

Northeastern University Press
An imprint of University Press of New England
www.upne.com
© 2011 Erin Aubry Kaplan
Manufactured in the United States of America
Designed by Vicki Kuskowski
Typeset in Sabon by Copperline Book Services, Inc.
5 4 3 2 1

University Press of New England is a member of the Green Press
Initiative. The paper used in this book meets their minimum
requirement for recycled paper.

For permission to reproduce any of the material in this book, contact
Permissions, University Press of New England, One Court Street,
Suite 250, Lebanon NH 03766; or visit www.upne.com

Library of Congress Cataloging-in-Publication Data
Kaplan, Erin Aubry.
    Black talk, blue thoughts, and walking the color line :
dispatches from a Black journalista / Erin Aubry Kaplan;
with a foreword by Michael Eric Dyson.
        p. cm.
    ISBN 978-1-55553-754-8 (pbk. : alk. paper)
    ISBN 978-1-55553-766-1 (e-book)
1. African Americans—Race identity. 2. African Americans—
Psychology. 3. African Americans—Social conditions—1975–
4. African Americans—Intellectual life. 5. African Americans in
popular culture. 6. Social psychology—United States. 7. United
States—Race relations. 8. Self-perception. 9. Kaplan, Erin Aubry.
10. African American women journalists—Biography. I. Title.
    E185.625.K29 2011
    305.896'073—dc23
    2011019309

TO MY FATHER, LARRY AUBRY

CONTENTS

An asterisk (*) indicates previously unpublished works.

FOREWORD

The Physics of Race

Two of the biggest names in the history of physics had an intellectual beef that went something like this: Albert Einstein believed that we can explain the universe in a single theory that unifies all the forces of nature; Werner Heisenberg believed that we can only say what's likely to be the case at any given time and place in the world. An overarching theory of the universe is impossible. Einstein chased a unified field theory for the last twenty years of his life with a monk's devotion. Heisenberg stuck to the principle of uncertainty. Einstein didn't like how Heisenberg hugged the notion of probability in explaining the laws of nature and shot back that God doesn't play dice with the universe. Not only did Heisenberg believe that God was a fan of craps, but he also insisted that the game's earthly participants, the scientific observers of nature, as it were, become part of the very thing they observe, thus changing its measure and value.

The same kinds of disputes have arisen among thinkers who try to explain race and the laws of black life. Debates about what black culture is and how race operates have been just as heated as those between Einstein and Heisenberg and their devotees. Afrocentric thinkers like Cheikh Anta Diop and Chancellor Williams might be cast in the role of racial Einsteins, smart people arguing for a single explanation of black culture's rise—its extraordinary black genius, for instance—or its ruin at the hands of white supremacy. And cosmopolitan critics like Zora Neale Hurston and Ralph Ellison might be cast as racial Heisenbergs, astute observers of identity and culture whose uncertainty about the things we're supposed to know about race and blackness brings us closer than ever to finding the truth. When it comes to race and blackness, Erin Aubry Kaplan is clearly in Heisenberg's camp, playing the role of a discerning critic of racial certainties and cultural absolutes. This may be her debut performance, but it's a star turn for sure.

Kaplan brings sharp intelligence to pop culture and politics. Few have pleaded as eloquently for the right shade of makeup in a culture that is still color struck in every way except any that help the complexions or egos of black women. Kaplan is soulful, yet analytical, about the problems that grab at the black female bottom. In fact, she has the sort of knowledge of her subject that philosophers call, drolly enough, "*a posteriori*," that is, knowledge grounded in experience and empirical evidence. Kaplan's butt becomes exhibit A, and as she lets on, she's got ample evidence to carry her argument about the black behind's splendors and trials. Kaplan also questions racial orthodoxies and the certainties of black life with irresistible logic, like some kinder, gentler Thurgood Marshall pressing for the truth of our culture under the oaths we swear by. That's especially true for black folk who've been forced into dishonest cultural meteorology by forecasting sun when we know the rain simply won't stop for a spell. Kaplan artfully examines the pressure to be positive in black life, and to barely acknowledge the vast sadness that clouds us into silent solidarity, a depression she bravely exposes in the first person.

Kaplan's courage is impressive because, as she notes, black artists are usually allowed to form only public identities. Private identities are off limits, the opposite of white artists who shape the larger world around their intimate reflections. Kaplan identifies with Randy Newman in a powerful essay here precisely because, in finding it difficult to expose himself in his art, he's thrust willy-nilly into the black musical tradition. It's just easier for him to inhabit somebody else's "I" in his songs. Kaplan's essay has the bonus of offering a precedent, perhaps even a justification, for rappers who refer to themselves in the third person. "Hov did that so hopefully you won't have to go through that," the artist Jay-Z raps about his drug-dealing days. His statement is trebly resonant: it's the third-person reference to the artist Shawn Carter whose pen name Jay-Z is suggested by yet another alias; "Hov," itself short for "Hova," is the shortened version of Jehovah, meant to suggest Carter's godlike skills on the mic. While Kaplan didn't intend an extended riff on the literary identities encouraged in hip hop—though she offers sophisticated spins on what hip hop makes of the world in several spots—her highly allusive work invites us to see the connections. But that's the case throughout this book: Kaplan clarifies a lot more than what she aims to make clear. It's one of the surest marks of her fertile intelligence.

Kaplan is open to a wide range of ideas when it comes to black culture, even as she eschews the rah-rah racial fundamentalism of strictly positive thinking. It's not that Kaplan doesn't get the need for black folk to combat negativity; her adroit dismantling of *our* habit of collecting mammies and other racially charged curios makes it clear that she thinks something bad has a hold on us, and it may just be that *we* won't let Pharaoh go, or Uncle Ben or Aunt Jemima either. But Kaplan knows that even if we could completely disown our fictive kin from the nation's racist past, our problems wouldn't go away. (Exactly whose aunt and uncle are they, anyway?) The cooning has gone high-tech, and the stereotypes have migrated from the rice box to the "idiot" box and are now broadcast in high definition. That's why Kaplan defiantly refuses to amplify the clamor for more black faces on television when more isn't necessarily better. Her luminous doubt and principled uncertainty serves her well in battling a unified race theory that measures progress by upping the body count.

The best deterrent to black buffoonery is black brilliance—but a brilliance that serves what's complex about black life more than what's positive. Kaplan shows that the most useful way to define black culture is not primarily in contrasting the positive to the negative, though that surely has its place, but in contrasting the simple to the complex. Kaplan makes it plain that getting caught up in the cult of opposition to the "negative" is not only imperfect (your negative could be my positive, as glimpsed in matters as diverse as styles of dress or sexual orientation), but it's often downright destructive. Bill Cosby's war against the poor was dressed up as a positive attempt to spread bootstrap wit and to get the poor to help themselves. But Kaplan's essay on the comic's tragic "call out" sessions to the poor shows that Cosby's rhetoric lurches in seizures of nonsense and malice. His attacks are a bad replay of brutal stereotypes, and Cosby syndicated those beliefs to all who would listen, including the poor themselves. Kaplan deftly reveals how Cosby's comprehension simply isn't big enough to match the bruising and bewildering complexity of black life. Cosby isn't just wrong about the poor; his vision is just too puny to grasp the forces at play in black life and the country at large.

Her treatment of Cosby and other subjects showcases a virtue of Kaplan's approach: by forsaking the certainty of a single, or simple, explanation of black life, she delves deeply into the robust complexity, and unyielding complications, of black life. In such a view, small gestures often take on greater significance, or at least they help explain bigger, more complicated realities. Kaplan is getting a facial when the Los Angeles rebellion of 1992 ignites. Her hot face becomes an unavoidable metaphor for the different sort of "facial" that L.A. will soon suffer—in basketball terms at least, one that is flagged by the lapsed defenses, blown coverage, and the embarrassing aftermath that the slang expression suggests. Sometimes it's what Kaplan doesn't say that's most intriguing and helpful: her take on Magic Johnson's populist entrepreneurialism never once uses the word *hustle*, but her essay skillfully parses the many ways the word can be applied: Magic's hustle as a player, the hustle he acquired when he was forced by illness to retire from basketball, his hustle to nobly serve the inner city, and politicians who tried to hustle Magic and ended up getting hustled themselves. Kaplan may never mention the word, but she defines the concept and thus helps to underscore the complicated way it, and Magic Johnson, operates. (And since Pulitzer Prize–winning historian Walter A. McDougall cites the propensity to hustle as the defining feature of the American people from the start of our history, Kaplan also helps to locate Johnson in the vast lineage of colorful figures who have made the nation what it is today.)

Kaplan's complicated view covers a generous swath of black life: interracial relations, family dynamics, genetic inheritance, educational aspirations, generational tensions, political conflicts, vistas of celebrity, the lure of neighborhood and geography, and the varied lessons of sports. Kaplan's take on Tiger Woods, or better yet, her being fully taken by Tiger, ambushed by a near total devotion to him, where the heroic and erotic merge, written a full decade before his self-immolation, shows why it made sense that he might have been vulnerable to the sort of female worship that later got him into trouble—except it's never directed at women of Kaplan's color, sparing her perhaps the embarrassment of being one of Tiger's conquests, but in the future, given her relentless intelligence, maybe not sparing him the sort of scrutiny that might make him her prey. Kaplan squeezes great insight from the controversy over Serena Williams's racy cat suit—and how gloriously it clung to the tennis star's beautifully sculpted physique. Serena's bravura knocks all parties from their respective comfort zones, while her unruffled demeanor is part of a racial etiquette that prescribes behavior rather than protests limits. There's revolution in her backhand.

There is also moral utility to Kaplan's beautiful writing and her brilliant thinking. Style is more than aesthetic choice, though it is surely at least that, which is important to say because some still deny the literary and intellectual effects intended by black past masters. Kaplan is a superb stylist and a new master of the essay, which means, at least in the black literary tradition she embraces, that she is, too, a superb moralist like her predecessors Ellison and Baldwin, and Walker, Hurston, and Morrison as well. That's not a haphazard list either, as Kaplan taps a vein composed of these scribes. She makes use of Ellison's broad learning and analytical acuity, and his grasp of the folkways and mores of black culture, Baldwin's redemptive eloquence and his moral outrage at the blasts on black humanity, Walker's humane lyricism in defense of vulnerable folk, Hurston's ethnographic scrupulousness in limning black existence, and Morrison's keen eye for the horrors than can only be tamed by resilient black imagination. Kaplan's resonant, luminous prose sings the black body eclectic.

It is poetically just that a writer of Kaplan's immense gifts emerges to assume rhetorical weight and do intellectual battle in the age of Obama. These are hard times for race—for its mention, for its temporary resolution, for its existence as an instance of national memory, for its relation to a blackness that is both evolving and shrinking before our eyes. Kaplan refuses to blink her eyes or to pretend that we're living in a post-racial nirvana where the black occupant of the White House has loosed magical healing and erased the nation's racial wound. Kaplan's meditation on Obama is remarkable. It measures his stride across the political landscape, fingerprints his influence against the culture that at once adores and indicts him, and empathizes with his huge difficulty in publicly identifying with black folk.

Yet Kaplan is instructive in her disappointment that Obama hasn't worked harder to achieve such identification. His failure of nerve means that he often turns manipulative and dismissive by turns, whether handling racial episodes like his administration's abortive firing of agricultural department official Shirley Sherrod or his stoic inattention to record levels of black unemployment. Kaplan beautifully narrates the Obama two-step: he appears to dance with black folk, with black interests, with black culture, only to abandon us as we hunger for the tamest reciprocity and the feeblest gesture of support. Black folk may have expected Alvin Ailey's *Revelations* but have ended up instead with Darren Aronofsky's *Black Swan*.

On the surface it appears that Obama is more Heisenberg than Einstein when it comes to race, more an adherent of the uncertainty principle than a unified field theory of race—less a fan of big fictions of race and instead an advocate of the careful consideration of race's undeniable dominion. Yet he has been devoutly resistant to grappling with the force of race, as if he were absolutely opposed to its appearance in any guise, under any condition, with any visibility or gravity. He seems to have subscribed to the fiction of racial control through complete racial absence, a fiction of the racial vacuum—a cultural black hole—that's just as seductive and wrongheaded as the belief in single theories to grasp the total sweep of black culture and identity. He has moved from principled uncertainty on the racial front, a position he staked out powerfully in his memoir, *Dreams from My Father*, to a harmful belief in the disappearance of race as a preemptive domestic doctrine every bit as destructive as George W. Bush's beliefs unleashed in the international theater.

Kaplan's complex, allusive, elegant book is a reminder of what we are made of, and what we can achieve, in a time of racial uncertainty. Her talents and outlook match the nation's needs perfectly. In her writing Heisenberg meets Tennyson and shakes hands with King. Kaplan realizes that what she observes she changes; the perceptions she shares also shape the realities she observes. But she is no distant observer; she is part of all that she has met. She is dissatisfied with how things are, and in no mood to be shallowly optimistic. Through her work she finds, and offers to us, a deeper virtue than optimism: a hope born of triumph over the despotic sway of bigotry and ignorance. It is not rooted in romantic notions of race. Neither does it depend on the willful denial of race in the public square. It echoes in the effort to tell as much of the truth as possible about the condition of black folk and the state of race in America and to let that truth outshine all our fantasies and fears.

—*Michael Eric Dyson*

ACKNOWLEDGMENTS

I am grateful to many people for their unfailing encouragement and support over the years of my journalism and of my writing in general. Howard Blume, Sara Catania, Joe Donnelly, Janet Duckworth, Sue Horton, Judith Lewis, Steven Mikulan, Steven Leigh Morris, Laurie Ochoa, John Payne, and Charles Rappleye, all made my years at *LA Weekly* productive and creatively challenging. Thanks to my first editor and dear friend, Edward J. Boyer, who encouraged me to pursue journalism back when I could hardly conceive of myself as a full-time writer, let alone a journalist. Many thanks to Brandy Underwood, who was unfailingly patient and invaluable in putting this manuscript together. My husband, Alan, always believed in what I was doing, even when I didn't believe or couldn't see. I am forever indebted to my mother, Gloria Olivier Aubry, who nurtured my love of reading and writing with regular trips to the library—it's still the best place on earth.

INTRODUCTION

Los Angeles, 1992. Opportunity was in the air, though it hardly appeared that way. The air itself was pungent with smoke; South Central was charred and skeletal after the riots of late April and early May, its sprawling but meager insides exposed block after block, intersection by intersection. But the shock had its benefits, as shocks always do. The truth was out. The injustice and imbalance that had long defined black communities burst the confines of gray statistics and became vivid photos and pitched voices that the country and the whole world could see and hear for days on end. The fact that this late-century discontent had erupted in L.A., a city romanticized for its opportunity and lack of urban stagnation relative to other big American cities, made the shock of post-riot truth that much more potent.

At the same time, it made the prospect of change in black places more real. That's how I saw it at the time. Like many people, I was angry at the not-guilty verdict of the Rodney King trial that had touched off the rioting, saddened by watching old childhood haunts cowed and desecrated by a week of looting and fire. But just beneath these feelings, I was thrilled. Here was a chance to expand the record, to deepen and change the story; here was my chance to raise my own voice and make a difference I didn't know I could make because I had frankly never known how. In 1992, though I had been writing for a small monthly black newsmagazine called *Accent L.A.* for years, I didn't really have a vocation. I cobbled together a living as a high school substitute and night-school teacher, the liberal-arts graduate's version of slacking. I also had a degree in theater and dreamt of being on a bigger stage of some kind but had settled into living in the wings. In L.A., living in the wings—in the permanent ether of potential, as I say later in this book—is very easy to do.

Then the riots thrust me into moment. I joined the *Los Angeles Times* as a beat reporter covering the predominantly black, southwest part of the city, otherwise known as the Crenshaw district. Though I wasn't conscious of it at the time, I set out to do something different—combine old-fashioned black advocacy with a point of view that was more intimate and participatory than I had been used to reading. The riots had broken black issues out of a glass case where they had been visible, but coiled and silent; I wanted to break out of the journalistic narrative of black people that was earnest but formulaic, almost like war reporting. This narrative had themes and issues but no individuals, only figures whose triumphs or tragedies (rarely anything in between) were used to illustrate the nature and depth of this crisis or that bit of progress. It was as if writers felt that focusing too much on black people would trivialize or distract from the "bigger picture" (the slavery question, the race issue, the color line) that have always had a life and a resonance much greater than our own.

I believed wholeheartedly in the bigger picture, but I thought it needed balance. So I wanted to marry the crucial narrative of black justice to an equally crucial examination of how living the justice narrative for so long (it has never resolved) has shaped black people as *people*. I wanted to describe how all the ongoing battles for equality and acceptance, from affirmative action to public school and police reform, have influenced who we are, what we expect from the world, how we shop for shoes, how we operate daily in this social experiment called America in which blacks are still the primary guinea pigs, despite modern arguments that blackness is passé and irrelevant (or if it actually isn't irrelevant, the argument goes, it should be). I wanted to ponder aloud questions like: In the amorphous but still oppressive racial atmosphere of the late twentieth and early twenty-first century, who are we? How are we feeling? What is the line between the battle and us? What kind of American is it possible for us to be? I am not saying that race is destiny. But there's no question that being black still shapes the arc of an American life more distinctly, and often more ominously, than being Irish or Mexican or Jewish does. Being black still requires constant negotiation, within ourselves and with the world.

This book is about that negotiation. It is a compilation of thirty-four pieces written over the last thirteen years that attempts to complete a single story, to forge a single new narrative, something Hemingway once said he was trying to with his novels. One of the earlier titles for this book, *I the People*, was not meant to be overly somber, sarcastic, or self-aggrandizing. It was meant to be truthful: I *am* the people I write about. Journalistic objectivity notwithstanding, I have never felt any separation between my fortunes and well-being and those of my mostly black subjects, whether they were stars like Bill Cosby, little-known community organizers, or government bureaucrats. What I have realized is that black folks in every place and station are intimately connected by history, experience, and socialization, whether we want to admit to that or not. This is not a new revelation, but in these racially atomized, class-obsessed times, it's a useful reminder; it is also, in my mind, a great relief. I am not as singular or as alone as my liberal-arts education and post–Jim Crow privilege would have me believe. When I am in the depths of depression or contemplating the shrinking percentage of blacks in Southern California and elsewhere, the fact I have company in that depression means there is always room for humor, irony, and reflection. A sense of community alone doesn't solve crises, but it does confer humanity and encourages humility. These are no small things.

These pieces are many facets of one conversation, so their arrangement into six themed sections is somewhat arbitrary. That said, the logic goes something like this: "Generation I"—as in "I am"—is intensely personal, a conversation held mostly with myself (and, hopefully, with anyone reading it) about the confluence of color, depression, appearance, body image, beauty, and identity. "State of a Nation" looks outward at politics and history, particularly watermark events that start with the 2008 election of President Barack Obama, and include the riots of 1992, the national debate over ebonics, and the ramifications of the civic and racial disaster that was Hurricane Katrina. "Starring:" includes interviews, essays, and commentary that look at how celebrities, media, and pop culture converge, or collide, with black issues and black people: sometimes the coming together is fruitful, sometimes frightful. "Stomping Grounds" muses about my somewhat improbable hometown of L.A., my nativist allegiance to, and frustration with, its myths of opportunity and transformation as the city increasingly shifts form and fails to deliver. That frustration and various other emotions are shared by my New Orleans–born, L.A.-bred father and the volatile former mayor of the city of Compton, California. "Mothers and Fathers" is a brief section that extends the theme of family with essays on parents and parenting. "Teach on *That*" is a group of pieces about public education and its central and still-unrealized role in racial progress; it's also about how I attempted to assume that role myself in small but significant ways.

None of these pieces were conceived as answers or counters to the very urgent problems posed by the "big picture." In each case, I was looking only to weigh in with my own experiences, to voice my questions, anger, and uncertainties about the state of things, to articulate my hopes and epiphanies, and to invite other black people to do the same. I confess: as a journalist, I have always been less of an observer than a fellow traveler. If this looks like self-indulgence or navel-gazing, well, that's the point. It's well past time that black people—starting with, but hardly limited to, myself—make the big picture that much bigger, and more generous and more *just,* by truly putting ourselves in it. We belong there.

BLACK TALK, BLUE THOUGHTS,
and walking the color line

GENERATION I

"The personal is the political," a phrase popularized by feminists in the '60s and '70s, argued that women's political issues almost always arose out of personal experience—oppression began at home. I agree that the two are inextricably linked, though in my experience as a black person, the equation is exactly reverse: it is the political that is the personal. But so long have we been defined and overwhelmed by the political, its effects on the personal have been minimized, sublimated, or ignored altogether. We as individuals have become less important and less visible—less real, in a way—than the racial crises we try to solve, generation after generation.

The pieces in this section try to locate the elusive "I" in that overwhelming "we." I'm not trying to separate the personal from the political. I don't think that's possible for black folks, or even helpful. I only want to stand up, stretch my legs, and define myself and my particular place in the wider black reality, which includes crises but is hardly limited to it. My initial crises may look odd or insignificant—obsessing about body parts and makeup choices—but that's the point. Any place I start, I end up at epiphanies of all sizes that surprise and encourage; I seek not resolution, only recognition. And that's no small thing.

THE BUTT

September 1997

Unlike the face, with its mixture of trickery and pretence, the behind has a genuine sincerity that comes quite simply from the fact that we cannot control it. —JEAN-LUC HENNING

I prefer myself a sistah/Red beans and rice didn't miss her/ Baby got back. —SIR MIX-A-LOT

I have a big butt. Not wide hips, not a preening, weightlifting-enhanced butt thrust up like a chin, not an occasionally saucy rear that throws coquettish glances at strangers when it's in a good mood and can withdraw like a turtle when it's not. Every day, my butt wears *me*—tolerably well, I'd like to think—and has ever since I came full up on puberty about twenty years ago and had to wrestle it back into the Levi 501s it had barely put up with anyway. My butt hollered, *I'm mad*! at that point, and hasn't calmed down since. But it is quite my advocate: it introduces me at parties, grants me space among strangers when I am too timorous to ask for it. It will retreat with me only when I am at my gloomiest, and even then it does so reluctantly, a little sullenly, crying out from beneath the most voluminous pants I own, *When can we go back*? It has been my greatest trial and the core of my latest, greatest epiphany of self-acceptance, which came only after a day of clothes shopping that yielded the Big Three—pants, skirts, another pair of pants. (Floating out the mall doors with bags in hand, I thought, *Veni, vidi, vici!*) I think of my butt as a secret weapon that can be activated without anyone knowing; in the middle of an earnest conversation with a just-met man, I shift in my seat or, if I am standing, lean on one hip, as though to momentarily rest the other side. *Voila!* My points are more salient, my words more muscled, and the guy never knew what hit him.

I have come to realize that my butt makes much more than a declaration at parties and small gatherings. Its sheer size makes it politically incorrect in an age in which everything is shrinking—government, computers, distances between people, car designs. In a new small-world order, it is hopelessly passé. Of course, not fitting—literally and otherwise—has always been a fact of life for black women, who unfairly or not are regarded as archetypes of the protuberant butt, or at least the spiritual heirs to its African origins. Now, many people will immediately cry that black women have been stereotyped this way, and they'd be right—but I would add that the stereotype is less concerned with body shape than with the sum total of black female sexuality (read: potency), which, while not nearly as problematic as its male counterpart, still makes a whole lot of America uneasy. Thus, an undisguised butt is a reminder of that fact, and I have spent an inordinate number of mornings buried in my closet trying to decide whether or not I should remind other people, and myself, of yet another American irresolution about black folks. On good days I can cut down anxiety with an almost legal argument (who defines "big"? how big is "big"?). But more often everything I put on seems to cast a shadow, and then I go back to bed, vexed for falling prey to this most opaque and mean-spirited veil of double consciousness. I am vanquished. Lying under a comforter with my head the only visible orb of my body, I have an éclair.

Women tend to talk freely about butt woes—they are simply another point along the whole food/exercise/diet continuum that dominates too many of our conversations, especially in L.A. But black women do not so readily consign their butts to this sort of pathology, because that is like condemning an integral part of themselves; even *talking* disparagingly about butts, as if they existed separately from the rest of the body, is pointless and mildly amusing to many. It sounds like this would be the healthiest attitude of all—but it's not the end of the story, says Gail Elizabeth Wyatt, an African-American psychologist at UCLA who authored the book *Stolen Women: Reclaiming Our Sexuality, Taking Back Our Lives*, about black female sexuality. Wyatt is pert and attractive, with a brilliant smile and impeccable suits. As you might guess from the title, her book—the first comprehensive study of its kind—is an all-out assault on a host of misperceptions and stereotypes about black women, many of which Wyatt believes are rooted in slavery and attendant notions of sexual servitude. Not to my surprise, one survey she cites found that the black woman/big butt association is among the enduring of female physical stereotypes; it was the only thing that a majority of the women polled—black, white, and other—agreed upon as being characteristic of black women. All right, I ask, but don't most black women have good-sized butts? Is that, in and of itself, a bad thing? Wyatt says no, explaining that what she objects to is not the butt per se, but how it is negatively perceived both by the mainstream and by ourselves. All of us, she says, have effectively reduced the black women to either the "she-devil," a purely sexual object, or the long-suffering "workhouse" and caretaking "mammy" types, who have no real sexual presence to speak of.

Wyatt insists there is a happy public medium, though she doesn't claim to have found it yet. Indeed, she herself speaks in the language of extremes: while she doesn't believe that "we have to give up our sexuality to be heard," she says neither can we afford to be oblivious about adding fuel to already in-cendiary notions of the she-devil, more contemporarily known as the skank, ho', or skeezer—that hypersexed staple of rap videos. It isn't fair that black women are held more accountable for the sexual impressions they make, but there it is. To complicate things further, Wyatt says that American culture is increasingly sexualizing its young. "Unfortunately, the very sexy image has moved from magazine pages to school campuses," she says. "But when, say, Madonna puts on that image, it's understood that it's an image. She can move between being a ho' and being a film genius. We don't move that easily." In other words, black women have little or no context to work with.

I recognize the truth of black women's unfortunate history, but I am none-theless dispirited. If in fact we spend so much time battling myths other peo-ple created, if we are always put on the butt defensive, as it were, we'll never have the psychic space to assess how we really feel about wearing Lycra—and a woman with a sizable butt must have an opinion about it. Another one of Wyatt's findings is that black women, when it comes to the body parts they like most, tend to focus on hair, nails, and feet; everything in between is vir-tually ignored. "We're not dealing with our bodies at all," Wyatt says by way of interpretation. "We're very conscious of the fact that our image is so bad. We're not dealing with ourselves individually."

It's as if we are still under the microscope under which poor Sarah Bart-mann found herself in early nineteenth-century France. More widely known as the "Hottentot Venus," the African-born Bartmann was the empyreal point of a European butt craze in which women wore skirt underpinnings called farthingales and bum-rolls to get the desired effect of an imposing rear and hips. The fantasy was made flesh with the exploration of Africa and the discovery of Bartmann and her voluminous butt, yet though she captured the erotic imagination of the Victorian age, she was also regarded as a freak, a curiosity: her butt was often depicted in the rotogravures as three times its normal size. She was paraded about and fetishized in public, and her body parts were dissected in private after her death. She was the tortured embodiment of the schism of thought about black women that is ruled by physiology and neatly avoids any discussion of heart and soul.

We all become, as Jean-Luc Hennig points out in his butt-history primer, *The Rear View: A Brief and Elegant History of Bottoms Through the Ages,* nothing but butts with heads attached. (France may have aggrandized the European fascination with the African derriere, but Hennig's book is disappointingly politic, not to mention incomplete. In the end—pun intended—the book is too stuffy for its own subject, too enamored of its own joke of couching lasciviousness in academia.)

The moment of butt reckoning always comes with a mirror—a three-way mirror—and you're pretty much standing at the gates of hell. It is a bad day. I freeze my eyes on a spot in the middle mirror that's well above my waist, with no more gut left to suck in or butt left to pull under. I'm trapped with my own excess, which commands my attention though I will myself not to look. The butt swallows up my peripheral vision and sops up reserve confidence like gravy; it doesn't merely reject my hopes for a size 6, it explodes them with a nearly audible laugh that forces the ill-fated jeans back into an ignominious heap around my ankles. My butt looms triumphant, like Ali dancing over a felled Foreman: *Don't you know who I am?* The genes whence it sprang have suffered too mightily for too many years to be denied a presence, again.

My butt refuses to follow the current trend of black marginalization, nor does it care that we are heading into the millennium with the most collective uncertainty as a people since we first stumbled up out of the dark holds of the slave ships and onto American soil. Oh yes, my butt sees things very clearly: *I* walk behind *it*. It dictates all my steps forward and the swagger that informs even the still, muddy sinkholes of depression. It proclaims from the miserable depths of the sofa where I lie prone, in a stirring Maya Angelou rumble: I rise! I rise! Still I rise! My butt has reserve self-esteem and then some; like the brain, it may even have profound, uncharted capacities to heal.

It also has a social conscience. When I pass a similarly endowed woman in public, I relax into the feeling of extended family; I know we are flesh and blood, not Frazetta cartoons. Recently I got a very gratifying bit of news from an African friend who called to say she had spotted supermodel Tyra Banks in the Century City Bloomingdale's. I was mildly curious; what was Tyra like?

There was a significant pause. "Erin," my friend said solemnly, "she has a *big butt*." "Oh," I said. "You mean, a big butt by model standards." "No, no. I mean she has a *big* butt." "What?" "Yes. Let me tell you." The finality in her voice had a residue of awe. "A. Big. Butt."

It took a few moments for it to sink in. Tyra was one of us. She was a famous model. *And* she was rumored to be dating Tiger Woods. I could have wept.

Black women are more monolithic than black men. This is what I realized as I sat through an L.A. Sparks game and thought what an astonishing array of black women there were: young, thin, wide, bony-kneed, sullen-faced, gazelle-graceful, hair braided back or flipped up or buzzed clean. Such publicly viewed variance is rare. As grievously stereotyped as black men are, they are more publicly visible — as athletes, politicians, ministers, musicians, businessmen — than women. The black male image is so charged, so undergirded with fear and secret fascination, that black men have sought vigorously to counter the bad press by raising profiles at every opportunity. Women, on the other hand, have long been regarded as the backbone of the race, as its uplift, and as such don't invite nearly as much public scrutiny or engender nearly as much debate. What black women lie between Angela Bassett (she kicks butt, rarely shows it) and the professionally scandalous Li'l Kim? In that great divide are plenty of women with heart, smarts, guts, supreme style — and, certainly not least, butts.

Ange Buckingham is one of those women. She's an aerobics instructor and personal trainer who wears Lycra, lots of it, though she hardly has the figure one associates with the job. Buckingham is African-American, admirably fit, but thick in the arms and legs, with a butt that curves up and out. "Do you think so? I never thought of it that way," she says cheerfully. She's a Detroit native with a head full of twisted braids and a raspy voice that's likely a product of years spent shouting instructions over dance music. She teaches at the Hollywood YMCA and has created a locally famous alternative to the aerobics regimen called Gospel Aerobics; one newspaper headline described it as "Sweating to the Holies."

"I don't look at myself as either big or small," says Buckingham, who at one point was two hundred pounds and still considers herself a work in progress. "I've always been athletic. But I'm no Barbie doll, never have been, and even if I could be that, I wouldn't want to." Buckingham's clients include Toukie Smith, sister of the late fashion designer Willie Smith. Willie, with

Toukie as his muse, made clothes cut generously below the waist. Toukie was a longtime paramour of Robert DeNiro and probably the most high-profile (meaning Hollywood) purveyor of the big butt. "Now [Toukie] has that bomb shape—small waist, big butt—but she never talks in terms of, 'Oh, my butt is big,'" says Buckingham. "It's more a matter of, 'I want to tone my arms.'"

Smith may be the exception; Buckingham admits black women tend to be unhappy with their butts, but it is often less a problem with weight than with self-image and expectations. "They tell me, 'I don't like my butt, and I want to lose weight,'" she sighs. "I tell them those are two entirely different things. The proportions of a butt are genetic." She's also watched potential clients eye her unfavorably before admitting that Buckingham doesn't reflect the physical ideal they had in mind: she is what they want to get away from. But Buckingham seems more struck by another memory: going to an African dance class for the first time with a friend, and having the instructor encourage students to employ their butts because they were aesthetically important to the dance, to the art form itself. "To hear someone say, 'No, don't minimize it, put it out there,' was startling," she says. "We were all, out of habit, doing small movements, trying not to stand out. We all looked at each other like, 'Wow.' Black women all have this mindset of not going out and shaking it, because we're taught that's uncouth or unproper or showy. It's a vicious circle."

By and large, it's too bad that black women seem to feel more need to turn down the volume than to turn it up. Between our collective ears, between the mother-earth church lady and the rap-video maven lounging poolside with Big Daddy Kane, is a certain wildness of spirit and imagination, an embrace of life that arcs above both the piety of church and family and the sexual kitsch of gold-painted talons and obvious hair weaves. It's a spiritualism largely missing from the text-based variety that we know. But when I'm hyperaware of my butt—body satisfaction is the most ephemeral of feelings—it can do no right. It is a sin. That's when I suffer through a day of what my sister calls the big-butt feeling, the primally strange sensation, like ears inexplicably tingling, of somebody you can't see watching you.

As has happened in many other instances, black people have taken a white-created pejorative of a black image—a purely external definition of themselves—and not only accepted it, but made it worse. Big butts thus offend a lot of black people as being not just improper, but low-class and ghettoish, the result of consuming too much fried chicken and fatback. "Look at that!" one black woman will hiss in the direction of another shuffling past, wearing bike shorts with abandon. "Mmm-mm-mmmh. Criminal. Now you know she needs to do *something* about that." In the minds of the black upwardly mobile, the butt may connote a dangerous lack of self-analysis (if you don't check yourself, the song says, you could wreck yourself), a loose, unrestricted appetite for food, sex, dances like the Atomic Dog. It's like having a big mouth or no table manners. Now we will all accept, even expect, generous butts in a select group of black people—blues and gospel singers, for example, whose emotional excesses can and should be physically manifest— but for most of us who are trying even modestly to Make It, butts are the first thing to bump up against the glass ceiling.

I have a friend who's been trying to elevate the butt's social status by publishing a classy pinup calendar called "The Darker Image." It's the black answer to the *Sports Illustrated* version—airbrushed skies, tropical settings— but its models are notably endowed with butts that Kathy Ireland could only dream of, butts that sit up higher than the surf rolling over them and render a thong bikini ridiculously beside the point. Ken said it was hell to get distribution from mainstream bookstores—black by definition is a specialty market, black beauty off the retail radar completely—but he finally got it with Waldenbooks and Barnes & Noble. It's a small but potentially significant victory for the butt, a commercial admission of its beauty and influence that hasn't been seen since the days of the Hottentot Venus. I want to give America the big payback: posing next year as Miss January.

Let's face it: sexual sophistication is one of those black stereotypes, like dancing prowess, that is not entirely without an upside. It implies a healthy attunement to life, a knowingness. At the same time I was growing acutely butt-conscious at thirteen or so, I also started recognizing that implicit power in a figure, how it shaped an attitude and informed a simple walk around the block. In sloping my back and elongating my stride, my butt was literally thrusting me into the world, and I sensed that I had better live up to the costume or it would eventually wear me to death. For me this didn't mean promiscuity at all, but a full blooming of the fact that I stood out, that I made a statement that might begin with my body, but that also included budding literary proclivities, powers of observation, silent crushes on boys sitting two rows over. Which is not to say—which is never to say—that my shifting center of gravity wasn't cause for alarm. I started a lifelong pattern of vacillating between repulsion and satisfaction: my butt branded me, but it also made more womanly, not to mention more identifiably black. I may have spoken properly and been a shade too light for comfort, but my butt confirmed for all my true ethnic identity.

As one of those physical characteristics of black people that tend to differ measurably from whites', like hair texture and skin color, the butt demarcates but also, in the context of the history of racial oppression, stands as an object of ridicule. Yet unlike hair and skin, the butt is stubborn, immutable—it can't be hot-combed or straightened or bleached into submission. It does not assimilate; it never took a slave name. Accentuating a butt is like thumbing a nose at the establishment, like subverting a pinstriped suit with waist-length dreadlocks. And the butt's blatantly sexual nature makes it seem that much more belligerent in its refusal to go away, to lie down and play dead. About the only thing we can do is cover it up, but even those attempts can inadvertently showcase the butt by imparting a certain intrigue of the unseen. (What *is* that thing sticking out of the back of her jacket?)

It was tricky, but I absorbed the better aspects of the butt stereotypes, especially the tootsie-roll walk—the wave, the undulation in spite of itself, the leisurely antithesis of the spring in the step. I liked the walk and how it defied that silly runway gait, with the hips thrust too far forward and the arms dangling back in empty air. That is a pure stand-up apology for butts, a literal bending over backward to admonish the body for any bit of unruliness. Having a butt is more than unruly, it's immoral—the modem-day equivalent of a woman eating a Ding-Dong in public.

And what about Selena, the Tejano superstar? Would she have been as big a phenom if not for her prodigious, cocktail-table behind, without the whispers of possible African origins surrounding it, the mystery? Mexicans complained when Jennifer Lopez was cast as the lead in Selena's biopic, but what else could Hollywood have done? A butt was of prime visual concern, and Lopez's butt, courtesy of Puerto Rican heritage, was accordingly considered.

What impressed me most was how Selena so neatly countered that butt— which was routinely fitted in Lycra and set off, like dynamite, by cropped tops—with a wholesome sweetness, a kind of wonder at finding herself in such clothes in the first place. She strutted her stuff, though more dutifully than nastily; she was the physical parallel but the actual opposite of young R&B singers like Foxy Brown and Li'l Kim, who infuse new blood into that most promulgated (but least discussed) black-woman image of the sexually available skeezer.

Grounded in butt size, this image is too potent to be complicated by wholesome sweetness or benign intent. No matter the age or station of the black woman who dares to wear revealing dress—Foxy Brown, Aretha, En Vogue, hell, even octogenarian Lena Home—they're all variations on a dominant theme of sexiness that is heard-wearing, full but embittered somehow, sexiness with a worldly sneer that dangles a cigarette from its lips and rubs the fatigue from its eyes before it is fully awake. It's Sister Christian versus the streetwalking Creole Lady Marmalade. Selena bounded from one end of the stage to the other ruminating on the grand possibilities of love as embodied in her boundless rear; Foxy Brown gyrates her hips and grinds all such possibilities to dust. One seeks knowledge of Eros; the other already, numbly, knows. To the world at large, the black butt tells the entire story.

I am entirely aware that my butt means different things in different contexts. At a private screening at an art house along the Beverly Hills strip of Wilshire Boulevard, at a gallery opening at the Westside Pavilion, I can wear tight clothes with impunity and no fear of reprisal. If the largely white crowd is looking, it is doing so discreetly, between bites of salmon tart. People may marvel, but always at a distance; the most appreciation I might get would be polite applause. But well south or east of there—in Inglewood, Crenshaw, or Ladera—my butt registers much higher on the social Richter scale. Even the possibility of butt described by a fitted coat or suggested by a hip-length shirt elicits catcalls, compliments, invitations to dinner.

Black men are famous for their audacity with women, even more famous for their predilection for healthy butts. The celebratory butt songs of the last ten years testify: "DA Butt," "Rump Shaker," "Baby Got Back," more brazen versions of such '70s butt anthems as "Shake Your Groove Thing," "Shake Your Booty," and of course the seminal narrative, "Bertha Butt Boogie." These songs are plenty affirming, especially the irreverent "Baby Got Back," in which Sir Mix-A-Lot rightly condemns *Cosmo* magazine *and* Jane Fonda for deifying thinness—but they are also vaguely troubling because most of the praises are being sung these days by rappers, many of whom are as quick to denigrate black women as they are to celebrate them; indeed, most artists rarely bother to distinguish between the two. Given recent cultural developments, butt devaluation was perhaps inevitable. As pop music has resegregated itself, the ruling butt democracy of the dance floor (over which the explicitly inoffensive KC and the Sunshine Band presided) has given way to a butt oligarchy run by self-proclaimed thugz and niggaz 4 life. Call me classist, but my butt deserves a wider audience. So to speak.

But sometimes all that matters is a captive audience, and black men rarely disappoint. Recently, as I was walking in comfortable anonymity through a clean section Hollywood, I passed by a homeless black man pushing a shopping cart. He took a look at me, stopped his cart in its tracks and shouted in a single breath: "Honey, don't let the buggy fool you! I got means! How about I take you to lunch? Are you married?" I didn't take him up, even after he had trailed me for half a block, but I had to admire his nerve; I was in some ways grateful for it. For all the much-discussed black angst about our war between the sexes, approbation from black men is still very much food for my soul, even from the ones with no means. It breaks the lull of assimilation and makes me remember that, for all the dressing-room nightmares I've lived and will live, I'd rather be successful at fitting comfortably into my own skin than into clothes meant to cover someone else's.

The late Gianni Versace was a champion of the bodacious woman: it was he who put Tina Turner in those rump-shaking minis, and a Versace memoir in *The New Yorker* had rapmeisters Spinderella and Salt-n-Pepa provocatively posing in similarly tight, butt-enhancing leather frocks. Yet this kind of self-affirmation veers close to whorishness in the eyes of the public. Tina and many of the young black nouveau riche buy Versace by the truckload; fashion insiders quoted in *The New Yorker* sniff at Versace designs as being a hair's breadth away from cheap and vulgar. The designer's sister and muse, Donatella (his Toukie Smith, as it were), with her shock of platinum hair, nightclub duds and profusion of gold jewelry, is really a Mediterranean Mary J. Blige.

But Versace was an exception; fashion, on the whole, assiduously ignores the butt. Tube dresses, hip-huggers, and shrunken T-shirts are touted as body glorifiers, but that claim barely masks their true fuck-everybody-else agenda. It is the season of the leg, the shoulder, the belly, the neck, but the body part that truly makes the clothes is left out—fabric must sweep down and past it, its path uninterrupted by an impudent behind with, God forbid, a life and a fashion statement of its own. Even the more corporeally accepting French have gone on the butt offensive, leading the way in attacking it as a chief "problem area." In the ads for Christian Dior Svelte Perfect anti-cellulite cream, a naked woman crouches demurely behind a cloud of pink tulle to hide a butt she doesn't have anyway.

In computer-idealizing the butt, we have left the ravishing behind behind. And it can't catch up; it won't. It doesn't want to. Feet were made for dancing, and the butt was made purely for indolence, which has no real place in this age of function and frightening efficiency. Buns of steel? To my butt's leisurely way of thinking, that ain't nothing but stale bread.

Some women consider fashion's disdain of butts the biggest urban conspiracy going. "It's butt discrimination! Butt segregation!" fumes Jan, whom I've known since childhood. Jan is short and compact, well-proportioned. I've admired her figure since the sixth grade, when she officially got one. "I mean, I had the first opportunity to buy a $300 pair of Todd Oldham pants on sale for $30," she says, recalling a recent trip to American Rag on La Brea Avenue in L.A. "They were my size, 6. I went to try them on. Everything was going well from the calves up to the thighs—then the butt screamed, 'Hell, no!' These were hip-huggers made for people with *no hips.* I was pissed. Then I realized that even if I had the $300 to spend, I wouldn't have been able to spend it. What is that about? Are they telling me I shouldn't wear high fashion?"

Designer Anthony Mark Hankins complains from the other side: "I'm a healthy black man, and I can't wear Gauthier," he laments. Hankins, based in Dallas, found a lucrative niche in designing an eponymous line of clothing with black women in mind. In the tradition of Willie Smith, he cuts roomier without cutting back on style. But for him, black fashion is less about butt considerations than about quality fabrics and Parisian sensibilities—in short, it's about marketing to women who feel they are too often kept at fashion's periphery when they want to be in the middle of it. "Black women are about being *stylish*," declares Hankins from his headquarters. "I'm so sick of black women being perceived as only wanting to wear loud colors."

Which isn't to say that Hankins doesn't have an appreciation of black women's particular sartorial inventiveness. "If you look at 1930s photographs, the sisters had it together. They gave clothes their own beat—but they've always had to make the look work. We've always had to take nothing and make something. Designing for black women keeps me on the cutting edge. We are *not* doing that one little sweater that pulls it all together. That isn't what we want."

Hankins also designs a Sears-distributed line called Sugar Babies, which emphasizes "sex appeal [and] shows a little bit of silhouette. We love a little bit of cleavage," he says, "a little butt." But the frankly sexy—what Hankins calls "hoochie-mama style"—is not what his customers want; the largest group of black women buying his line are Southern, with tastes that tend to the conservative. "That doesn't mean you hide the butt—it's there, bam, it's beautiful—but don't go showing it with a G-string," he says with a laugh."

Like Gail Wyatt, Hankins has no real maxims about how black women should look, other than that they should fundamentally embrace however they look. "Clothes are our spiritual armor. Self-adornment is *so* important for African-American women. Why should we dim our natural lights? We need to accept who and what we are. If we don't celebrate our own diversity, we're right back to the 1950s."

Hankins is optimistic. "The veil," he says, "is coming down."

I was taking the second-biggest butt challenge (jeans being the first): shopping for a bathing suit. Suits have stretch, sure; they'll get up over the hips but will throw a butt into horrific relief. I hadn't shopped for a bikini in a few years. The one rolled up in the corner of my bureau drawer was a cotton, daisy-print, cornflower-blue affair I had snatched off a Gap sale rack, ostensibly as an afterthought ("Heaven forbid this girl makes a bathing suit a *priority*," I imagined one salesclerk smirking to another after I left the store). But this day, wandering the sunny, sexually denuded Westside Pavilion mall in West L.A. with my twelve-year-old niece in tow and scores of puffy matrons bolstering my courage by the minute, I felt reckless. Dez and I went into a shop called Everything But the Beach. Against the scrubbed white walls hung multiple rows of suits made of neon-bright nylon matte jersey and something that looked like fur. I went straight for the Gilligan's Island number, a lemon-yellow two-piece printed with giant tropical blossoms. In the dressing room, Dez stood by the mirror like Carol Merrill from *Let's Make A Deal*. As casually as possible, I suited up and thought, Here we go. Is it door number one, door number two, or door number three?

I looked in the mirror and started with surprise. The thing fit. I didn't look gross. The colors complemented the brown of my skin. I looked round but strong and capable, a somewhat augmented Angela Bassett by the sea. The bottom half was conducive to my butt, which looked at peace. I could get away with exhaling and stooping normally. Dez looked approving. I had another epiphanic flash: my figure is still the soul of the feminine ideal. It *has* been through the ages. In the '90s it merely ran afoul of this trend of casting what is good and perfectly logical as something without currency, something that was once a nice idea, but . . . (cf. affirmative action, civil rights statutes, TVs without remotes).

I'll admit: for all of my hand-wringing, I'm growing accustomed to my butt. It's a strange and wonderful development of the last six years or so—as I've gotten heavier I've actually gotten more settled with how I look. Perhaps it's function of maturity or a realization that fashions aren't likely to bulk up anytime soon, but I'm much more inclined to reveal myself now, at thirty-five, than I ever was before. I've finally concluded that there's no clever way around my butt, as there never seems to be a clever way around the truth—whatever you try only leads to the most fantastic lies. In the interest of honesty, my butt now gets accent—a lot of stretch, slouch pants, skirts that fall below the navel, platform shoes that punch up my walk. I don't do big and shapeless anymore, not even in the complete privacy of home. I have finally glimpsed the full, unadulterated length of me and don't want to obfuscate the image any more than I already do on bad mornings. I must burn myself into my own memory; my butt is more than happy to help.

So what if America, in its infinite wisdom, wants to perpetually help rid me of this bothersome behind with its *Self* magazines and *L.A. Times* "Celebrity Workouts" and the demonizing of complex carbohydrates? More and more, my response has been: I *am* going to eat cake. I *will* wear that things that fit—whatever ones I can find—with impunity. I don't have an issue, I have a groove thing. Kiss my you know what.

BLACK LIKE I THOUGHT I WAS

RACE, DNA, AND THE MAN WHO KNOWS TOO MUCH

October 2003

Wayne Joseph is a fifty-one-year-old high school principal in Chino whose family emigrated from the segregated parishes of Louisiana to central Los Angeles in the 1950s, as did mine. Like me, he is of Creole stock and is therefore on the lighter end of the black color spectrum, a common enough circumstance in the South that predates the multicultural movement by centuries. And like most other black folk, Joseph grew up with an unequivocal sense of his heritage and of himself; he tends toward black advocacy and has published thoughtful opinion pieces on racial issues in magazines like *News-*

week. When Joseph decided on a whim to take a new ethnic DNA test he saw described on a *60 Minutes* segment last year, it was only to indulge a casual curiosity about the exact percentage of his black blood; virtually all black Americans are mixed with something, he knew, but he figured it would be interesting to make himself a guinea pig for this new testing process, which is offered by a Florida-based company called DNA Print Genomics Inc. The experience would at least be fodder for another essay for *Newsweek.* He got his kit in the mail, swabbed his mouth per the instructions, and sent off the DNA samples for analysis.

Now, I have always believed that what is now widely considered one of slavery's worst legacies—the Southern "one-drop" rule that indicted anyone with black blood as a nigger and cleaved American society into black and white with a single stroke—was also slavery's only upside. Of course I deplore the motive behind the law, which was rooted not only in white paranoia about miscegenation, but in a more practical need to maintain social order by keeping privilege and property in the hands of whites. But by forcing blacks of all complexions and blood percentages into the same boat, the law ironically laid a foundation of black unity that remains in place today. It's a foundation that allows us to talk abstractly about a "black community" as concretely as we talk about a black community in Harlem or Chicago or L.A.'s South Central (a liberty that's often abused or lazily applied in modern discussions of race). And it gives the lightest-skinned among us the assurance of identity that everybody needs to feel grounded and psychologically whole—even whites, whose public non-ethnicity is really ethnicity writ so large and influential it needs no name. Being black may still not be the most advantageous thing in the world, but being nothing or being neutral—the rallying cry of modern-day multiculturalists—has never made any emotional or real-world sense. Color marks you, but your membership in black society also gives you an indestructible house to live in and a bed to rest on. I can't imagine growing up any other way.

Wayne Joseph can't either. But when the results of his DNA test came back, he found himself staggered by the idea that though he still qualified as a person of color, it was not the color he was raised to think he was, one with a distinct culture and definitive place in the American struggle for social equality that he'd taken for granted. Here was the unexpected and rather unwelcome truth: Joseph was 57 percent Indo-European, 39 percent Native American, 4 percent East Asian—and 0 percent African. After a lifetime of assuming blackness, he was now being told that he lacked even a single drop of black blood to qualify. "My son was flabbergasted by the results," says Joseph. "He said, 'Dad, you mean for fifty years you've been passing for black?'" Joseph admits that, strictly speaking, he has. But he's not sure if he can or wants to do anything about that at this point. For all the lingering effects of institutional racism, he's been perfectly content being a black man; it's shaped his worldview and the course of his life in ways that cannot, and probably should not, be altered. Yet Joseph struggles to balance the intellectual dishonesty of saying he's black with the unimpeachable honesty of a lifelong experience of *being* black. "What do I do with this information?" he says, sounding more than a little exasperated. "It was like finding out you're adopted. I don't want to be disingenuous with myself. But I can't conceive of living any other way. It's a question of what's logical and what's visceral."

Race, of course, has always been a far more visceral matter than a logical one. We now know that there is no such thing as race, that humans are biologically one species; we know that an African is likely to have more in common genetically with a European thousands of miles away than with a neighboring African. Yet this knowledge has not deterred the racism many Europeans continue to harbor toward Africans, nor the wariness Africans harbor toward Europeans. Such feelings may never be deterred. And despite all the loud assertions to the contrary, race is still America's bane, and its fascination; Philip Roth's widely acclaimed novel set in the 1990s, *The Human Stain*, features a Faustian protagonist whose great moral failing is that he's a black man who's been passing most of his life for white (the book was made into a movie that was released in 2003).

Joseph recognizes this, and while he argues for a more rational and less emotional view of race for the sake of equity, he also recognizes that rationality is not the same thing as fact. As much as he might want to, he can't simply refute his black past and declare himself white or Native American. He can acknowledge the truth but can't quite apply it, which makes it pretty much useless to other, older members of his family. An aunt whom he told about the test results only said that she wasn't surprised. "When I told my mother about the test, she said to me, 'I'm too old and too tired to be anything else,'" recalls Joseph. "It makes no difference to her. It's an easy issue."

After recovering from the initial shock, Joseph began questioning his mother about their lineage. He discovered that, unbeknownst to him, his grandparents had made a conscious decision back in Louisiana to *not* be white, claiming they didn't want to side with a people who were known oppressors. Joseph says there was another, more practical consideration: some men in the family routinely courted black women, and they didn't want the very public hassle such a pairing entailed in the South, which included everything from dirty looks to the ignominy of a couple having to separate on buses and streetcars and in restaurants per the Jim Crow laws. I know that the laws also pointedly separated mothers from sons, uncles from nephews, simply because one happened to be lighter than the other or have straighter hair. Determinations of race were entirely subjective and imposed from without, and the one-drop rule was enforced to such divisive and schizophrenic effects that Joseph's family—and mine—fled Louisiana for the presumably less boundary-obsessed West. But we didn't flee ourselves, and didn't expect to; we simply set up a new home in Los Angeles. The South was wrong about its policies but it was right about our color. It had to be.

Joseph remains tortured by the possibility that maybe nobody is right. The essay he thought the DNA test experience would prompt became a book that he's already 150 pages into. He doesn't seem to know how it'll end. He's in a kind of limbo that he doesn't want and that I frankly wouldn't wish on anyone; when I wonder aloud about taking the $600 DNA test myself, Joseph flatly advises against it. "You don't want to know," he says. "It's like a genie coming out of a bottle. You can't put it back in." He has more empathy for the colorblind crowd than he had before, but isn't inclined to believe that the Ward Connerlys and other professed racial conservatives of the world have the best interests of colored people at heart. "I see their point, but race does matter, especially with things like medical research and other social trends," he says of Connerly's Proposition 54, the much-derided state measure that sought to outlaw the collection of ethnic data. "Problems like that can't just go away." For the moment, Joseph is compelled to try to judge individually what he knows has always been judged broadly, to reconcile two famously opposed viewpoints of race not for the sake of political argument—he's made those—but for his own peace of mind. He's wrestling with a riddle that will likely outlive him, though he doesn't worry that it will be passed on to the next generation—his ex-wife is black, enough to give his children the firm ethnic identity he had and that he embraced for most of his life. "The question ultimately is, are you who you say you are, or are you who you are genetically?" he muses. The logical—and visceral—answer is that it's not black and white.

FIRE AND ICE

MAKING IT UP

August 2001

Like a lot of women of my age, fashion sense, marital status, and middling economic strata, I have conflicted feelings about Lancôme. Ambivalence about makeup is rampant among my sex for all sorts of reasons—why a nude or natural "look" has nothing to do with a nude or natural face is a good place to start—but for the moment let's focus on one factor of that ambivalence that itself remains eminently unambivalent: skin color. Barely prosperous black women such as myself like to imagine ourselves ideal Lancôme customers, but Lancôme and its department-store ilk—Chanel, Clinique, Christian Dior—generally do not make products for anyone darker than a paper bag. Yet I can't seem to pass one of those counters without pausing to look; women like me are not so much ambivalent as we are in denial. This is one of those rare instances in which I regret that race matters. I truly wish we could all wear the same foundation, not because I'm a proponent of cosmetic multiculturalism—a mirror-compact version of CK One—but because I like to buy nice things that announce *I Belong.*

I am an American marketer's computer-generated ideal, a willing sucker, a discriminating but ravenous shopper for whom nothing feels more like possibility than swinging open the heavy door of a Macy's or Bloomie's and, after the initial head-rush of air-conditioning, bobbing through a sea of makeup and skin-care counters. Makeup is most often a shopper's port of entry into recreational buying, yet it is also where race immediately thwarts that lovely sense of possibility. I want foundation by the latest maker, but it's all too ashen or ruddy for my brown, yellow-undertoned complexion. I want that damn-near-white eye shadow that promises to contemporize and brighten any face; not mine, because the stuff doesn't show up on my lids at all. In the end I buy a pot of clear gloss—colorless!—and move on, sour. I feel ripped off and want money back even though I've spent hardly any. Which is exactly the point.

I know what you're thinking: But isn't there makeup made expressly for women of color? Of course there is. Barbara Walden, a black woman and former actor, started her own company back in the '50s. Then came Fashion Fair and Posner and dark-pigmented versions by mainstream outfits like Avon, right on up to the turn of this century and the more racially understated, globally cast Iman and Interface lines. Yet these triumphs seemed somehow compromised; they were not victories for black women so much as they were victories for the big, luxe companies that have long enforced a kind of beauty segregation. Iman should at least have a spot at Barney's, but she sells at JCPenney; we do not have our place at the table. Higher-end lines like Barbara Walden are relegated to department stores that serve communities of color, a retail species rapidly approaching extinction. (The demise of Macy's and the tenuous status of Robinsons-May at the Baldwin Hills Crenshaw Plaza are recent evidence of that. In all of L.A., you can find Barbara Walden and Fashion Fair at two, perhaps three shopping malls.)

For all these caveats, the black offerings certainly have their merits. In addition to providing practical alternatives, they inspire ethnic patriotism and a sense of empowerment and choice, if not buying frenzies. They highlight (excuse the pun) racial uniqueness in an age when everyone seems anxious to blunt as many racial differences as possible and get on with their lives; not even the most rabid multiculturalist would argue that black women don't require different makeup shades than white women. Actually, the irrefutable primacy of skin color in the makeup trade makes it a much more honest American business than, say, government contracting or commercial lending. Its separatist tendencies are insulting at times, unprogressive to those of us seeking sophisticated evidence in this century that We Belong, but it is also reassuring in its affirmation of racial differences that we're increasingly told don't exist anymore.

I'm not suggesting that makeup take its rightful place alongside the civil rights movement in the scheme of social justice. But it does assume more significant dimensions when you consider that it reflects, and protects, the hard core of American beauty standards—why else is one always able to find lipstick in a million variations of pink, blush in the same variations, concealer meant to graduate those dark under-eye circles to the same shade of pale as, er, the average American face? Most makeup cooperates with a certain pallor, proceeds from it: light colors are for everyday, intense colors for evening or more exotic occasions. Those of us who already have color, meaning we are more exotic than everyday (not as good as it sounds), obviously decry this logic, but the fact is that we often have very different intentions when it comes to makeup. Denied beauty affirmation and primping rights for generations, women of color are more apt to take glamour literally. We may yearn for the acceptance conferred by Lancôme, but not necessarily its aesthetics. Not for us the minimalist look, the subtle-eye/strong-mouth balance of power—power as we've known it has extracted the price of our restraint for too long, and it can go to hell. What better way to send it there than with palettes conceived with us and our liberation in mind—sunset-orange lips, russet cheeks, glittery gold eyelids that show? What more resonant way to say I Am, which after all is more fundamental than I Belong?

But it is possible to say, in our own voice, both things. In the pages of a recent *LA Weekly*, a style maven remarked that the most inspired and inspiring tableau she had seen recently was a youngish black woman getting her nails done at a swap-meet salon on Slauson Avenue. The woman was a courier, dressed in UPS duds and sensible shoes—and "she had this makeup, I know she meant it to look natural, but it looked like Divine's. And she had this gigantic hairdo, and was getting these long nails printed gold with rhinestones on them . . . It was so cool." She took work and glamour equally seriously—I Belong and I Am. Her appearance posed absolutely no contradictions in her mind. She was, of course, entirely out of touch with the Lancôme-Luxe trend of makeup as mute button, as an agent of irony, as a subverter rather than a supporter of beauty: the pages of *W* and other magazines have lately been featuring models with greasy faces, eyes done up in what looks like aerosoled graffiti, lips so undone and underdressed you can see the cracks. This is in keeping, I suppose, with the anti-fashion mood of fashion that has gripped the '00s as we have moved steadily away from excess and proper glamour since the '80s.

Black women have paid little attention to all this grappling with the existential and political meaning of beauty and sexiness—we've been victimized by exactly that, and don't care to repeat the experience. We're still fighting for popular regard as those elusive, highly evolved beings called "ladies" and so prefer to look pretty rather than post-punk; for us, beauty still is the revolution. We don't go in for the psychological teasing that makeup colors have become—Coy, Naughty Feather, Trailer Trash, etc.—remaining content to call a red lipstick red. Black lines like Barbara Walden and Fashion Fair might throw in an adjective like hot or sizzling or cherry, but rest assured that if you're looking for coral, you'll find something in that name. We want to clarify, not complicate, beauty; soften, not sharpen, its edges.

But this is an era of sharp edges. In public repose, without any makeup at all, scuttling from one shoe rack to the next, black women are statements, political declamations. Makeup can't help in this regard (neither, for that matter, can shoes). It does get confusing at times. In this age of diversity campaigns and fashionably minimized expressions of wealth, *Allure* magazine recommends that the more hip and adventurous American woman look to the black makeup lines for real options. Makeup artiste Kevyn Aucoin says the typically saturated colors favored by black brands can be diluted with gloss or water and used very effectively on *any* skin tone! Though of course this is but a pleasant diversion from the staple pinks and beiges, something cheap to try if you ever make it to Penney's, or the Baldwin Hills Robinsons, or the makeup aisle of a demographically accommodating Sav-On. Me, I'm still looking for something expensive to try.

BLACKNESS ITSELF

September 2006

In these days of polarizing, pulverizing debates that make it almost impossible to describe what it means to be African-American anymore, I find it's better to simply describe a day in my life:

It's Thursday. I drive to Locke High School to teach a weekly poetry workshop to a group of tenth graders. Locke is a terribly underperforming, occasionally violent campus in a poor, significantly black neighborhood in South Central. It is not fifteen minutes from my more middle-class, significantly black neighborhood in Inglewood. The campus is clean and putty-colored, if somewhat bare. The black girls in my group are reserved, but not sullen; they are willing and often eager to write. The boys tend to speak out of turn, though mostly in service of questions I ask about poetry — volunteering answers, ideas, reasons why something is a metaphor or why it is not. They write, too, though not always well, technically; no one's grammar or literary analysis is perfect or even halfway conventional. But that's hardly the point. I leave Locke after only an hour feeling buoyed, reconnected, hopeful. I think: *So few of us can save so many.*

I stop at a gas station and switch almost unthinkingly to a grim face because some young black men loitering near the pumps, men who resemble the boys I just left, are looking at me hard, too hard. Caught between ethnic fear and familiarity, I go with fear; I learned much too early in life that at moments like these I must survive first and reason later. Back on the road, a black motorist in a gleaming SUV has the hip-hop music, droning expletives and all, turned up to a deafening assault, shivering everything within a four-lane radius from the tires up. The hopefulness of the morning fades like dew, and I flash on a well-worn anger: *Why we got to be like this?* Later on I drive into Hollywood, an area flush with stores, condos, construction, and other earmarks of a budding new population that's mostly white; I can't help but notice that nearly every homeless person I pass is black, male, and broken-looking. The anger flares again, this time more sorrowful indignation tinged with embarrassment: *Why we got to be like this?*

By the time I get to work—an office in which I am the only black person doing what I'm doing—I've recast my response to the state of the race for the third time in as many hours. I'm sure that what I do at Locke means almost nothing at all, that however willing the students, they will eventually be swallowed whole by a monster that has stalked us from one generation into the next, a ravenous chimera of lesser schools, lack of trust, indifference, idleness, fury, low ambitions, and low-hanging pants that sag like eternally unrealized freedom dreams. I put myself beyond that monster's reach decades ago and am relatively safe; many, many other black people are not. Yet however prudent it may be to not go back to Locke, to cut ties and close my eyes against a mounting sea of troubles, I know it is not possible, because in spite of the miles and sensibilities that separate Hollywood from South Central and South Central from Inglewood, we—me, the students, the SUV driver, the gas-pump loiterers, and the homeless—are all somehow in the same place. A place in which there is no retirement for paying your dues and no consequence for never paying them at all; a wide but narrow, endless but circumscribed, rocky but maddeningly even plane on which we all stand at any given time. It's a point in space that will outlive all of us, that terrifies as much as it inspires: it is where we always are and all that we ever have. With a mix of weariness and wonder that I can't characterize at all, I think for the last time: *Why we got to be like this?*

So as much as I chronicle blackness, I am confounded by it. Contrary to conventional post-millennial wisdom about race in America, black means everything and almost never means nothing. That is not a boast or a declaration of permanent victimhood or a blind refusal to let the 1960s rest in peace: it's the truth. The daily, overwhelming truth of black significance makes a joke of modern, minimalist notions of race and racism that tend to take an almost commercial view of things—race and racism as new and improved products that cost less and are less filling than they were forty years ago. But that's a theory, while black significance is reality. All black people live it, and everyone else is witness to it. It is still being the only black person in the room at a party, the only voice raised against police abuse in a polite, presumptuous conversation about crime and taxes, the only black customer in the fancy boutique. It's the deafening, faux-deferential silence that greets the story I tell at that party of how *my* people came to California—not via the Dust Bowl or the Gold Rush or the suburban housing stock boom the 1950s. Black significance is up to the minute, as chic as it gets, but it also has the creaky, enormous weight and breadth of four hundred years of American history behind it; it's larger than life-size and can't be broken down into small pieces, no matter how much the race modernists insist that's exactly what must be done in order to "get past" the whole black thing for good. (Curiously, I don't see any other group being encouraged to "get past" themselves— Asians renouncing Asianness, Jews renouncing Jewishness. Whether recent immigrants or fourth-generation Americans, they tend to draw their identity closer to better understand and appreciate its strengths and subtleties, not push it away in a kind of horror that, sadly, blacks have learned to associate with *their* identity. The current campaign to overcome blackness in order to overcome is proof enough of its significance.)

Take Bill Cosby and the remarks he made in 2004 at an NAACP commemoration of the fiftieth anniversary of *Brown v. Board of Education*. Cosby declared to the well-dressed audience that it was more or less the poor and ghetto-dwelling who were holding back—well, holding up—the progress of the race. He excoriated "these people" for a dirty-laundry list of things that have become quietly synonymous in many people's minds with the black condition: bad parenting, bad English, unplanned pregnancies, imprisonment, gangs, high school dropouts, even singular names like Shaniqua and Shaligua that attempt to reach back to Africa via a classic American capacity for chutzpah and self-reinvention, but that to Cosby and others are simply more bad English. So vexed was Cosby at this kind of black significance that he went out and spoke against it in town-hall meetings across the country, meetings in which the Shaniquas and Shaliguas actually showed up to hear what he had to say. The truth was, they did need help, none seemed forthcoming, so why not listen to Cosby? The black masses were looking for deliverance, even from a man who had insulted them; he was a famous man, a celebrity, at any rate smarter and more successful than they were. Watching one of these town halls, it struck me that whatever virtues black people lack—starting with the ones iterated by Cosby—forgiveness and fairness of mind is certainly not among them.

After minutes of anticipatory applause, Cosby spoke. But what came out was not revolutionary, or even very useful. Random admonishments to parents to care for their kids, think of them as precious saplings that can grow into trees, give them a good breakfast, tell them pull up their pants. There was no ten-point plan, no greater agenda. Even the question-and-answer session was less question or answer and more opportunity for Cosby to pontificate; when one mother, poised on a razor's edge of reverence and desperation, ventured to say that Cosby hadn't exactly addressed her question, he cut her off and glared at the rest of the audience as a warning. Here was not a sympathetic figure or a compatriot in the struggle, but a stern and wrathful God that the black middle and moneyed class has most often become to its lower-class counterpart.

Yet even the class issue is tiny compared to the greater, enduring truth of black significance. This is not just our truth, by the way, but everybody's—white, brown, Asian, poor, well-off, immigrant, citizen. It shapes the entire country from the bottom up: blacks are at the lowest rung in too many ways, but it is from this position that we reverberate all the way to the top and always have. Without our legacy of slavery and oppression, there would be no way to measure everyone else's freedom; without our falling short over hundreds of years—abetted by American laws and social customs, of course—there would be no way to appreciate the inspiring success of other groups over just a generation or two.

Those reverberations from the bottom up are also positive. An obvious example is music. But even the triumph of our music is diminished by the fact that, from the standpoint of progress, it hasn't seemed to matter all that much. Jazz and blues and rock and hip-hop are American institutions that have been institutionalized worldwide, and *we* are still on that bottom rung, still in search of a good breakfast, still scratching out day hustles to make a dollar out of fifteen cents. To much of the country we are not common folk to be admired for our efforts, but a cursed and vaguely corrupt people whose failures are never honest. We can't be trusted with opportunity or good luck, and therefore can never represent a country that reveres the abundance of both. We will always be the damning, countervailing force to the whole American can-do mythos: slothful, bitter, foot-dragging, impudent. The middle class may speak and dress better than the poor—no sagging pants or enormous T-shirts—but underneath whatever we're wearing, we are considered the same. At this point in history we are no longer openly terrorized; we are tolerated or left alone. That is the sum total of our freedom so far. We are mimicked and discussed but almost never encouraged or invited into or made a part of. We are, as we have always been, on our own.

Dire as all this feels sometimes, I'm not sure that I want to feel any other way. I am in a position that's utterly unique. I carry a movement on my shoulders, like a dragon half alive: part monster-stalker, part magnificent, the dragon is always formidable. It's also ugly and ungainly; it spits and grumbles, kicks at the moments when ı want most to lie still and go to sleep. Yes, it's a burden that sometimes feels like the weight of a dead man. But just as many times it's heavy like riches—I am lucky to carry it. I was destined to carry it. The unfinished black movement, the restlessness carried forward over generations, is the essence of black significance, the heaviest part but also the most kinetic, the force that animates our anger and optimism in the same moment, even our disaffection and silence. Wherever we are in history, the movement is the sum total of who we are so far. It is us. Like all movement, it makes us appear blurry in other's people's eyes, unfixed, possibly dangerous. When people meet me—that includes many fellow black people—they anticipate the dragon but strive to ignore it. They hope I've left it at the door. They hope I'm not one of those black folk who insist on keeping it close year after year, like an expired coupon or an outgrown toy. They try talking down to it. "Oh, you don't *agree* with the Supreme Court's compromise on affirmative action?" they say casually, wine glass at their lips. They're speaking not to me but to my significance. They act as if it's a tantrum thrown in polite company to get attention, when in fact it's the fire under their feet they're trying hard to tread so lightly over. It's fire that burns all the time, all around them. They would like to reduce affirmative action and other nominally racial subjects to cocktail chatter, move it all permanently into the category of Things We Can All Talk About.

But they need my consent to do that. They hate that they need my consent, but there you go: it's one of very few things that America still needs black people for. They can go ahead and declare affirmative action and the racial justice movement that gave rise to it irrelevant—indeed, they did that years ago. But without black consent, it is not the expression of power and dominance they would like it to be. Without consent, it is just one voice rising louder than another, like a six-year-old's; and when they raise that voice, it becomes clear that it's them throwing the tantrum, not me. Not us.

And what about us? What about that troubled "we" all black people like to fling around but most are loath to hold too close for too long? Holding my own as the lone African-American in a crowd is one thing, but I have communication problems with black folks too. Among each other we are all Significant, which is not wrong, but it takes up a lot of space. There is simply not enough space for us all, space for all that accumulated significance for which there really isn't a vocabulary to describe. There are not enough words to describe us, never enough words (the words we tend to use are, in blues fashion, generally opposite of what we mean: cool, smooth, okay, straight, wack, alright). But we all want to have our say, offer our life in words for the first time, which is why we all tend to squeeze to the front row at public meetings, hold forth on radio call-in shows, sit too long on the microphone whenever and wherever it's passed. We are all guilty of announcing to each other, I can fix things if you all let me. I and only I have the answers . . .

And we all believe we have answers, whatever our class or station. It's part of a psychic legacy that includes, among other contradictions, having both great certitude and gutting self-doubt; having brazenness born of a feeling that there is nothing to lose, and mute despair born of the same. When I interview an average black person on the street about anything, he or she tends to say, "Let me tell you something . . ." and he will, for an hour or more. All of us need to talk, to advise, to describe destiny and why it will be so, to be the sage or authority we assume we will never, ever be; this is what burns in us and has burned for centuries. That's Cosby's dictatorial hubris, and we all share it at times, the notion that we can *all* lead any time we like by virtue of stepping up and stating our case (Cosby's celebrity gave him extraordinary stage and microphone time, which he took full advantage of.) It's ironic that we bemoan the lack of black leadership when in fact we have tons of it—not from politicians and famous people, but from the people on the ground. The leadership is never organized or mined for anything, and that's the real problem: as significant as we all are and have always been, we are not taken seriously as a group. It's the most grievous contradiction of all. It is why virtually all black public dialogue is exhausting, erratic, tedious, and tangential—but also shimmering in spots with energy and poetry and purpose. It *moves*. It never rests, least of all when the meeting's adjourned and everybody puts on their coat and prepares to go home. Our parting greeting is always along the lines of "to be continued." Closure is one of many American traditions that rarely make sense to us, that make us feel less American than we are. But of course blacks are more American than anyone, and not only because we're more willing to show the flag than history has a right to expect. It's because we believe in an America that hasn't even *happened* yet. The civil rights movement was a big enough movement to warrant a name and a thousand accounts by a thousand authors, but it was not the end point. The dragon lives.

And this is Cosby's problem. He was not angry about schisms of class or culture or dress or language: he is angry about blackness itself. He is angry that it takes up so much of his time, that it does not seem to be self-sustaining and that it needs so much, too much, to grow and prosper and to get right. He's angry that at the moment blackness, for all its outrageous ubiquity and for all its significance, is also declining into a kind of quiet apocalypse. Never a settled matter, blackness today feels inefficient, slippery, not our own, wandering off in a wrong direction the moment we take our eyes off it, falling out of the census here, ballooning to grotesque proportions there. Deep down, we'd all love to ignore color, as we're admonished to do. But he can't. We shouldn't. The world, and our own sense of incompleteness—which Cosby has, else he wouldn't have bothered to say anything at all—won't let us.

Yes, there's fatigue. Yes, there are days when we'd all like to shuffle off this marked skin that constantly demands a coherent position and point of view, whether we've got one or not. The difficulties of black identity are ancient, and ageless. We are always evaluating where and who we are, and it's inconvenient. Entirely un-American in the land of convenience above all things. But that evaluating and reevaluating is, in fact, who and what we are. We are a people in process, with little idea of where or even if the process ends; because of that, we are still the best measure of democracy. College grads, under-educated high school students, thugs, bums, big mouths, conservatives, radicals: we all measure it together. Whatever we do, wherever we call home, we're all walking down the same street.

DOWN AND DOWNER

August 2010

Little frustrates me more on a daily basis than the notion that I should be, must strive for, and must remain at all costs, positive.

Positive is a word that connotes anything good and encouraging, but its sunniness is often wrapped in tyranny. I've lived with that tyranny all my life, but was sharply reminded of it when writer and critic Barbara Ehrenreich published *Bright-sided*, her 2009 examination of the great American obsession with positive thinking. Ehrenreich was inspired to write the book after she got breast cancer a decade earlier and tried to connect with similarly afflicted women online. The overwhelming feedback she got was to be positive. Being angry or resentful or even annoyed wasn't an option; the tragedy of breast cancer itself, Ehrenreich discovered, had been recast as a life-affirming experience that would make the afflicted a better and wiser person in the long run. That view has been reinforced by the pop-culture embrace of breast-cancer research, with its walkathons and pink ribbons and campaign posters of women of all colors and persuasions standing shoulder to shoulder, wearing encouraging, slightly satisfied smiles—we've overcome, and you can, too! To Ehrenreich, breast cancer was portrayed as almost a welcomed opportunity to get healthy, informed, focused on your priorities, and so on. (Menopause, a universal female experience that is not a disease and that affords a logical opportunity for women to do all of the above, never had it so good.) Of course, the not-so-shiny implication of brightsidedness is that if you don't subscribe to it, as Ehrenreich did not, you are not considered a team player or truly interested in your own well-being and the well-being of others. You are a cancer on the group spirit.

I know all about prescribed positivity. Like Ehrenreich, I resist it, though not as a cancer survivor (thank goodness) or as a critic. I resist it as an ordinary member of the black community, both the actual community I live in and the much wider one to which all black people belong. I'll preface my complaint by emphatically saying this: I understand. For black people, positivity is terribly serious business and always has been. Far from a fad or a marketing campaign, positivity—the belief that, however bad things are, they'll get better by and by and you *shall* overcome—is a tool that's helped blacks survive the sickness of racism for hundreds of years, racism that has created a long and open-ended history not only of injustice but of personal disappointments, thwarted ambitions, isolation, repressed anger, and dispiritedness too wide and deep to measure. Remaining positive often means simply remaining upright in a country that's spent the vast majority of its history trying to knock us down and keep us from getting up; positivity is a coping mechanism that's the psychological equivalent to civil disobedience. On a personal level, positivity is also the best deal we could make for ourselves—to sublimate our own doubts and troubles in order to keep moving forward as a group, or at least to preserve the appearance of moving forward. The trade-off is not really a choice, though Americans presume that choice—also known as empowerment—is the very essence of being positive. Quite the opposite: blacks are always called upon to be positive in the face of no choices, to keep faith when there's almost none to keep, and that goes for everybody, even the religiously disinclined—positivity is our mandatory church without the Bible or the building. To be black is to believe that things are never as bleak as they appear, and believing otherwise is a drag on our own group spirit that we can never afford and certainly can't afford now, not in the time of Obama. Not because he's such a potent symbol of positivity that we have to live up to, but because his prominence obscures the decidedly negative state of so many other black people and the still-urgent need for progress that was fading from national view long before he showed up.

Positive isn't just hazy, Oprah-like affirmation that's good for the collective soul. It's self-defense, both body armor and weapon in the bloody fight against assumptions of black failure that have become synonymous with the race. Cornel West once said that blacks in America have been wrongly labeled a problem people, fraught with pathologies and perpetually viewed as more broken than whole, with achievers like Obama (and West himself) the exception, not the rule. Positivity is at the root of all the ideologies developed to refute that image of brokenness, to undo the white-man brainwashing, as Malcolm X would say—ideologies like Afrocentrism and the Nation of Islam. (It's funny that whites and plenty of blacks associate these beliefs with black hostility, when in fact they are fundamentally optimistic, even romantic). Yet West is a humanist who doesn't believe any of these ideologies alone can cure the "problem people" syndrome—they are too narrow, he says. And they are too unwilling to address the nihilism and self-loathing among black people that are byproducts of racism that have become a very real part of us. To declare that all blacks are proud African kings and queens ignores this reality for a good reason, but ignoring it as a matter of principle acknowledges the power of the black inferiority myth more than it refutes it; wearing kente cloth and dismissing all of Western culture signals not triumph, but a kind of defeat.

Yet West believes that strategies such as Afrocentrism are important pieces of a bigger effort to restore us all, black and other Americans, to sanity and full humanity. That can only happen if we tell the whole truth and collectively face up to the race-based problems American society has either ignored or exaggerated in every generation, with disastrous results. Yet West is firmly on the side of positivity. Like Martin Luther King and other thinkers, he is a realist but ultimately an idealist who knows change and deliverance is not only possible, it is imminent. The necessity of positivity for black people is a given; it needs no discussion. It is the point from which we all must proceed, and after making even the most scathing inventory of all that's wrong, the point to which we must return. To stray from the course is to slip backward; slip far enough, and you self-erase.

I completely agree with West about the importance of examining the entire picture, and admire his tireless optimism in the face of it. My problem with positivity, other than the fact I'm not really wired for it, is that it simply can't do the job. It's overworked and spread too thin. The brightsidedness Ehrenreich talks about is a big phenomenon that takes specific and sometimes subtle forms—in politics, in consumerism, in breast-cancer research campaigns. It's diverse, adaptable. But black positivity is a single-ingredient corrective, a topical applied to everything that ails or derails us, and it isn't enough to keep us going. It's a salve on our wounded image attached to an even more wounded psyche that goes layers deep and never heals; it doesn't begin to get at the density and complexity underneath that we must get at if we are ever to make positivity something more than treading water while the ocean rages around us. Focusing all of our positive energy on repairing image, while understandable, puts us in a new set of shackles: if being racially progressive means always putting on a resilient face, how do you really argue for your humanity? Without the freedom to express doubt and insecurity, fatigue and even fury, how can black folks truly be equal? How can we be our *selves*?

In America, the self is the smallest unit of power that has enormous politi-cal meaning and cultural resonance. The self is the foundation of our unique sense of entitlement that says individuals have the right to expect that they will be protected, listened to, taken seriously—in a word, valued. Education, employment, income, and all the rest are only affirmations of that right. That blacks are so consistently at the bottom of these indices says clearly that, as far as America is concerned, we are still a long way from being valued for ourselves, for being Americans. I know that positivity keeps despair about all the grim statistics at bay and reminds black people that we are, of course, hu-man. We are worthy. We know that. But at some point we do need everybody else to agree.

Journalists are expected to foster that agreement by putting black folk in the best light possible. From my first days as a reporter in Crenshaw and South Central, people expected that I would carry the banner of racial posi-tivity as a matter of professional common sense; my chief but unwritten job description was to counter hundreds of years of media distortion of blacks by publishing stories that were positive. I knew what that meant. I perfectly un-derstood the role of advocate, and was more than eager to fill it and to make a difference (a phrase that was drummed into me at least as much as the impor-tance of staying positive). But I had a slightly different take on things. I saw the battle lines drawn not so much between positive and negative portrayals of black folks, but between complete and incomplete. I saw myself as less of an activist and more of an artist who was filling in a minimalist sketch with gradations of color and light: I was making three-dimensional a formerly flat Earth. But that kind of aesthetic approach to racial improvement proved a tough sell to blacks who looked at big papers like the *Los Angeles Times* and only saw an agenda of crime and ghetto narratives. I had to fight fire with fire, or something even more potent. If I couldn't or wouldn't do that, then what good was I?

For the last twenty years, the mortal enemy of black positivity in the minds of many has been hip-hop, specifically gangsta rap. This culture/image war has flown mostly under the radar of Americans too busy tracking abortion rights and gay marriage, but make no mistake, it's been a war—for blacks, a war within a war. Anti-gangsta-rap factions see NWA and Jay-Z as forces bent on severing the tough but tenuous links of black positivity. To critics, glorifying gang and street life and egregiously boasting about killing other blacks is nothing less than self-destruction—and that's "self" in the biggest sense of the word. Blacks advertising contempt for each other via popular music is suicide that we all informally agreed never to commit, the nuclear option that we wouldn't take. Yet that stance is certainly too cataclysmic; much of hip-hop is not gangsta, and even some of the roughest stuff reflects a very real mood out there in the 'hood, a justifiable feeling that the fortunes of poor black urban places have been abandoned by everyone, that positivity is an illusion and it's every man for himself. It is simply telling us that truth we don't want to hear. And too, focusing on one genre of music as *the* problem tarnishing our bright side, rather than on bigger though admittedly more amorphous problems like poverty and lack of jobs, is easy. But even those who acknowledge the validity of all those factors remain convinced that gangsta rap and other mainstreamed approbation of thug life has had a devastating impact on our image, the state of our own positivity, and our general state of mind. Technology has multiplied that impact exponentially: a couple of homies rapping on a globally watched YouTube video are dragons that can slay a thousand stories about black college students, set back dozens of proposed domestic policies aimed at helping the black poor. The real problem is that the black gangsta/bourgeois binary is too simplistic; the picture of blackness is incomplete. There is not enough choice, so the gangsta has disproportionate influence on how the rest of us are seen.

But the questions remain: Why the disproportionate influence? Why *don't* the college students hold the popular imagination? The answer is that America likes its black people simplistic, which is by definition negative—criminal, clown, sass, loudmouth. The black gangsta image has become so familiar now as to be almost neutral. I've worked on an overwhelmingly white college campus where students play thug rap not like it's something exotic but as background music. In the twenty-first century, the black outlaw is the norm, his ubiquity and predictability almost comforting. The gangsta goes deep.

Among the most un-positive characteristics of gangsta rap cited by critics is its profanity (especially the word "nigger"), its uncritical embrace of consumerism—bling—and some elements of misogyny. But that's only touching the surface. The deepest anxiety about the gangsta narrative is that it seems so willingly, almost gleefully, to broadcast to the world a me-first, don't-give-a-shit attitude that positivity is meant to counter, or to cover. It gives aid and comfort to the enemy of stereotypes and to the belief that young black folks not only can't achieve, they don't want to. It also breaks with a long tradition of black music serving as an antidote to the hardship and meagerness of everyday black life. Spirituals, blues, ragtime, jazz, gospel, and soul all offered poetry that transcended bitter reality; with hip-hop, that reality (or authenticity, a very problematic notion and usually a fiction when applied to black folks) is the point. Black music has functioned through the ages as a kind of talking drum, a way for us to encourage and celebrate each other even as we entertained white folks. More often than not, hip-hop tells us to back up or fuck off. It isn't encouraging.

Critics also see hip-hop as a kind of non-music that sullies the important role of black music as an agent of positivity by virtue of the fact it's good art; in that sense, everybody from Duke Ellington to Chaka Khan represents us well. I certainly grew up believing this in the '70s, when R&B was king, disco was heating up, and the talking drum was still very much in force. With an innocence that seems unimaginable now, black pop singles routinely urged us all to move our feet, strive, and never look back, or look down: "Keep On Truckin'," "Keep Your Head to the Sky," "Love Train," "Lovely Day," "Wake Up Everybody," "I'm Every Woman," "Ain't No Stopping Us Now," "Don't Stop 'Til You Get Enough." Simplistic, perhaps, but to my adolescent ears the songs were all powerful messages of can-do. The artists who delivered them were cool, too, funkmeisters that my friends and I all aspired to be, and the altruism in their music was part of that aspiration. The cool in hip-hop lies not in its altruism but its chaos; artists dare you to look them in the face, let alone like them. The irony in all this that hip-hop has always been beholden to R&B—producers have sampled its lyrics and beats from the genre's beginning. Rap enthusiasts call that veneration, and say that, far from breaking with black tradition, hip-hop (even gangsta) is keeping tradition alive. That's hard to argue. But sampling is also deconstruction—taking what you like or find useful and leaving the rest, slicing up an originally sunny tempo and shaping it into something cryptic or darker. I'm all for artistic license, but I'm also for integrity, and gangsta ultimately feels more like racial propaganda than art, or even than plain old-fashioned commercialism. Far from casting any new light, it puts black folks in the social margins where the media has kept us a long time. That doesn't mean hip-hop should be banned or even modified because of a lack of positivity; positivity has no claim on hip-hop or any other kind of entertainment. Modifying it to fit our morals or sensibilities would simply make it propaganda of another sort. I can only say that the genre could benefit from a thorough soul-searching, musically and otherwise.

For all of my issues with positivity, I don't like the idea that I'm failing it. I don't like the thought that on any given day I may be falling down on the job of lifting up others. My failure is more acute because I'm educated (not moneyed, but educated) and therefore more responsible for being a live example of the kind of achievement most black people still don't attain these days. I have an image; it is mine to uphold or not. This is Du Bois's vision of the "talented tenth," which, though Du Bois himself eventually discarded it, still fuels a popular concept that the more fortunate among us are the leaders charged with bettering everybody else. So I've done lots of workshops and career days in public schools, not quite believing but always hoping that young people find some measure of inspiration in anything I've done in my life so far. But something slightly miraculous always happens. When I get up in front of the fifth graders, I feel in the presence of, for total lack of a better phrase, a higher power. I feel that I have no *right* to sully their inspiration or obstruct their hope; my persona, my *self*, belongs to some greater cause. At these moments, far from feeling the usual drag of obligatory positivity, I get inspired in very unexpected ways. I see a community assembled before me that I'd forgotten existed; toiling alone over a computer, endlessly trying to write into existence who *I* am, community is an easy thing to forget. In that classroom I don't need words at all. I am literally made whole.

Because of moments like these, I try to practice positivity even though I'm an agnostic at best, even as I feel hope and sanity slipping off the table. I try in small and daily ways to channel Baldwin and King, and when that feels impossible, I try to channel my father, an activist now in his late seventies who still labors tirelessly and unapologetically for racial justice that in some ways feels less attainable now than it did forty years ago. As I said before, I admire that very much. I admire all the people who've come before and made my doubts and my somewhat boutique lifestyle—a choice!—possible. But my post–Jim Crow sensibility argues that the positivity that's been such an essential part of our survival is out of date. We have now absorbed just enough of that larger American culture of self to seriously ask questions like, Why aren't things better? What *hasn't* happened? Have we maintained a good outlook at the expense of action?

But we still need that high note to end on. We've earned the right to critical reflection, but it's a luxury we can't afford to use quite yet because black history isn't done; our biggest problems have not resolved to the point where we can indulge in hindsight. Unlike historians of the Holocaust, blacks cannot yet look back and assess, sum up, figure out what happened and what to do better next time. I thought in the late '70s that we might be reaching that moment of assessment: with things cracked open a bit by affirmative action, I thought that positivity might help black people actually get somewhere instead of being a cruelly inadequate protection against the cold climate of segregation and separation that had always made a mockery of a sunny outlook. Positivity—and its modern and more sensitive cousin, self-esteem—looked like it was going to be rocket fuel in our shiny new engine of success.

But we all realized soon enough that much more was required for change than a good attitude. Jim Crow was gone, yes. But its deep-rooted legacy of discrimination, crappy schools, and circumscribed opportunity didn't exactly go with it. When I was bused to a largely white school in 1973, all the swagger in the world didn't blunt the inadequacy and uncertainty I felt around white kids, whose enormous and casual sense of entitlement was almost frightening; it made my own homegrown positivity seem small and quaint. Years later, as I battled depression, positivity as a reference point and especially as a solution to what I suffered from—to say nothing of what ailed other black friends of mine who never got as far as college—felt less satisfying than ever.

These are strange days. The American empire is dismantling itself, piece by piece. I don't have a job, and the last one I had, the one that promised the kind of career zenith I had dared to expect on my good days, disappeared before it could ascend at all. And there are so many other, bigger things to worry about these days, from creeping fascism in this country to climate change spreading over the globe like the wings of a giant vulture. And yet I feel confident. Why not? Or more precisely, what other feeling makes any sense? I am let down, but that hardly surprises me. I am where I always half-thought I'd be, where history predicted I'd be: further along than my parents' generation got, but unfinished. Not there yet. In retrospect I can see that I was prepared for this all along, have been preparing for years, bracing for the blow of irresolution that is cyclical for black folks, a fact of our lives since we've lived here. I tally up the good things: I'm still standing, and most improbably yet most importantly, I'm expecting progress against the worst of odds, maybe in the worst of times. The defiance amid disintegration feels good and hallowed in a way I can't describe. Positively crazy.

BLUE LIKE ME ▰▰▰▰▰▰▰▰▰▰

ON RACE AND DEPRESSION

August 2000

The problem of the Twentieth Century is the problem of the color-line. —W.E.B. DU BOIS, 1903

The overriding experience of the black American has been grief and sorrow and no man can change that fact. His grief has been realistic and appropriate. What people have so earned a period of mourning?
—GRIER AND COBBS, *Black Rage*, 1968

Today blacks are as religious, socially conservative, and patriotic as any other ethnic group, with a deep belief in the goodness and inclusiveness of American society and, despite the popular perception that blacks blame whites for their problems, a willingness to shoulder a large amount of respon- sibility for the present condition of their brethren. Values supposedly matter in America, but if black people have these values and are still not fully welcomed into the mainstream, it is fair for them to finally ask whether anything they do will ever make a difference. —STEINHORN AND DIGGS-BROWN, *By the Color of Our Skin: The Illusion of Integration and the Reality of Race,* 2000

I Feel Good—Not

About a year and a half ago, a thought struck me with unprecedented force: life sucks. Overall. I had become acutely aware that I hadn't been feeling good in years. Not physically, but psychically, and in a way rather worse than the modern miasma of inner perplexity and urban wariness that we call depression, a condition we've grown almost fond of because we've grown so fond of countering it with the latest wrinkle creams and poetry workshops and such. This despondency was different, and felt completely above, or beneath, any self-actualization remedy. The usual miasma was there, but surging beneath it, like oil stealthily darkening a floor where you thought only water had spilled, was a sense of brokenness that felt vast and familiar, lived in; it had the wonderful and terrible assurance of a thing that had long been alive, much longer than I had been myself. This great anxiousness seemed to speak, much better than depression could, to all the manifestations of my lacking life: the bills that couldn't quite get paid, the boyfriend who seemed a permanent fixture but was always passing through, and most of all a weary acceptance that this would be about as good as things would get. Everything and everyone felt ephemeral, so what I was most attached to, what gave me the most comfort, also felt the most ominous. Each day I had to invent the world and appoint its order, try on attitudes like suits of clothes, discard them in heaps, finally bolt out the door with invariably ill-chosen feelings: life was making me not sad so much as exasperated and pissed off. Nothing fit the occasion of my life, whatever that was. I had decent-paying work, a roomy place to live in a decent part of town, a car, no family-household obligations, license to shop when I wished. What gave? Why did life so often feel like a football pass thrown to the wrong player, something I had been bobbling in my hands ever since the happy mist of adolescence lifted twenty years ago and I balked because I could no longer reasonably live under the auspices of naiveté and preposterous expectation? How and why were my blues not like everybody else's? Eventually all these questions slowed to a freeze. I spent three lost days holed up in my apartment without a telephone or any other form of quick communication, moving about as little as possible. After I thawed I decided, with the help of a few friends and family members, that some therapy might be in order. Quite inadvertently, this decision began unraveling the mystery of my inertia. I had always lauded therapy in theory but discovered I scorned it in private. Therapy was for wimps and complainers, or at least for people who had sufficient leisure time and money to take up a talking cure in the first place. In other words, therapy was for white people.

When I first sat before a therapist, a very pleasant white woman of unsparing insight, I realized there was far more to it than that. I am black and, as such, had never been disassembled as an individual. It had never really seemed necessary, or even practical. In the course of life I had concluded that history had never taken much note of Negroes who were not iconic or tragic figures, or some combination thereof. They were symbols to admire at best and loathe at least, but not people to embrace for their vulnerability and personal explorations and resonant existential crises in the way that, say, Anaïs Nin or Albert Einstein were embraced for theirs. Our people, I had learned over and over in so many ways, are not like yours. We are not so finely calibrated, or so emotionally instructive; the world is more interested in how heavy a burden we can shoulder than in our capacity for curiosity, for observing the stars or walking a beach and collecting shells and bottle caps (which I did as a kid, alone, vaguely embarrassed by the lack of a larger point to it all). The world recognizes our capacity for resistance, and that's the best it can say about us. That's the best we can often say about each other; that is the best I can often say about myself. We are thus forever defined by the tension of standing opposite to something; in the absence of such tension, we are the trees that fall in a forest and that nobody hears.

But the therapist was listening. I was a tree in full view and hearing range. I began talking, but after five minutes or so I felt I had said too much. Here the mystery unraveled further: I found that I didn't want to offer myself up. I was nobody's business. In the environment in which I was raised, character was built not on exposure—that was foolish, if not dangerous—but on a certain imperturbability. You could shore up weakness, but you could never be weak yourself. Being sympathetic and considerate was good, Christian if you looked at things that way, but the sympathy and consideration were supposed to emanate from a rock. It was especially important to be a rock in front of whites, who were all too eager to consign you to dysfunction anyway. So were black people, though for entirely different reasons: they didn't mind you being drunk, strung out, or ranting—that was common enough—but you must never admit that you couldn't be something *else*. One's eyes must always be on a prize or a better life; hope is the cornerstone of blackness still, and to not invoke it is considered treachery and a waste of precious psychic resources. Melting down emotionally for the mere sake of release therefore never felt like an option for me, even though I longed to do it. Like voting and free speech, it's practically an American birthright, but another one reserved for Americans of certain birth. There were smaller-scale but no less weighty considerations. I wouldn't be exposing just myself during therapy, I would be exposing my whole family, my progenitors, my race, my—and our—still unformed legacy. This thought unsettled me far more than the thought of being colossally depressed — that was just me, after all — and so my next move with the therapist was to launch into a passionate defense of my father, whom I had always admired from a distance. I explained to her that he was peerless, that he had kept the wolves from our door even as he struggled to find his place among the wolves in the larger world. He had done battle, he was as rock-like as they come . . .

The therapist listened. She nodded sympathetically. "All right," she said when I was done. "Now tell me how you really feel."

The Third I

Such schizophrenia is really a postmodern elaboration on what W.E.B. Du Bois described one hundred years ago as "double consciousness," the state of being black and American but never both at once, because society had deemed it eminently undesirable. Du Bois talked about this double consciousness as the Negro people's greatest curse, because it meant that as long as they weren't reconciled in society's eyes, they could never reconcile themselves in their own. At the turn of the twenty-first century we still struggle with reconciliation in a vastly different but no less crippling context. We are entirely free to be agitators and voting blocs and gadflies — we are reasonably certain we won't be arrested or shipped off to Liberia — but being agitators has not humanized us, and therefore it has not meant real freedom. We are free to not agitate at all, to populate suburbs and remain conspicuously silent, but that extracts a price of self-denial and psychic compromise and isolation, and has not meant freedom either. That there is virtually no middle ground between full resistance and slack-jawed acquiescence speaks to how embryonic freedom still is for us. In the meantime, our greatest commonality is the very bipolar condition that describes our separation. Depression struck me as being real but ridiculous. To be black is to inherit conditions that are well beyond depressing — I couldn't imagine recalling incidents of racism and then confessing, "Doc, I've got this little self-esteem problem; can you help?" There's little documented evidence of such psychic quandaries but plenty of concurrence. Victoria Pratt of Virginia Union University concluded in a newspaper story on blacks and depression that "we kind of accept that depression is a part of our reality and accept that we have to deal with it the best way we can." Even trying to describe our troubles through the model of depression is ludicrous, a bit like the famous conciliator Booker T. Washington characterizing, as he did more than a century ago, the uptick of lynchings in the South and Midwest as the result of a few offending people's "bad habit." James Baldwin remarked some seventy years later that to be black and conscious of what that meant was to be "in a constant state of rage."

That is more intensely true now. The American cult of the individual has reached a zenith, and we assume we are a part of this movement, with its spiritual impresarios and gated communities and cell phones on every table. We are not. Take the ongoing conversation about the angst of the baby boomers. Boomers have had their long days in the sun as they've protested, prospered, and now, passing into old age, contend with crises of purpose and spirit. Black people, even the most resolutely middle-class among us, are at a very different point along the arc of social evolution; our crises are still chiefly those of deprivation, not abundance, and so our experiences are not considered germane to the boomer discourse at all, which cuts us out of yet another great American cultural moment. The book *By the Color of Our Skin: The Illusion of Integration and the Reality of Race* (2000) concludes that while blacks may be earning comfortable incomes in record numbers, they are not really considered part of the middle class, with all the affirmation that phrase confers upon its members. "The virtual absence of blacks from middle-class iconography has led a number of writers and scholars to view them as the 'invisible men' of the 1990s," write the authors, Leonard Steinhorn and Barbara Diggs-Brown. They go on to say that President Clinton's chief pollster, Stanley Greenberg, reported something even more diminishing: for whites in focus groups, "not being black is what constituted middle class; not living with blacks was what made a neighborhood a decent place to live." Beneath our plenty runs the cold undercurrent that being black is still the least advantageous and most repugnant state of being, the thing we all so concertedly run from and measure our misfortunes against. If you do happen to be a Negro, the best solution is to look determinedly over your shoulder in another direction. Ignore the feet and keep your head straight and fixed; the heart that sits equidistant between the two will have to get along on its own.

Equal and Opposite Reaction

I am *not*, therefore I am. On balance, I have always been much less concerned with what I am than what I am not—not uneducated, not uncouth, not socially unaware, etc. It's why I got gold stars on my papers in grade school, not for being an original thinker but for being above the reproach meted out to black students like daily gruel. My personal triumphs never proceeded from that point of youthful narcissism the psychiatrists Price Cobbs and William Grier defined, rather wistfully and improbably, in their seminal work *Black Rage* (1968), a collection of case histories; like so many other things, that narcissism was something fundamental to the American worldview and something blacks were never supposed to express, much less feel.

My earliest recollection of acting with confidence involved somebody's backyard birthday party, where I sat in a wooden picnic chair, in a straight pink dress and ruffled ankle socks; I was six. A portable record player was spinning Stevie Wonder's "My Cherie Amour," and I was almost faint with eagerness to show everybody how I had learned to do the cha-cha. I got up and started to dance. It was my grand entry into the world. For the length of the song, at least, I stood in opposition to nothing and led everyone to my particular enlightenment. From that point on, life became less and less like that.

Slipping into Darkness

Depression as it's been clinically defined has been on the rise among blacks, though what might look like an overnight phenomenon is more likely an admission of what's been true for a long, long time. The National Mental Health Association (NMHA) says in an online fact sheet that there's been a historical "underdiagnosis" of black depression (though, interestingly enough, an overdiagnosis of schizophrenia, suggesting that our madness is easier to fathom than our middle ground). Surveys conducted by the NMHA show that blacks more than any other group view depression as personal weakness, that they are most likely to believe they can "handle it" by turning to prayer, family, or community. Yet the rate of depression among black women is now estimated to be nearly 50 percent higher than the rate among white women. As they are so often, blacks are behind the self-help curve in that they are only now beginning to feel that depression is fit for public discourse: the Magic Johnson Foundation, which has addressed a host of health concerns, affirmed that shift in 1999 by teaming up with the National Medical Association and Pfizer Inc. to start a public-awareness program on depression in the African-American community.

I Been 'Buked

One component of depression is a fatalistic acceptance of a circumstance you know is harmful but you are convinced you cannot change. What if you know in your bones that you can't change it, that it will take oh so much more than you to change it, and so in the meantime you ignore the brittleness of your teeth and smile? Is that courage, confusion, battle fatigue, all of the above?

A dozen years ago, I traveled to New Orleans and to ground zero of the Big Uneasy. I took a bus ride out to a plantation in steam-iron heat that fairly hissed, with a contingent of white folks armed with cameras, brochures, and carefully concealed expectations. They avoided looking at me. We were greeted by women in gay ruffled skirts offering mint juleps for sale; they took us from room to Victorian-style room, declaiming about the nature of the goods, the exotic origins of the wood, the pianos, the dining-room columns. I felt vaguely stupid, and vague period, as though I was there but fading by the moment, like a ghost who adamantly refuses to accept death even as death is doing its fiendish business. There was no mention of blacks on the tour; the guides referred to folks who worked in the mansions as "servants." That blithe upgrade of status somehow riled me more than the epithet "nigger." I finally raised a hand and inquired, too loudly against the high ceilings, about the slaves' quarters: Where were they? "Oh. Those," the guide said with practiced patience, "blew away in a hurricane."

No one asked a similar question. I was scornful but curiously uninflamed, because deep down I accepted this omission as the natural state of things. It would never matter how well my own story turned out, it would always be trumped by this plantation story, this no-story; this story was the one that had to change.

From Slavery to Eternity

The book *Black Rage* argued in the 1960s with scientific eloquence that blacks had been shut out of the American culture of individualism and self-determinism just as they were shut out of the founding American culture of democracy. It implied that they would not, could not be shut out forever, but it also acknowledged the killing effects of slavery and how those effects were still reverberating loud and clear in the late '60s. It hardly needs to be said—well, perhaps it does—that they resonate now. We still wait in the wide gray gulf between annihilation and actualization, where we have been waiting for several hundred years; Cobbs and Grier say that it was really after slavery ended that our psychic troubles began in earnest, for it was then that white America had no more use for us, laborwise or any otherwise, and so, they write, "Negroes drifted into a nonexistence which they still occupy."

Slavery should be entirely passé in 2011, in the so-called era of Obama, the first black president, but it's not. It's still the ultimate American denial, on both sides—whites want to forget about it for obvious reasons of incrimination, and blacks are at the very least torn about remembering it because they would really rather reach past it, around it, forgo the happy-darkie and yassuh-boss cultural paradigm that they feel has kept them down for so long. But: denial, however understandable, is denial, and it leads nowhere good (just ask my therapist).

There is at least an ongoing movement to accord slavery its proper place. Randall Robinson of the organization TransAfrica and author of *The Debt: What America Owes to Blacks*, has campaigned hard for reparations for descendants of slaves—that's us—though he and his supporters are not fundamentally talking about money. More than cash disbursements, Robinson wants recognition from the government of the oppression that slaves endured. He wants everybody to mourn. He wants an official monument, like the ones that pay homage to Washington and Lincoln and to Holocaust survivors and the Japanese citizens who were wrongfully interned on American soil during World War II. Yet beneath the academic polish and impeccable reasoning of Robinson's arguments and editorials is a plea that is touching and saddening—and angering: here we are, hat in hand, still seeking at-large affirmation while the rest of the world is busy shifting borders, spinning deals around the globe, merging, making websites faster than you can spit. (The House and Senate did pass resolutions apologizing for slavery in 2008 and 2009, but the authors of the resolutions made it clear they were not making a case for reparations. Robinson called it a "confession," a beginning.) We're weathered rocks in the middle of a fast-moving stream, and the world is flowing around us without breaking pace. We're still steeped in what historian Orlando Patterson, in his book *Rituals of Blood: Consequences of Slavery in Two American Centuries* (1999), calls "natal alienation," permanently wrought by the fact that slaves had no legally sanctioned or recognized family structure. Continuity has therefore always been tough to come by, like standing on the shoulders of someone who's been cut off at the knees, and the only thing that persists generation to generation is the need to create a new coping mechanism for being both extant and extinct.

Wanna Take You Higher

I borrowed my father's old hardback copy of *Black Rage* hoping only for a side comment or two about the black psyche, some incidental insight that might prove useful in writing about race and depression. The title seemed quaintly dramatic, overwrought, of another age and arc in time that had once glowed hot with color and then vanished like a rainbow. But when I started reading, it felt not quaint at all but immediate, devastatingly relevant. Here were the million points of connection among ethnic, social, and individual dynamics that I saw daily but, despite the vast array of media outlets at my disposal, never heard or recognized in words. This was analysis, epiphany, prophecy. I took many notes. I avidly followed stories of former patients like Bertha, a woman whose keen intelligence and curiosity seemed to have been neutralized by the fact that she'd also been born with dark skin and a flat nose; John, an executive torn between corporate assimilation and ethnic identity; Booker, a doctoral candidate who struggled with the lingua franca of scholarship and clung to his Southern-patois rap like a security blanket. Like Randall Robinson's explication of the merits of slavery recompense, the book is at once logical and supremely impassioned, and it rings with truth and condemnation. It draws its subjects cleanly and objectively but does not worry about maintaining academic distance—it in fact uses academics with a vengeance. The unexamined black life gave Cobbs and Grier all the drive and indignation they needed, and all the proof I needed to know I wasn't alone with my sense of being chronically out of focus.

Check the Black Box

When Census 2000 proposed a new racial category, "Other," I felt equally furious and hapless—that is, depressed. (By virtue of being black for thirty-eight years, wasn't I already Other?) It was the damned ease with which the establishment assumed it could redraw boundaries of color and identity and cultural orientation, like congressional districts, in the same way it did last century when it decided who was black or white enough for polite society, and who wasn't. I know what some folks are thinking: But don't you *want* to be free of those categories? Isn't it exactly those categories that have bound you for so long? To the multiculturalists who've been multiplying since the early '90s like maggots, I say no: what has bound me, and binds me, is an inchoate self that can be made whole only by effecting inclusion—retroactively, please. Eradicating race is not a postmodern version of enlightenment to me but self-annihilation, even if it's done only on paper. (After all, the most damning and lasting edicts are just that, ink on paper.) Neither do I view myself as merely a figment of race, but I cannot and do not separate race from Me. Why would I want to, anyway—to blur the few lines of distinction that I and everybody else recognize? And if I were to cast out the "old" paradigm of black, as I am regularly encouraged to do, what new one would I embrace? Full-blooded American? Why isn't anyone in my vicinity casting off old paradigms of white, Thai, Chinese, Latino? No one else seems to be in such a hurry to depluralize themselves. Assimilate, adapt, yes; give up a defining culture, however in flux, no. In fact, the *more* put upon and oppressed a people, the less likely they are to lay down traditions and the more likely they are to thrive. The problem is that we consciously fail to recognize what our traditions are, though we are certainly reminded daily what *we* are. As pioneering publisher Earl Graves remarked a generation ago, "You can graduate from Harvard and Yale, but you can't graduate from blackness." Even if I could, would I want to?

Maulana Karenga, executive director of the African American Cultural Center in L.A. and a locally famous figure from the Black Power '60s, waves such questions away like an annoyance, so much cigarette smoke. In his modified boom of a voice, he touts the importance of thinking in a new box, an African one. He calls it *kawaida*, principles similar to those of Kwanzaa (also his creation) that stress a constant connection to African culture in order to carve meaningful spaces for ourselves in the world. Karenga calls them "free spaces." "Self-assertion in the world is dependent upon self-understanding," he declares. His office is cozy, stacked with books, woody and inviting, like a rectory. The noise and hectoring of 54th Street seem miles away. An enormous, very handsome atlas with yellowed pages and intricate pictures sits open on a lectern. "We don't turn to Africa for answers, because we're Europeanized, so we've turned historically to Greece and to Israel," he goes on, "but how do you reconcile being African with this acculturation?" I have no idea. I want to listen, that's enough. "But look at all the things we've done," says Karenga, sweeping out an arm. "I'm very impressed with black history. We've suffered a holocaust, but we've achieved tremendously. No one gave us that—we carved it out of the hard rock of reality. We did things the founding fathers"—whose?—"never dreamed of. I've been saying this since '65: we must fight a cultural revolution for ourselves, for the hearts and minds of our people, a revolution that will grow a collective self-conscious. Kawaida says we must constantly recover and put forth the best of what it means to be African."

Karenga rails against the current black intelligentsia—chief among them Henry Louis Gates, de facto leader of Harvard University's black academic "dream team"—for deconstructing black people, criticizing them into irrelevance. "They're always looking for the stitch and stain of blacks, peeling paint instead of providing the masses with models of possibility, of human excellence," he says emphatically. "Blacks are greatly in need of *possibility*. If not that, what?" What, indeed? I second Karenga's motion, and in the pit of my stomach I am guilty. Am I needlessly unraveling thread, as he accuses Gates of doing? Should I keep my doubts to myself? But if I had, I would not have been led here. And if I were only ministering to myself, I also would not have been led here.

Karenga, too, seems to have been reviewing the puzzle-box questions of I and We, of I and Me, Me and We. He sighs. "Black indignity and indivisibility," he says. "They're inviolate, inseparable." He chuckles ruefully. "When you hear a gangsta rapper denigrating the ho's, that's you. He doesn't say, 'Everybody's a ho' except Lakisha.'"

Mad, Mad, Mad World

I'm depressed because I can't merely be mad, and my anger therefore wanders around aimlessly in a kind of emotional cul-de-sac. If you're black and mad, you are never assumed to be merely black and mad: you are in the throes of Black Rage. However inalienable a right this rage is, it is viewed as fearsome, tedious, wearying, an impediment to progress. I claim black rage, but I hardly exploit it in the way people like to think it is routinely exploited by, say, Al Sharpton. That presumption is why people around me back up when I glare at a mall cashier who's telling me my credit card's been denied. No matter that I'm really only concerned about my checkered financial past; at bottom it must be black rage that's turning my face into a hurricane threat. In fact, I don't often know which parts of my anger are which—am I mad at Visa, at the humiliation of it all, at yet another instance of being denied? Sometimes I don't even try to untangle things, from which I get a grim sort of satisfaction in being the unruly Negro the world figures we all carry around with us like an inner child, the one that makes its appearance sooner or later and trumps everything—reason, job, straightening combs, everything.

The Truth Will Set You Free, Or Kill You

Admission of depression is certainly liberating, but its consequences are proving deadly: black suicide rates are soaring, particularly among the young. According to the Centers for Disease Control and Prevention in Atlanta, the suicide rate among blacks between ten and nineteen years old more than doubled between 1980 and 1995, and for males between fifteen and nineteen, the rate increased an astounding 146 percent. Unlike whites and Latinos, whose suicide victims tend to be poor and disadvantaged, black victims tend to be equally distributed across the economic spectrum. Carl Bell, a psychiatrist at the Community Mental Health Council in Chicago, believes this points to unique psychological pressures borne, but hardly acknowledged, by the black middle class. "Many blacks no longer accept you, and whites don't want you either," he said in a recent *Essence* interview. "As for young black men, society definitely doesn't have any place for them—except prison." Stephen Thomas, director of the Institute for Minority Health Research at Atlanta's Emory University School of Public Health, says suicide among the privileged class and homicide in the ghetto may be two singular expressions of the same kind of despair. "The kid who walks out of the house with a semiautomatic gun and confronts another kid armed with a weapon—we don't call that suicide," he said in *Essence*. "But it's self-destructive behavior that has a place in the same debate."

I Remember David

Self-knowledge is assumed to provide us with those moments of pure, unalloyed happiness that are rare but, like love, terribly potent and necessary in any life. But what if the self is always at odds with its environs, if it turns and turns but finds no berth or welcoming place? Then it becomes a kind of antimatter that may spontaneously combust or collapse into itself like a black hole. I think David died like that. He died no place, on the side of a freeway, and no one was saying how he got there.

We grew up together on a generously tree-shaded block in South L.A. in the late '60s, and David was my best friend. He wasn't supposed to be; for one thing, he was a boy, and for another, he was an oddity among those boys in our surrounding blocks who learned fast and early the art of cool. They knew how to stick blades of grass in their teeth and look both languid and menacing, how to do a slow, foot-dragging rooster strut even if they were late for school or their mothers were standing out on porches strenuously calling them in to dinner. David didn't play himself like that, because he didn't seem to care, and didn't know how anyway. He liked to pretend and play make-believe, to assume various superhero identities and make up games and rules and puzzle through all these things aloud. As we grew up and parted company with childhood and its exigencies of imagination, he drifted into drug use and never quite found his way out. He had no idea where to put himself as an adult, certainly not in the scheme of black male adulthood. I think he jumped, from an overpass or a car, or he got loaded and let things take their course. Or maybe, as his family theorized, he was done in by one of the seizures that plagued him in the final years of his life. Nobody raised the specter of suicide at the funeral—few things are more anathematizing to the core black belief of hope and betterment—but we all moved about the chapel weighted with the sadness that David bore, that of a soul that knew itself early on but left life unlived, by the side of the road. Several years before he died, I wrote a story about my old block and wanted to talk to David, but he refused me an interview. He didn't want to talk about what hadn't happened, what he was not. He sent an adamant message through my brother: I don't want to see her. I've done nothing with myself, she can find a better example of what shines, of who matters . . . He was wrong.

The Entertainer

I started playing piano again after years of languishing, and though I read sheet music like one blind, I still gravitated toward what had vexed and enthralled me most: Scott Joplin. His ebullient ragtime described America around the turn of the century and foreshadowed other music genres that would describe it: jazz, R&B, rap. It was also the tragic beginning of the American practice of appropriating black culture and ignoring black *people* as personally and culturally unworthy. Joplin fought this, and lost. He dreamed of completing operas, crafted rags in the spirit of classical waltzes and rondos and quadrilles, and got nods—bare nods—for writing black barrelhouse, whorehouse, cakewalk piano rolls. His syncopations were genius, and exactly what exiled him: the sociopolitical metaphor of black rhythms laboring to break free of, and enhance, and conform to—all at once!—an unbending 2/4 beat was too much for America to bear, black or white.

At the turn of the century, we all listen to black, dress black, walk black, step to the real, etc. In fact, we've all rather publicly decided that rap, hip-hop, and their a innumerable spin-offs are acceptable fun in a corporate sort of way, a way of getting dangerous without getting hurt, like Nintendo or a theme-park ride that offers a near-death experience. The book *By the Color of Our Skin* elaborates on this malady of delusion in its discussion of "virtual integration"—the idea that whites (and blacks, to a degree) see far more integration in the media than they see in reality, but believe the mediafied version because it makes them feel better about themselves and about racial progress in America. Virtual integration also dictates what gets integrated (*The Cosby Show, Fresh Prince of Bel-Air*, the WB) and what doesn't (gang activity, black suspects on the five o'clock news). Psychologically speaking, it makes perfect sense to take something feared and make it something appealing: so it is that blacks are the nation's bogeyman and also the nation's greatest entertainer.

I know now why Scott Joplin admonished musicians in his sheet music, "Do not play this piece fast. It is never right to play ragtime fast." It was a small but persistent entreaty that we all read between the lines: smell the roses, make distinctions. As I stumble over "Gladiolus Rag," "Bethena Waltz," "Solace," I am grateful that I cannot do otherwise.

Rage Redux

I never caught up with William Grier, though he's in Southern California. (His son, I discovered, is the comic actor David Alan Grier, whose career in Hollywood would be a study in the abuse and neglect of full black talent, and in any case an appropriate subject for this story.) Price Cobbs lives in San Francisco now, works primarily as a coach of business executives, has an office in a lovely part of town that feels like Larchmont Village but newer and not so hip yet, twinkly and inviting in a middle-class kind of way. He answers the door immediately. He is grayer, of course, than in his photo on the dust jacket of *Black Rage*, taken thirty-two years ago. He's dressed in the Dockers and leather sport shoes of his active but listing-toward-retirement generation. He understands perfectly what I'm trying to write about, but doesn't know what I want. On matters of black behavior and psychology, he is both clinically brusque and deeply feeling in the way his book is. He is kind to me, like family.

Cobbs agrees with the notion that, socioculturally speaking, it's still very hard for blacks to exist as individuals because our group sense is so fragmented. And this fragmentation is not well understood, or even regarded as a problem; the world at large, which in its most magnanimous mood paints blacks with the broadest of brush strokes, has increasingly little patience with our postmodern angst or the new nuances of black consciousness. "There's a sense of 'Damn, you got all those civil rights laws, of course the playing field is level now,'" says Cobbs. "We get unfavorably compared to model minorities, like Asians. The problem now is that issues are for us much broader, deeper and more diffuse. They're much harder to mobilize around than, say, 'Get out the vote.' While there's a more visible and bigger middle class, the problems are much less tangible—problems that are economic, psychological, social."

Has there been net progress? Cobbs says yes, but guardedly. At points he vigorously refutes his own examples of progress. "We're more aware of black history," he muses, "but on some level it isn't really substantive awareness. It's put on, trivial, commercialized by Black History Month . . . But I think that whatever our degree of pessimism, we're still optimistic about how things could change." That optimism has also undone and undermined us, by glossing over where it should illuminate with the light of truth. "It's most important now to know where we are, but we use these PR campaigns in real attempts to negate what's going on," Cobbs says, animated but fuming now. "When we first saw black people in ads back in the '60s, we thought, 'Great! This is cool!' But later we thought, 'Wait a minute, this is bullshit.'"

Speaking of which, Cobbs believes that we are deep in an age when things are not what they seem, as well as an age of comfortable, and comforting, denial. When it first found public voice, black rage seemed like a clear, straightforward, albeit taboo concept; in the new century it is still as potent, but expressed so differently that people are willing to assume it has percolated down to nothing. Cobbs says nothing could be further from the truth. "One of the reasons we wrote *Black Rage* was this notion we had that seemed to make sense: the angriest black person is the one most deprived," he says. "But we found out that the angriest black people were those working at a major liberal metropolitan paper, or the suburban schoolteacher. They had no way to talk about the rage, to feel it. They had no context. I've seen people in corporations who are there to represent blacks, but they have as many hang-ups and self-image problems as any black person out there. What to do?" Cobbs wishes he knew—he, after all, *should* know. His coaching job has called for him to convince black executive types that they belong, that they have as much of a stake in their outfit as anyone else. "I'm supposed to help them see that they could be everything they wanted to be," he says, half wistfully, half caustically. "But I talked to them individually and realized they had risen as high as they could go, and now it was, 'Now what?'" What to do, indeed.

Another conundrum that has worsened considerably, perhaps fatally, since the '60s is that of authentication. In another modern-day complication of double consciousness, blacks—especially middle-class blacks—devote so much energy to squaring themselves with an authentic black mode that they find little time and space for individuality. Cobbs says that mode defines being black as "deprived in terms of housing, economics, jobs, money." Black is still the culture of have-nots. If someone has all these things, then they are not black, and they are lost. That's very difficult.

"I can't tell you," he goes on, a bit mistily, "how wonderful it was to hear in a meeting, years ago, 'Black is beautiful.' You could hear a pin drop. The ledge that we stood on had been broadened. But once it was broadened, the question was, 'Well, who's black enough and who isn't?' Rather than giving us more room, it gave us less room on the ledge. The *Washington*

Post ran a story recently that wondered aloud if the new mayor of D.C. was 'black' enough. The very new definition that 'expanded' us has actually narrowed us."

We've all had a hand in the narrowing—black and white, corporate tiger and street-corner rapscallion alike. Cobbs puts aside the growing vexation for a moment and focuses on me. "Do you collide with the ledge?" he asks. "Do you write about something non-black, like French cinema, and broaden the ledge? You've got to do those things. You've got to follow the beat of your own drummer. You're grounded in who you are, which means you can go off on as many tributaries as you want and it augments you; it doesn't limit you."

I am starting to feel distinctly charged with something, a mission of renaissance. Cobbs grows more agitated, his eyes brightening behind thick glasses. "You're in a process of liberation," he says. "I went through it too, as a psychiatrist. I was seen as too bourgeois, or too militant. All you need to do is be yourself." I feel in the middle of a mildly fantastic journey. I've come up north seeking the great and powerful Oz and found instead the man behind the curtain, in a nice cubbyhole of an office, with an air of fatigue and no answers but perhaps with something better, more empowering. He is seeking something in me; I've got the deliverance all wrong, and that's good. Maybe. Cobbs walks me out into the blinding sun, down the street to a deli, where we sit with coffee, soup, sandwiches. He's eager to know what's going on in L.A., the town where he grew up: Who's up and coming in leadership? What's promise look like?

What can I tell him? What can I give a back? I search my mind, knowing I don't have to, shrug elaborately. "There's nobody," I say. "Nobody I know of."

Back to the Couch

I stopped going to the therapist eventually because I couldn't afford it. I had grown rather used to the confessions, the onion-peeling, even liked the process, my induction into the whole wonderful gestalt of being listened to—for no reason! It was 180 degrees from "not" and all the tensions of opposition and authenticity. At the therapist's, I floated on a current that carried me wherever I wished. I could talk about why I overspent on shoes, why I liked solitude so intensely, why I had stuck with a lousy relationship for so long. I found I could very neatly separate these issues from those of race, and I tacitly decided to talk about the former and not the latter. I was hardly aware of this decision, it seemed so natural: race would upset the balance of this new relationship that was forming comfortably. It was forming, I reasoned somewhere deep within myself, precisely because I wasn't leading with experiences tied to color. If I invoked blackness I would become something less vulnerable and more belligerent: she wouldn't like me anymore; she would regard me less as a person and more as a political malcontent. I was enjoying the luxury of being listened to too much to risk any less listening on her part.

But that became the problem: here was a mother confessor, finally, to whom I was free to tell all but couldn't, for fear of retribution. And I was withholding perhaps the most important information of all about myself. I might as well have been a serial killer with a great secret of having buried five bodies in four counties. Yet discussing myself as a black person navigating the world—which is fundamentally what I was, what I am—felt somehow more foreboding than discussing myself as a failed pianist. My feelings about shoes felt more appropriate for these chaise-longue discussions than my feelings about race and my conflicts with loyalty and displacement, with family and a larger collective. Certainly all these things were making me more subtly crazy than the shoes or the boyfriend, and I felt increasingly guilty that I was holding back with a woman who seemed to want to know everything and would seemingly wait forever to know it. But there it was. I couldn't quite integrate myself in her presence and didn't want her to know, yet worried she would never get to the bottom of me, that she would never surmount what I couldn't surmount myself. Therapists are of course there to do what you cannot do yourself, but believe me, she needed my help on this one. And then the situation suspended itself rather abruptly when I ran out of money. I yearned to go back—depression lurked always, and partial disclosure turned out to be vastly better than none—and when my finances and insurance limits improved several months later, I did. But I went back resolved to tell all; my fiancé, to whom I had confessed this racial reticence, declared that I must make exactly the same confession to the therapist if I was going to make real breakthroughs. That's how the stuff worked. Her reaction, my fiancé said, would be critical: "Then you'll know if she's really any good or not." Really? I was distraught about putting the therapist in professional jeopardy, because I really did like her and didn't want to make her responsible for setting right what I essentially felt nobody could set right, not now. Not after New Orleans and David and realizing over and over how enormous this thing was. What could she do about it?

I did tell her. After a deep breath and a preface that I'm sure sounded like I was going to announce I had terminal cancer. She listened, as always. She nodded gravely, as always. She put an index finger to her lips. Then, for the first time in the year or so since we'd met, she spoke about herself—to let me know that, all along, she recognized the whole of my self, at its most certain and most chimerical, even if I couldn't. "Did I ever tell you," she said, "that I'm married to a black man?"

But maybe, after all, the Negro doesn't really exist. What we
think is a race is detached moods and phases of other people
walking around. What we have been talking about might
not exist at all. Could be the shade patterns of something
else thrown on the ground—other folks, seen in shadow.
God made everybody else's color. We took ours by mistake.
—ZORA NEALE HURSTON, *Dust Tracks on a Road,* 1942

In my writing, America is a recurrent character that is alternately a villain, a casual acquaintance, a frog prince, and a bully with a heart that it fears showing more than it fears anything else. A racial incident or plot development—the L.A. riots, the ebonics debate, Hurricane Katrina, the election of President Obama—always reveals America most clearly, down to its roots, and in that awful clarity I always have to decide how to proceed. Wash my hands of the country? Give it another shot? These feel like serious choices. The pieces in this section describe those emotional crossroads, how and why I, and we, arrive at them again and again.

BARACK OBAMA

MILES TRAVELED, MILES TO GO

I. 2009

It hits me most when I'm in the car. At the top of the hour, any hour, on any day of the week in the wake of January twentieth, the newscast leads with a report of President Obama. What he said or did, what he's thinking, or what issues he's grappling with in the near future. I stare at the dashboard: President Obama! *Who?* I almost laugh in astonishment. I thrill with a feeling, too rich and heady to contain in the small space of my Chrysler, at having gotten away with something I had no right to get away with; it feels like getting a shot of pure oxygen when you've been breathing bad air so long, the good stuff almost kills you. I would die happy breathing this, so happy it wouldn't feel like death but a kind of effortless transcendence that religion always promises but that reality has slyly delivered ahead of it. I'd be damned happy to be dead. Maybe I am.

Who in the hell would have thought? Who would have thought at all that they'd be here for *this?* President Obama. I sigh big, adjust my grip on the wheel, shake my head to clear it. But I'm eager for it to fill up again. Eager to contemplate, again, how Barack was close to me forty years ago in ways that I couldn't have imagined until today. Yes, he was there all along. But for a quirk of geography (I was in L.A.; he was five hours across the water in Hawaii), he could have been in third grade with me, one smart, unbottled black boy among many in the very early '70s, one of relatively few boys who succeeded, one of even fewer who made it big. But never mind—in the beginning, Barack Obama was Gerald, was Gabriel, was Dwayne, was Stephen, Joe, David, Kevin, Patrick, and Derrick. They were all there, and all equally possible. Wherever they are now, I hope they burn with the old sense of open road as much as I do when the realization of *President Obama* lands on me in the middle of traffic, as it does routinely. I almost have to brake from the impact. It makes me remember. It is glorious.

And then it passes. The newscast segues into a talk show or a song, and then I'm simply in the car, driving. I'm going along a boulevard toward home, a largely black neighborhood on the outskirts of South Central. Almost against my will, I look at what I'm returning to. I reluctantly take stock of the red graffiti that cuts across pale brick walls like flesh wounds, idle storefronts, young black men congregated around the open door of a tattoo shop like it's a church hall. The distance between all of this and Barack and the new way he's supposed to be showing us is frustrating, crazy-making. Does no one see? In all the praise, and even in the doubt of Barack, there has been almost no acknowledgement of this whole black netherworld of grinding sameness, non-movement, hope gone slack. It's a world that belongs to all black people, wherever they end up, and to the rest of America, this world of weak schooling and even weaker job prospects and prison stints that have threatened black people always; this generation is no different. The burden and blame for this state of affairs is all of ours. This is what we are loath to admit, to see, that Barack is extraordinary, but he is not our difference. Not yet. For black people so hungry for victory, the most I can say is that Barack is certainly *of* us, a shining example of us, but he is not all of us. The strange truth is that we secured a black president before we secured justice for the vast majority of black people; of course, nobody thought things would happen in this order, but they have, and now we are groping for the way forward. Some say that there is no more need for a way forward, that a particularly murky chapter of black struggle has finally come to an end. What struggle is that? The struggle to become president? There was never any such thing. In the scheme of things that had to be done, it wasn't important.

There are reasons for that. I count those reasons in my last mile home: grown men half-heartedly selling chocolate bars out of boxes on street medians, tough boys mincing along like geishas in pants with waists pulled low, girls indifferent to each. None of them have what Barack and I had—an absolute belief in possibility and, consequently, in ourselves. We never divested ourselves of that belief, it never left us, whether we left the communities we grew up in or whether we stayed. I'm still here. I am not the difference, either. I would like to be. I would like President Barack Obama to make my difference possible. In those moments in the car when the radio seizes me and I'm wonder-struck for thirty seconds out of the day, it doesn't seem like much to ask for at all.

II. 2010

Obama is shrinking. It started happening the moment he took office, when he officially crossed over from the airy magic of the possible to the dirty, deoxy-

genated, thoroughly racialized workaday grind of American politics; all those
new white converts started falling away from him like party confetti falling
to earth. In the harsh light of the morning after, Obama looked suddenly out
of place. It was obvious. The natty suits and close-cropped hair, the practiced
thoughtfulness, the measured rise and fall of his voice meant to give shape to
the vague chaos of two wars in the Middle East and the much clearer chaos of
a failing economy, the way he lifted his chin during public addresses and press
conferences as if trying to literally put himself above it all—all the things that
had stirred people's imagination became, on the other side of the inaugural,
targets for doubt and derision. It's all been exhausting to watch. Of course,
there was no way for a black man to look in place as a president, because
there had never been one before. I expected that. But I also expected the nov-
elty to wear off fairly quickly and for "Obama" to become synonymous with
"president." It had happened for everyone else who'd held the office in my
lifetime, even for the short-lived and unremarkable presidents like Ford and
Bush II: like them or despair about them, Americans accepted them as their
leaders. The acceptance starts with the title "President," but it goes much
deeper than that. An agreed-upon sense of collective investment in the person
in charge is what makes a nation—to say nothing of a democracy—possible.

But what's happened, and not happened, in the very brief era of Obama
is unprecedented and unsettling. In some ways he is still not really president.
Rather than fusing, the words "president" and "Obama" have only become
more estranged over the last year and a half as it's become increasingly clear
that that the *idea* of President Obama is more powerful and persuasive than
Obama the man could ever be. There's no comparison between the two, and
likely never was. It's true that a campaigning politician is a much more romantic figure than that same politician after he's elected; it's also true that
almost nobody expects that politician, especially one gaining an office for
the first time, to fully measure up to the pre-election magic. But Obama is a
marked exception to this. Eighteen months on, it turns out that people not
only wanted him to measure up to the magic, they wanted him to improve
on it—in retrospect, the much-analyzed "hope and change" campaign was
taken by the public as a reasonable starting point, not as the usual overreaching that new presidents are allowed to adjust downward, to a certain degree.
Obama's goldenness wasn't supposed to tarnish even a little; it was supposed
to spin itself into platinum. In a country that's been worshipping at the altar
of individualism for the last forty years, Obama's political fortune was widely
viewed more as a privilege given to him by a generous (and anxious) public

than a right made possible by his innate qualities. Even among his supporters, the attitude was therefore: he owes us. Starting *now.*

High expectations are fine, necessary, especially in bad times. But they often mask resentment or a fatal skepticism, and this is the wall—the barely concealed flip side of hope and change—that the post-candidate Obama ran into. The wall is that much more formidable for anyone or anything that challenges the racial status quo, and Obama does that simply by being black. He was always a paradox: the man whose ascension to the presidency was either going to resolve or resurrect for a new century the whole matter of racial justice. As a country, we much prefer resolution. We like events that dramatize racial resolution in memorable ways—for example, the 1954 *Brown v. Board of Education* u.s. Supreme Court decision. We think of this as one of the finest hours in our judicial history, a sweeping application of hope and change that finally retired the era of Jim Crow. But that decision was a comma, not a period. What we never talk about is the fact that after 1954 public schools across the country desegregated very slowly, and integration in many ways never happened at all. Brown precipitated a big shift, all right, but it was a shift away from the spirit of the ruling, not toward it. Whites fled public schools before desegregation had time to take root as a new reality; conditioned by years of black fear and loathing, they refused to submit to what they saw as a radical experiment, and so deserted their own places and even their own self-interest rather than allow the experiment any real margin of error. The same thing has happened with the first black president. From the beginning of his time in office, Obama's declining poll numbers have shown that non-black voters are simply not willing to grant him any margin of error. Of course, that stinginess is partly due to circumstances: Obama arrived with more major national and international crises to fix or deflect than any other president in history. He was expected to quell rising anxiety from all quarters—Democrat, Republican, liberal, progressive, conservative, pacifist, hawkish—about the ultimate fate of a country that everybody wants to believe has unlimited capacity to heal, recover, and progress. The expectation that Obama, or anyone, could right this long-foundering ship in a year's time, or four or even eight years' time, is absurd.

But the other part of the public's unforgiving attitude is tied to ancient reservations about color. In the real world, blacks in charge are given little room to fail, even less room to be mediocre; the sanctioned margin of error for leaders is tiny, and for black men it's nonexistent. People of color are not really people in these situations, but symbols—question marks representing whether the race has the right stuff or not. President Obama in the White House, the seat of American power, is that symbol writ about as large as possible: he is a president operating constantly under the hot lights of both celebrity and racial scrutiny. It's a burden he was bound to carry. But being a symbol has also dehumanized and diminished him, even among his admirers. This is not a new dynamic, or a new effect. We're all guilty of dehumanizing black people, even in good times; we distance ourselves from their complex reality by seeing them first as constructs and symbols described by the hopes, fears, and fetishes we project onto them. Dictating who blacks are and what they should be allows whites to retain their cultural supremacy and to contain their eternal fear of blacks as the ultimate other, likeable, maybe, but unknown and unknowable. Those blacks who don't fit the preferred construct—welfare queen, hip-hop thug, college grad, post-racial redeemer—are marginalized or ignored. It's all part of a psychological and spiritual inequality that has always defined race relations and that black people continually struggle against, whether they're a prisoner on death row or president in the White House. And the higher they rise in modern times, the closer they come to white folks and the greater their struggle—and the less they seem able to fight.

I watch Obama battle his own symbolism on a daily basis, watch him trying as artfully as possible to counter the notion that he's either a hero or hedonist (post-election, it's mostly hedonist) that people infinitely prefer to flesh and blood. It's interesting to compare this treatment to that of Obama's predecessor, George W. Bush. For eight years Bush, despite being widely despised, was granted plenty of latitude, shades of gray, and even forgiveness by media and by the voters, including those he made steadily worse off with his policies. Why? Bush was familiar. Maybe he was an idiot, but to many voters he was *their* idiot, the underachieving fuck-up that everybody knew in school and could relate to as such, even if they didn't invite him to parties. The bottom line is Bush was a recognizable entity to a majority of Americans; Obama is not. People don't talk about Obama's personal quirks or life philosophy or vulnerabilities, nor do they seem interested. A deep identification between voters and the person in charge is the real power in politics, and Obama doesn't have it by virtue of his color. This doesn't mean he doesn't have admirers. Lots of Americans were suitably impressed and even moved by his bootstraps success story and how he came to terms with his own racial history, but few people have lived that story. Others were moved by his charisma and exotica (a black American man without the freighted black

American name of Johnson or Jackson), and on that basis alone gave him a chance. But—would they have had a beer with him? Could he have lived in their neighborhood with ten other families that looked like his? Those whites who hated Bush as president likely wouldn't have objected to him living in their midst.

Obama is not Bush, and that was, and in some way remains, as much of an obstacle as it was a political advantage in 2008. Yes, against immeasurable odds and against the lessons of our own history, he did become president, and I suppose we can be proud of that. But we have misread the depth and nature of our act. America hired Obama; it didn't take him to its heart or invite him into where it lives. We feel about him pretty much what we feel about other black people in workplaces where they are scarce or, as in Obama's case, where they are the pioneering First One—we give them a chance, applaud ourselves for our vision and generosity, and then settle quickly into watching them for missteps. It's a schizophrenic attitude: we are encouraged by the black person's potential enough to give him a job, but are ever wary of giving him power. This is why as soon as Obama stepped into the White House, he had to be punished. Whites are used to controlling black opportunity, to giving and taking it as they see fit. President Obama in that way was never president-in-waiting, he was an opportunity—the bright and capable intern who deserved a shot. But being in charge was not part of the deal.

It seems ridiculous to have to keep asserting this, but Obama's election did not put the finishing touches on racial justice. America hasn't achieved nearly enough racial justice to even think in such terms. What Obama and the new century have really given us is a third run at Reconstruction (the second being the civil rights era of the 1950s and 1960s.) But this one is going sour much more quickly, in part because news cycles and event cycles move much more quickly. But it's going sour also because a black man assuming national and international power at a moment of such great national fear and uncertainty is proving to be a noxious mix. Fear and uncertainty have moved steadily from the margins to become full-time occupations, and discrediting President Barack Hussein Obama has become so common a practice, it's a whole new discipline unto itself, complete with on-the-job training and benefits. Critics are quick to say they're not just unhappy with Obama, they're unhappy with the whole federal government he represents. But in the minds of too many, Obama and the sins and excesses of government are inseparable; in fact, they're the same thing. We've all been trained to see the fed as the main helpmeet of undeserving blacks, so a black man actually heading the whole government is, for conservatives and lots of others who lean that way, a nightmarish conflation of race and politics (for those somewhat less conservative, including Democrats, it may not be a nightmare; but it is at the very least unappetizing food for thought). Obama's smallest move to help or empathize with the needy is openly challenged as a liberal impulse, but subliminally, and more importantly, it's challenged as a *black* liberal impulse, which we all understand is the most unrestrained kind.

In this new era of Reconstruction, the reinvigoration of a states'-rights, anti-central-government movement has found expression in the so-called Tea Party, which is not the Klan of old but has quite comfortably harbored elements of it. This being the twenty-first century, everybody denies being racist—the label is hopelessly old-fashioned in the high-tech age of Twitter and Facebook. But how else to explain the pettiness and distortions that have characterized so much anti-Obama-ism? Hysteria about Big Government is one thing; that goes back centuries and rises and falls on a historical continuum. But there has been equal hysteria about manufactured, race-driven controversies about Obama's American citizenship, his shadowy Muslim-ism and sufficient lack of Christian faith, his emotional opaqueness (betraying the preferred stereotype that blacks should be cool on the surface, but volcanic underneath), his mother-in-law moving into the White House, his daughters' hairstyles, his wife's gall in taking a European vacation. The political opposition that I knew would be fierce has been beyond reason. Calling the modest steps Obama has taken toward health-care reform socialism, fascism, and the end of America as we know it was so absurd I have to assume that what really offended people was not the reform at all, which we didn't actually get, but the fact Obama carried it out against the wishes of those who didn't approve of his hiring. This is why the fight against "Obamacare," etc. dug in deeper by the week and was animated by such fury: he had broken the rules of black opportunity. He is that worst of all things, an arrogant black man. Protesters didn't quite feel free to say that, but they did the next best thing by waving signs that depicted Obama as dastardly figures such as Hitler, Osama bin Laden, the bloody-mouthed Joker from the "Batman" movie. One irony among many is how the epic fight against health-care reform played out so personally against Obama, when it was really all about what he symbolizes. Media painted the fight as a segment of the American people against one man, but it wasn't. It was the opposite, or something more complicated than that—the American people against their better angels.

This is painful to say, but none of the racial oppressiveness excuses what

Obama is doing wrong as president, or not doing enough of. Call me naïve, but I expected more of him (did I have a choice?). Yes, he came to office a career centrist Democrat, but it's disappointing to see that his presidency has not yet unleashed or substantially encouraged a progressive side many of us thought we had glimpsed beneath the mask of racial accommodation. (Certainly I thought the progressivism was there, was sure I had seen it when Obama visited Los Angeles way back in 2006. He came to a park in the core black neighborhood of Crenshaw; I drove down there to pick up some bath towels at a store near the park and to see what all the fuss was about. By the end of the rally, listening to Obama rail easily against the injustice of too many people of color being in prison, I nearly swooned. He made his points with his suit jacket off, chin up, white business shirt rolled up at the cuffs and gleaming in the sun. As far as I know, he never made them again.) He has shown himself to be more manager than leader, more married to the status quo than his rhetoric had us believe. He even expanded on the status quo in unnerving, Bush-like ways: bailing out giant corporate miscreants with taxpayer money, casting the disastrous war in Afghanistan as a moral under-taking the same way Bush cast the invasion of Iraq. And there is Obama's failure of nerve in taking and holding a position on smaller but still significant issues—racial profiling, equal treatment of Muslims. Too often he's taken the right stance and then, after some hasty temperature-taking of public opinion, backslid into a compromised space that ultimately gets him nothing. He is not able to trust own assessment of things, and that undermines him most of all. Obama doesn't seem to know how far he can or should go, what he can get away with; it's as if he is testing various facets of himself to see which will work best in the uncharted territory of being a black president. But this kind of tinkering is disastrous. It doesn't achieve change. It was obvious from the beginning that certain folks would hate him for whatever he did—so why does he not lead and make a difference? I don't think Obama would mind making a difference. But I'm not at all sure that he wants to make a difference more than he wants to secure a legacy at the table of American power. The best scenario I can concoct at this point is that he wants to do both, fulfilling an old black-empowerment adage that you can do well for yourself and do good at the same time. But Obama doesn't seem to understand, or he refuses to accept, that doing well for himself and doing good for the people isn't possible in the divisive, disillusioned, almost radioactive climate in which he became president. It may never be possible.

One more thing: What about black people? What about us? Obama may turn out to be the strangest bit of black history we've ever had. He is without a doubt the most spectacular example of black achievement to date, but his impact on the distressed state of black people in the twenty-first century will be almost nil. That's disorienting, a giant vacuum of a fact that no black person dares to go near lest he or she get sucked into a void of disappointment we have not known before—and we have known disappointment. Since the ecstasy of the inauguration has faded, black people seem to have no idea how to feel about Obama. Our votes helped carry him to the promised land, but now he is gone from us, or we have let him go. We are listless and depressed, left to wonder: Is Obama proof that the system works, or evidence that it has outfoxed black people yet again? Is the joke on us? I realize that, since the inauguration, I have not talked very extensively about Obama with other black people. There seems to be not much to say. He is not in our running conversations in the way that Martin Luther King or Jackie Robinson or even Malcolm X was; we recognized those lives and those fates as our own. Obama's life in many ways is *his* own. His presidential run was a singular vision, a challenge he set for himself, not an outgrowth of black discontent or an affirmation of black resolve. Such is the individualism we are privy to now—selfhood that Martin and Malcolm could have hardly imagined.

Obama may not be a reflection of us. But he *is* us. He knows we're here, just beyond his presidential reach. He signifies it constantly with that stern, preacherly stance, with rhetoric that lingers in sing-song when he wants to make a point, with eyes that habitually rove over an audience while he talks—seeking out a witness—with the way he consciously clasps hands together or folds arms across himself when he's exasperated with white folks but can't show it. That is surely us. We have all stood where he stands now. But as president, Obama stands in another country. At this point, black folk can only observe him from miles away and wish him the best and hope that whatever good he does, we will benefit too: we pray that where he goes, we will be able to follow. This laissez-faire wishfulness is so far the extent of our hope, and it isn't much. It ought to be more, much more. We thought our store of hope would get a fresh infusion from Obama's triumph, but instead it has rendered us oddly helpless, more at a loss than before because deliverance looks tantalizingly near. Obama has come at a cost. He has achieved a great height that required that he officially separate himself (if he hadn't done it already) from the daily cares and concerns of other black people, as though shrugging off unnecessary weight as he moved further up a mountain. Will-ingly or not, he's done that. What do the rest of us black folk do now do with our strangely resilient faith in the American system and its promises of equal consideration? Even the most cynical among us have never known how *not* to believe.

The anemic state of black hope, briefly resuscitated by the events of 2008, has been years in the making. Hope has decreased in direct proportion to the growth of our middle and educated classes and the occasionally spectacular success of one of our members. Between the '60s and now we convinced ourselves that we don't need it anymore, that collective black energy and self-interest eventually had to go the way of hippie communes. We've grown to accept as a price for being comfortable the stigma of empathizing with other, less fortunate black people who are not. Obama understands that stigma, and though he may not agree with it, he abides by it. He is not a black politician because he cannot be. Though even if he were, black people would still expect him to do little for us, so accustomed have we grown to black elected leader-ship giving us platitudes and performance, but not leadership. Like tolerance built up in the blood over many years to certain viruses, we have developed a great tolerance and even affection for all the brave talk about the primacy of community; we are used to our politicians sounding radical on our block and then blunting the message in another part of town because, we're told, that's how the game is played, that's how we can get over. Except that com-promise and selective brave talk have never gotten us over. Our needs are not only not taken seriously by our own, they're not *taken*. We have seen this so regularly in the last fifty years, in the long, sustained golden age of black representation, it's hard to feel any outrage now about what Obama is not doing for us. We have long understood, even if we don't officially accept it, that self-suppression and abandonment are key and unquestioned ingredients of modern black success, like literacy in the home and algebra before eighth grade. So of course blacks don't really talk about Obama or keep close tabs. But even at a distance, it's hard to watch a black man in charge handling his own people and his own history with rubber gloves like it's all one big infec-tion, some kind of hazardous waste that has to be detoxified with words and declarations before it can be buried underground in concrete. Obama is not the first to do it, but he's become the most skilled at appealing to blacks at certain moments while simultaneously keeping them at arm's length, reaching out but not daring to risk an embrace of any kind. For Obama to be "outed" as a black sympathizer would be in a way worse than being outed as a gay man or as a Muslim. Being perceived as truly black would mean defeat, pure and simple. So, once again, we have lost.

In the summer of 2010, the *Los Angeles Times* described Obama as a kind of Velcro president when it came to race—despite his attempts to treat it like any other issue on the table, racial questions (starting with his own genetic makeup) and controversies were sticking to him like flies to flypaper. When he did say something, it was invariably characterized as radical or inappropriate, and he and his administration overcorrected to an almost embarrassing degree—hastily modifying a remark Obama made about a cop who arrested a well-known black scholar in his own home, preemptively firing a black government bureaucrat who had allegedly said bigoted things about white folks (she hadn't). What's really been happening is that Obama is still trying to climb out from under the shadow of Jeremiah Wright, his former pastor and black activist who stirred the wrath of the anti-Obama critics early on. Obama quelled racial fears enough to be elected, but he is still tarred him with the sin of Wright, who he can't shake as a doppelganger even though whites applauded candidate Obama's eloquent 2008 disquisition that was meant to pit racial reason and circumspection against Wright's narrow-minded racial madness. That speech was almost for naught. As president, the new neo-cons, led by sportscaster-turned-anti-Reconstructionist Glenn Beck, lost no time in calling Obama a racist who hates white people and possibly white "culture"; Tea Partyers felt free to call him every bad name—fascist, socialist, Hitler, Joker, Muslim/non-American terrorist—except nigger. But that is often what they meant. They meant a misbehaving, thieving, silver-tongued trickster nigger, a modern-day Br'er Rabbit trying to best the farmer while appearing to be his friend. So obsessed are the neo-cons with the idea of this deception, racial fury is building in the country as swiftly as funnel clouds, though the media tends not to remark on it. At a rally held in New York City to protest Attorney General Eric Holder's proposal to try terrorist detainees in criminal court, rather than detain them indefinitely in Guantanamo Bay, one of the more agitated protesters at the rally suggested that Holder, a black man, be lynched. I read about this terrorist threat in the leftish but evenhanded *New Yorker* magazine. Though it shocked me, the story didn't remark on it; it was simply presented as one detail among many in the fight to try, or not to try, Muslims detained for terrorism. I didn't read about the lynching remark anywhere else.

But my apprehension isn't just about would-be lynchers or Tea Partyers or devotees of Glenn Beck. It's also about plain Americans, even liberals—

especially liberals—who help to corrupt the legitimacy of a President Obama with their silence and indifference. I'm sure they don't see themselves as racist and probably consider the very word distasteful. But they feel no compulsion to speak out against the racial hostility and resistance that Obama attracts. That lack of compulsion is most glaring in the president's fellow Democrats, who talk plenty about unity and respect, but who are leery of even raising the vote-losing idea that some of their constituents might be racially unenlightened. And while Obama has lots of hard-working hires in his administration, none effectively represent him; no one feels like his proxy. George Bush had Cheney, Rumsfeld, and Carl Rove, but Obama has no one. Every bad moment sticks to him because there's really nothing and no one between him and all the inclement political weather out there, no barrier islands to break the hurricanes. Obama has been to the mountaintop, and it is raining. It's been raining there a long time. James Baldwin said as much forty years ago when he responded to Robert Kennedy's suggestion that someone like Baldwin might be elected president one day: "What really exercises my mind is not this hypothetical day on which some other Negro 'first' will become the first Negro president," said Baldwin. "What I am really curious about is just what kind of country will he be president of?"

Still: I'm furious Obama can't represent me in the way I wanted him to, expected him to. Who else *but* him? He is me, as well as David and Joe and the rest of us who were solemnly handed off the dream in the '60s and '70s; we took it without much idea of what to do with it, but now—well, now we have the most high-profile black American leader in history, more watched and studied than Martin Luther King, and I am not a priority? It's an abomination. And yet I understand, we understand. Black people understand without wanting to or agreeing to. We close one eye, shift Obama away from the raging center of things, and we instantly see what kind of cul-de-sac he's stuck in. Anybody black with any kind of ambition has been stuck like that, boxed in, arm twisted up behind the back. For all my reservations about Obama the president, my heart can't help but go out to Obama the man on this one; he tries so hard to duck under the razor wire of prejudice and difference, but he keeps getting cut. None of his maneuvers matter. He stands up straight and holds his head high, does all those things we were told to do when we were kids, back when the 1960s lit the torch and we were its flames finally being blown upward by a new breath of freedom and self-determination; all that unequivocal *Hell yes, we can!* was our new half-patriotic, half-defiant pledge of allegiance. But we look back and see that a lot of that was just brave talk;

Yes, we can was fine for us, but it didn't have a lot of takers in the real world. Many of us in Obama's generation and generations after remain in the stuffy ether of potential, convinced that we might still set the world ablaze with a new consciousness and finally purify it of its sins, set it in a new direction. We are still waiting.

But of course it will take time. Black folks will give Obama time; we are used to things taking indefinable amounts of time, to seeing time as almost biblical when it comes to improvement for us. Meanwhile, we content ourselves with the fact that Obama is our brother—not in the details of his personal narrative or even his philosophy, maybe, but in the historical, quasi-biblical black struggle for acceptance and true equality that other Americans expected Obama to put to rest. He has not, and we're glad of that. Of course we don't want him to fail—or, God forbid, to be mediocre. But I am nonetheless relieved that his incomplete story, and ours, are joined together.

One of the more memorable discussions about the logistics of black American success happens in a scene that comes late in the Michael Mann movie *Ali*. As the Champ, played by Will Smith, prepares for the famous Rumble in the Jungle in Zaire, he argues with his wife about his friendship with boxing promoter and hustler extraordinaire Don King. His wife snaps that King doesn't give a shit about Africa and black empowerment, that he's a capitalist who "talks black, lives white, and cares about green." Ali doesn't deny this, but he defends King by saying that in order to accomplish what he, Ali, wants to accomplish, he's got to use everybody who's willing to go along with some piece of his vision, "honkies and bad-ass niggers, too." That reminded me of Obama's multicultural approach to his campaign; he learned early that the South Side of Chicago, or the east side of Oakland or the central part of L.A., could never get it done alone. He had to enlist anybody who would go along with some piece of his vision. This is what initially filled me, the idea that Obama could point all these anybodies in a single direction, get them to actually follow him and people like him—David and Joe and Derrick—instead of fearing their intentions or freezing them in a construct that forever puts them at the margin of things. The rub was Obama's goal in bringing us all together. Ali's larger goal in Zaire was clear: to bring some uniquely American uplift to a country and a continent that that was struggling to stand on new legs of post-colonial freedom. I'm not sure what Obama's goal was. I'm still not. What I do know is that the time in which he came to power does not belong to black folks; the moment is not ours. Nor can President Obama, a presence that is flawed but still intoxicating, make it ours. *We* have to do that. He is not the best we have, though he is the highest, but even from that lofty height he has made it clear that we have much more climbing to do before we finally get over.

LOSING NEW ORLEANS

August 2006

I never knew how much I needed New Orleans until it was gone. "Gone" is too dramatic a word to describe what Hurricane Katrina did to the city, I know. It is still on the map. The French Quarter keeps regular hours. But emptied of half its people, dark and paralyzed and trash-strewn on streets where houses are moldy husks and dead bodies are likely still unexcavated, it is severely and permanently diminished, like a person who's suffered a major stroke. There may be rehab, and it may even be successful. But the city's speech, the thought process, the unbridled attitude, the life force that emanated from the grass roots up that gave New Orleans its character and connected it to a grand and troubled Southern history that it increasingly didn't want to face—that has changed. That consciousness that was as big a part of New Orleans as po' boys and Mardi Gras has been desiccated, blown away like the fearsome floodwater debris that dried up in the post-Katrina sun and was eventually reduced to dust. The focus has rightfully been on the black poor, but make no mistake: everybody displaced by Katrina has gotten poorer. We've all lost, and not just those in Louisiana, but all of us who held it close as an emotional and familial touchstone in a country where black demographics have been shifting rapidly under our feet for years now. Once a place where its majority black natives mostly stayed put, New Orleans is now a place of very unlikely return. It will never be the same.

This has terrible consequences for me. I am not from New Orleans. I'm from Los Angeles, a city as undefined and as untraditional as New Orleans was circumscribed and steeped in the vinegar of history. But I always claimed New Orleans. Both sides of my family, from my parents' generation back, hail from the 7th Ward, for generations the most intensely Creole part of town. Most of them migrated west between the 1930s and '50s, lured out of the South by prospects of better jobs, better weather, and the absence—well, the smallest presence possible—of Jim Crow-based segregation. But though they were eager to free themselves from New Orleans, they also brought it west. With typical immigrant gusto, they remade a good bit of L.A. into a lively if somewhat deconstructed Creole enclave spread out over blocks, at points over city limits. And it was this that I grew up with and assumed as my past, not the past of Los Angeles, which is almost impossible to visualize and makes no impression on people anyway. "I'm from L.A.—but my family is from New Orleans," I always say to someone I'm meeting for the first time. "I have people there." Their eyes invariably light up in recognition—ah, New Orleans. It explains everything.

It still does. Most critically, it explains me to myself. But in its crippled state, and with all the friends and relatives I used to visit and still hoped to meet now dead or driven out—including a cousin, Helen, the oldest living relative on my mother's side who perished in a nursing home that sat power-less for five days in the hellish post-Katrina heat—New Orleans is already different. I felt the difference immediately here on the West Coast, where I had to admit that L.A. is at best a spirited approximation of New Orleans, but it has never been its equal. I had never been to Mardi Gras in New Orleans because I felt I never felt the need to—after all, L.A. has the largest population of Creoles outside of New Orleans itself, a distinction the Creole population claims among the many immigrant groups that comprise the city. Americans in Boston don't travel to Dublin to celebrate St. Patrick's Day because there's long been enough Irishness in Boston to justify its own celebration—indeed, Boston Irish is practically an ethnic group all its own. I felt the same arrogance and assurance about Creolism and Creoles holding down Mardi Gras in L.A.; if we could not do it here, we could do it nowhere. Statistically speaking, we were safe.

We were not. I should have known. With black folks, the most promising statistics can be deceiving, even imaginary: when New Orleans fell, L.A. teetered. We realized what we had known but not said for years, that the transplanted population that had once flourished easily in enclaves like Leimert Park had long since moved on and moved out, part of the general black flight that forced central L.A. into an uncertain age that is still unfolding. The new Katrina-fueled flight intensified that uncertainty, and when it was clear that Mardi Gras in New Orleans would make no sense in '06, I assumed it would make even less sense here. What would we celebrate? What would we, should we, approximate for the mother country this time? Suddenly we had no navigating compass, no north star. The soul of New Orleans is durability and staying put—unique among big Southern cities that lost so many people to out-migrations in every other direction—but the flood unleashed by the broken levees had gravely wounded the city, not simply at its asphalt core, but at its soul. The compass was cracked, unusable. Katrina was the watery grinch that would finally cancel Christmas this year.

It wasn't canceled, though it was toned down. The New Orleans tragedy turned out to be strangely good timing for my family, which had suffered a tragedy of its own. My cousin Errol, the most faithful keeper of New Orleans traditions of the last decade, our reliable second-line parade marshal at weddings and parties and even a funeral or two, had also suffered a sudden, initially debilitating stroke—like New Orleans itself—just before the holidays. Unlike New Orleans, he made a remarkably steady recovery that was almost complete by February, Mardi Gras season. He and his wife decided to have a party at home to commemorate several things: his birthday, recovery, Mardi Gras, the fact that New Orleans hadn't been destroyed entirely (black folk are good at venerating what *hasn't* happened, at honoring whatever is left standing after the damage wrought by nature, by public policy, by white-folk anger that could surely decimate everything, but doesn't quite; hallelujah.) We were happy for the invitation, and grateful to Errol for giving us the occasion to celebrate something outright. Errol was the man for the moment: graying and slight, but a hopeful symbol of an improbably stricken New Orleans that might rise again despite the odds, as he had done. This would be not a party so much as a motivational seminar.

Despite some winter bluster and cold, the party came off. Rain drummed on the roof of a backyard tent, but the tables were dressed in shimmery purple, gold, and green. The evening was distinctly un-raucous, with the emphasis less on the usual Mardi Gras fete and drinks, and more on family and counting ranks. We talked gravely about New Orleans and didn't bother to try to articulate a strange mix of anxiety and relief we felt about being nestled deep in the affluent West San Fernando Valley, half a continent away from the swamp of New Orleans's misery—a mix that could only be described as survivor's guilt. When we gathered in the kitchen to sing "Happy Birthday" around an elaborate cake, Errol's eyes widened in a kind of wonder and, fleetingly, distress: he would normally be back home this time of year, reabsorbing his beloved New Orleans for the benefit of uninitiated kin like me. For a moment his own tragedy edged back to the surface, and he looked tired, done. Then he recovered—again. With some effort he blew out his two candles, and amid the clapping, thanked us all for coming. He urged us to have a good time, and urged us again. His few words were met with more vigorous applause that matched and then outdid the sound of the rain that still fell; Errol had beaten back something terrible, possibly fatal. He was the stroke victim who got lucky and then got tough. Not so New Orleans. Not yet.

Then there's my cousin Shirley and her husband, Ed. Shirley was among the relatively few in my mother's family who had their criticisms but who never left the complicated embrace of New Orleans and of the South. She lived for some twenty-five years in a handsome two-story brick house in New Orleans East, a big, rambling place that had plenty of room for company and visitors from out west. It's been difficult to imagine New Orleans without her and that house. When I came, she cooked—gumbo, jumbalaya—and told me stories over the dinner table that my mother, her first cousin, never had. One of the many things I asked Shirley was why she didn't follow her people out to L.A. She laughed. "Oh no, you all got earthquakes out in California," she said. There was never any L.A. to New Orleans folk, or San Francisco or San Diego: just California. I pointed out that she had to weather bad hurricanes much more frequently than I had to weather bad earthquakes. She was unmoved. "They're not bad," she said of the hurricanes. "They don't really come up in the gulf that far. When it gets to raining you stay inside and wait till it passes, that's all." In 2005, the hurricane didn't pass New Orleans without doing its best to bury it. And Shirley, who had mostly hunkered down in her house during storms for all of her seventy-one years, left this time. She and Ed evacuated first to Baton Rouge, where a hotel insisted she leave after three days, though they had nowhere else to go. They managed to get a room a Little Rock; landed next in Santa Clarita, a craggy, carefully ordered suburb of L.A. where one of her sons and his family lived. The last stop was Las Vegas. Something sealed up in Shirley in the months between fleeing waterlogged New Orleans and landing in the arid Mojave Desert; she told my mother that whatever happened, wherever she ended up living, she was never going back. Back home. New Orleans had gone cold for her, like a corpse. My mother the longtime L.A. émigré—pragmatic, almost Zen in a Catholic kind of way, detached when the occasion called for it—understood. But the New

Orleans nativist in her took it harder. "That's it for Shirley," my mother told me on the phone one morning, with a sad finality.

My mother and Shirley were close. They grew up together on and around Roman Street in the 7th Ward, for generations the most intensely Creole part of town. In 1956 my mother left to get married and settle in L.A., like her other, older relatives who had been pulling up stakes year by year. Shirley stayed. When I was growing up, I studied a sepia photo of this faraway New Orleans cousin, a somber-faced girl of about seven dressed in Sunday clothes, with hair curling to her shoulders and a deeply weary air that seemed to me terribly Southern. I knew nothing of New Orleans, not geographically anyway, and Shirley helped me place it and put it somewhere. She was the muse of a past I didn't know, that I could only really guess at—my mother, preoccupied with her increased freedom that included the advent of shopping malls, wasn't much help that way. I finally met Shirley during my first trip to New Orleans in the 1980s. She was short and coffee-colored, with glasses and long, dark hair that wasn't quite curly but, because of its sheer length on a woman well over fifty at the time, recalled the girl in the photos.

Shirley was happy to see me, but not overwhelmed. I was Gloria's daughter, the family she already knew; we had been neighbors all along, albeit neighbors living a couple of thousand miles apart. She took me around town, pointed out the Lafitte projects where she grew up, a place she insisted in a wounded voice "used to be real nice." Like most other projects, Lafitte was very poor and populated by black people of a certain shade, a hard truth not lost on me. I was not from New Orleans but I was Creole, and I knew the color-coded realities of the city—of the whole South, the whole country—all too well. Lafitte was a mini-city of dilapidated structures that looked like they'd been standing since the Civil War. I loved New Orleans, but instantly got the difference between it and L.A.; compared to this, the projects back home—Avalon Gardens, Imperial Courts—looked like resorts. On that first New Orleans visit I finally understood why Shirley stayed, and why my mother and others had left. For black people of all castes, New Orleans was home in the most irreducible sense, but it was also a place that shut them out. The shutting out was only a matter of degree.

Of course, many Creoles preferred to shut out the shutting out entirely, to jut out their chins when asked about segregation and declare it didn't happen (well, it happened to Negroes, not to them). Denial required that the fabric of family and friends be knit tight enough to keep the anger and humiliation inevitably visited by the outside world from bleeding through. Creoles were clannish almost by psychological necessity; they were very mindful of New Orleans traditions, and downright protective of those they considered to be exclusively Creole. They refashioned them all in L.A. with restaurants and social clubs and service clubs and hangouts and Mardi Gras and Feast of St. Joseph observations, all of which operated within a couple of square miles and kept the patchwork Creole community in central L.A. from flying apart and resisting the gravitational pull of the suburbs. My family was a big part of that community: a co-founder of the annual Louisiana to Los Angeles festival—LALA for short—was my Uncle Leon, who also had a barbershop on Jefferson Boulevard, the main thoroughfare of repatriated Creole life.

In 2004, the year before Katrina, thanks to Errol's dedicated planning, my father's family gathered for its annual reunion in vast Kenneth Hahn Park, off La Cienega Boulevard. There atop a hill, in the breeze and benevolent sun, we toasted New Orleans with a usual second-line dance, waving fringed and spangled umbrellas, napkins that served as handkerchiefs, electric-colored beads borrowed from those who'd been to the last New Orleans Mardi Gras and brought them back. We pored over a massive family tree drawn meticulously on cardboard, pieced together and laid across two large picnic tables; as we did every year, we studied connections, haggled over their accuracy like money, passed around ancient never-seen-before photos somebody had brought—more studying and haggling. It was exhilarating in a completely ordinary way, and it was as much back-home as many of us got, these remnants of ritual and preservation standing in for the true New Orleans experience that was evaporating now before our eyes. Well off as we were, New Orleans could only save us; we could not save it. We could only watch and remember what we saw.

Part of that remembrance will certainly be politics, and all the connotations of race therein. The bitter truth is that Katrina was a human disaster that struck humans the federal government in 2005 cared little about, except as a chip in a voting bloc that could swing a close election in its favor. During the first long week of the flood, I imagined George W. Bush and his advisors huddling daily and then hourly, calculating precisely how many Negroes (Creoles included) could die before they needed to appear concerned and before the non-Negro population—the *real* swing voters—started getting uneasy enough to affect poll numbers. Certainly this is why Bush kept lurching from one bizarre position to another: first condemning the thugs for looting unsalvageable Wal-Marts, then declaring New Orleans would rebuild into something bigger and stronger (I very nearly expected him to say that Amer-

ica would not rest until it brought *democracy* there), next encouraging us to
buy less gasoline, and at last admitting, in a much smaller voice than the one
he'd started the week with, that perhaps all the governments involved had not
acted swiftly enough. He seemed drunk, not with drink but with ignorance
and confusion; minus the scripted, simple messages about Iraq or social security, Bush lost his famous false equilibrium before our eyes. I felt not contempt
this time for him, but sorrow for us all. That we were morally sinking as a
nation—and no one escaped that "we"—hit me like never before. New Orleans had lost its wetlands, its natural protection against the fury of hurricanes that could now ravage it clean in a matter of hours. America had lost
something similar, something that for years had protected it from the consequences of its worst impulses and most corrosive, exclusionary beliefs. Like
New Orleans, we had come to the point of being completely vulnerable to
violent attacks of nature—our own. And as with hurricanes, the attacks were
happening with greater frequency and denuding us year by year, incident by
incident. Soon we would be below sea level, too.

I don't know what will happen, but for now—perhaps forever—New Orleans is no longer a living place to me. It is a museum, a hologram, a Pompeii
eternally frozen in the moment that tragedy hit. From now on, I will have to
content myself with memories of visits with Shirley and Ed. Their wonderful
house was ruined by roughly eight feet of water, a fact revealed to Shirley as
she sat in the lobby of the Baton Rouge hotel, trying to settle on what to do
next; the TV news was on, and somebody sitting next to her, a fellow evacuee
in equally dire straits, nudged her and said, "Isn't that your neighborhood?"
Shirley cried then, but silently, and only once. After several months of limbo,
she and Ed ended up settling—very gingerly—in Henderson, a suburban
boomtown on the outskirts of Las Vegas. I was speechless. Vegas the city is
everything New Orleans, and even Los Angeles, isn't—dry, brown, and very
recently invented. Tract housing as far as the eye can see, all with standard air
conditioning and attractive low-water shrubbery that looks like art and helps
everybody forget they're in the middle of one of the most merciless deserts
on the planet. I am happy Shirley and Ed survived Katrina; I am heartsick
that they wound up there. I can visit them, but that no longer means visiting
my past. They now have to do what I've done all my life, claim New Orleans
from an unlikely vantage point hundreds of miles away, keep the faith of
home in a place that wills them to do otherwise. I feel for them. Their new
house is fine, but it is boxy and bright and has none of the shadows or intrigue
of New Orleans. When we all walked through the Henderson house before

they moved in, there was little to say beyond, "This is really nice." It was nice, without being anything else. I knew then, as Shirley and Ed lay down tentative new roots, that I would finally have to cast L.A. in my mind and heart as the place where I'm from. New Orleans, the place I loved and venerated but never quite got to know, is gone.

My mother agrees. She had packed up New Orleans and put it away long ago, expected little of it over the last fifty years as it slipped into a future that looked more ominous than the impoverished past she'd shut up like a locket. But its misfortune made her see that had been more forgiving of the city than she realized; it had become an old person to her, frail through no fault of its own and given to stubborn illusions of grandeur that were best tolerated, even encouraged. Living in L.A. had taught her that much about dreaming beyond your means—in the end, why not? Who did it hurt? Now the dreamer she had watched over for much of her life had vanished, gone to sleep. "Poor New Orleans," was all my mother said in the end. "Poor New Orleans."

I know what she means. Here in the splendid desert of my own native town, free from the violent storms and strictures of New Orleans of reality, of history, of memory, I am more homeless than she'll ever know.

THOROUGHLY MODERN MAMMY

OF COONS, PICKANINNIES, AND GOLD DUST TWINS: WHY DO BLACK CURIOS STAY CHIC?

December 2002

The most memorable Christmas gift I ever got was from my best friend about six years ago, an old-fashioned pegboard listing stock grocery items one needed to be reminded to buy week to week, such as flour, sugar, and bread. The board itself wasn't memorable, but its particular old fashion seared my consciousness and then some: at the top was a decorative ceramic of a grinning, coal-black, red-kerchief-headed "mammy," a reproduction of one of those Jim Crow—era advertisements that have come to be known as black memorabilia. Beneath the ceramic was written, "Fo' da kitchen we needs."

I put the board in a closet and thought, without much conviction, that I'd find a place on the wall for it later. I strove to be heartened by the knowledge that my friend was among the most politically enlightened and erudite black people that I knew, and therefore the pegboard had a redemptive quality that would reveal itself to me in time. But quite the reverse happened: stashed out of sight among the other questionables in my front closet, the peg board bothered me like the invisible pea bothered the princess. Its presence in my apartment began to feel like an affront to many things in it that were meant, I realized, as affirmation—African wood carvings, a framed college degree, family photos, even fashion magazines. Whenever I thought of the mammy pegboard or spied it inadvertently, I shrank from it like Kryptonite. At last I dug it out and offered it to my downstairs neighbor, also a good friend and a highly conscious black person who nonetheless pronounced it "cute" and took it away. (It must be said that she is also a longtime curio collector especially fond of kitchen things—chili peppers are her favorite motif—so her apolitical assessment of the pegboard didn't exactly surprise me.) I was still left with the same deep-down bad feeling bordering on heartburn that black memorabilia always leave me with, and the same nagging question: Why do we keep this stuff around?

I mean we in the strictest sense. I know why whites keep it in circulation— to begin with, they *put* it in circulation, the black grotesquerie of the Gold Dust Twins and Old Black Joe that branded cleaning powder and tobacco and lots of other goods, as well as many more generic images of watermelon-gobbling pickaninnies that accented everything else from watches to wall clocks. After such stuff fell from popularity at about the middle of the last century, it was relegated to antique-store Americana that, however awkward it might have always been to display, nonetheless fetched a price for rarity and quality of condition. There is always a pure-market argument shop owners can make in defense of having black memorabilia on the shelves. But what, really, is black people's excuse? Why have ceramic-mammy vendor tables become de rigueur at ethnic-pride or even nationalist streetfests like Kwanzaa and Juneteenth? How are big lips and bug eyes, not created for us or by us but entirely against us, even remotely empowering or aesthetically pleasing?

The most common response I get is a vaguely militant claim that we're "taking back" something meant to be sabotaging by embracing it—that is, defanging the wolf by inviting him into your house and hanging him on your wall. Another common rationale is that these black distortions are history, albeit a nadir of history in which naked racial oppression ruled the day, and that we must preserve it as such. I would say that's fine for books and monuments and historical societies, but I hardly see the point in propagating the mammy in the modern consciousness. (Jews have their Holocaust museums and their memorials, but you never see Nazi-created caricatures of Jews rendered on mugs and placemats.) Whenever I go into any antique shop anywhere in the country, along the central California coast or New Orleans, my stomach kinks into a knot of apprehension over the blackface I know I'll come across, usually in the back of the store, placed not too discreetly in a corner. No matter how quaint or refined the place, among the first-edition Cole Porter sheet music are versions of "My Old Kentucky Home" with a cover of a big-lipped buck seated by a river, strumming a guitar. I have smothered many an impulse to complain to the proprietor or storm out, knowing how right and how utterly senseless it would have been to do so—here indeed is Americana, whether I like it, or buy it, or not.

I am not entirely without empathy. I understand the urge to mark the bad times lest they be forgotten, which is largely the purpose of blues and spiritual music. But rest assured, we are in no danger of gross black stereotypes becoming things of the past; to the contrary, today they retain a sophisticated power well beyond the subliminal or the nostalgic. Aunt Jemima may have traded in her head rag for a suit and pearls back in the 1980s, but she's still selling pancake mix. Uncle Ben still beams from boxes of rice. In the ever-more-insidious realm of entertainment, Bernie Mac may have an innovative television series, but his trademark pop-eyes are anything but. The recently released movie *Friday After Next* is the urban equivalent of a traveling minstrel show, a contemporary black commedia dell'arte of hustlers, ho's and ne'er-do-wells that, when this history is all said and done, will sit very comfortably next to the mammies and Black Joes. Progress for African-Americans is increasingly becoming less than the sum of its definitions: the NAACP fought to ban screenings of *Birth of a Nation* in 1915; eighty years later, mammies, coons, and other early relics of high bamboozlement are not only not bannable, but *collectible*.

Cultural undermining notwithstanding, blacks in theory have the right to use the commerce argument as much as whites. Memorabilia sellers are running legitimate businesses, and perhaps their profit-making even redresses some of the wrong done by whites who benefited financially for so long from what was essentially the stylized fear and mockery of black impoverishment and under-education, conditions that were (and still are) painfully real. But money, of course, was always only part of the story. Mammyism was also about perpetuating a national negrophobia to keep the American social order intact after the end of slavery threatened, however modestly, to change it. It was about a decades-long PR campaign for the constitutionally reprehensible Jim Crow laws that were enacted around 1900; it was about preaching, through primary colors and snappy logos ("Dat sho' am good!"), the absolute sanctity of keeping the races apart.

The whole trade wouldn't bother me nearly as much if I could believe that black consumers were pointedly taking the stuff out of circulation and routing it to places like Museum in Black, a local curatorial treasure in the black arts district of Leimert Park that documents in artifacts our worst of times, beginning with slave manacles and auction notices and winding up with the Gold Dust Twins. It sells things, of course, but it's primarily a museum, and in such a context the collectibles truly do have power, as unsparing reminders of just how deep the American race animus has run, on permanent display in a hall of shame. But I think it'll be impossible for me to ever regard mammy as a gift, even if blacks at this point had evolved completely out from under the weighty issues of representation. Long after Christmas, when I finally told my friend somewhat guiltily how I felt about the pegboard, he waved his hand airily and said, "Oh, it's no big deal. Take it back and get something you like." I wish that had been possible.

The complicated coda to all this is that blacks never quite divested themselves of their own vicious parodies, even when they freely had the right to do so; no doubt we were hampered by a lingering slave mentality, but the quest for Americanness and true self-determination often makes it hard, still, to know whether declaring "sho' is" is affirming or embarrassing. One could argue that blacks never really had such a right at all, that corporations continue into this century to mercilessly appropriate blackness as selling points—I dare anybody to drive down Sunset Strip and not agree. But when we are at home with ourselves, with the television off and only the pegboards and the clown faces to examine, surely we must *know*.

BEHIND THE AMERICAN-
HISTORY CURTAIN

WASHINGTON, D.C., AND THE LESSONS OF MEMORY

August 2003

This summer, my husband and I went to Washington, D.C., for the first time. I had never approached a visit to a city with such leeriness; flying past Texas to Washington felt like sailing into the heart of darkness. My lifelong curiosity about D.C. that began with that serene postcard picture of the Capitol building in childhood had evolved over the decades into a cubist mixture of ancient awe and modern disdain; by 2003, Washington conjured up plenty of feeling, but no images at all. Still, wary as I was of Washington, I wanted to get the picture. Not CNN's piecemeal offerings of the White House lawn, but the sense of a fairly small town that held a whole fractured country inside of it and always had. As much as I held D.C. and its symbology at arm's length, I was *in* there somewhere. I wanted to go looking.

I found myself instantly. The postcard part of D.C. was ringed with cherry blossom trees and luxe hotels, anchored by that surreal view of the Capitol that seemed visible from nearly everywhere we walked. Drifting amid the splendor were black people, chiefly men, ranging from poor to homeless, so much apart from the sparkle and bustle they appeared to be ghosts; I knew they likely lived across the river in the Chocolate City part of D.C., the less visible but nearly as famous half, but that they so clearly had no place in the other half riled me. Urban segregation is commonplace, especially in the South, but that the capital was no exception and made no attempt to be was, in spite of everything I knew and had braced for, disappointing. I carried that disappointment around the rest of the time, like a souvenir purchase in a plastic bag that you don't really want to schlep but you don't want to put down and lose either.

We went to the National Mall and started with the war memorials—it seemed as good a place to start as any. I was somewhat mollified to see that neither the Korean nor the Vietnam memorial glorified war in the name of liberation and democracy nearly as much as it simply recalled the dead (Vietnam had no glory to speak of in its day, much less any to remember now). The bronzed soldiers of the Korean War, frozen in flight across a treacherous enemy field, looked weary and uncertain, and that moved me. (I have always been moved by the less glamorous and more ambiguous aspects of militarism; when people proposed changing the national anthem after September 11 from "The Star-Spangled Banner" to "God Bless America," I seethed. Francis Scott Key may have been writing about the glory of war, but it's no accident that the whole account starts and ends with a question.) Walking past the engraved names of the Vietnam dead, I asked my husband, who teaches American history, where the Civil War monument was; it felt like an obvious omission. Here was a war, *the* war, in which over half a million people died and that made the country possible at all. Was the government, in its infinite wisdom, working backward from the twentieth century to the nineteenth? My husband laughed ruefully. "This whole city," he said, "is a monument to the Civil War."

Nothing was more satisfying or disheartening than visiting the Lincoln and Jefferson memorials. Lincoln's legendary troubled face, his bony hands gripping the armrests of the marble chair not in power but in a kind of panic, his words about slavery endangering the soul of the republic inscribed in the walls around him—this was the mecca I had hoped for, the place I was content to see myself in. Jefferson stood erect, but expressed the same caution and seemed no less troubled. These were true temples of American idealism that in 2003 were rife with thieves who were quartered in the White House and Capitol just down the street. Sitting in the blessed shade offered by the memorials—the weather was tolerable, but stultifyingly Southern—I felt the ghosts of both men and the reluctant acknowledgment beneath their golden words that America was fluid by nature and design, and therefore it was inevitable that it would be led at times by people who had no interest in furthering the principles they had set forth, principles that make such disinterest possible and even sanctioned by the public. Among our freedoms is the freedom to discard and reinvent, whether we do that for the common good or for the individual benefit of fat-cat campaign contributors. But I left the acropolises on the hill feeling nevertheless enriched: what can't be bought can at least be taken by whoever deems it valuable. Small as it seems today, democracy lives.

In the sea of museums dominated by the Smithsonian, including one under construction detailing the history of Native Americans, there were none dedicated to blacks (the Frederick Douglass site and the Museum of African American Culture are, predictably, across the river near Chocolate City). Blacks appeared incidentally in places like the postal museum, which mentioned about three quarters of the way through that most blacks got their first federal jobs with the post office (yes . . . *and?*). I expected more in the Museum of American History, a straightforward-sounding place that, though interesting, turned out to be the most glaringly subjective memorial of all. Past the grand exhibits of guns, presidents, and first-lady fashions was a corner chronicling the great Negro migration from South to North. It looked and felt spare and dusty, all shacks and ploughshares, which was fitting to a point, but it dawned on me this was an acknowledgment only of poverty, and scant acknowledgment at that. The exhibit was ill-attended, and the people there breezed through and barely watched the introductory film that played in a loop. They didn't know what to make of this particular history, which saddened and incensed me; I sat through the film with a mix of defiance and dejection, the lone member of the choir.

That experience stood in great contrast to our visit to the Holocaust Museum, which ensures that we will remember the Holocaust and its wider meaning to the same degree that the relative absence of blacks in museums ensures we will forget there was any Holocaust at all. Yet this museum, after the anger and resentment and inspiration that kept me charged and jittery for four days, was the place where I broke apart. Toward the end of the tour, among the footnotes of the exhaustively documented history, were small iron bed frames that once held mentally disabled children who were lethally injected (a fate nominally kinder than the ovens) because their faulty genes, of course, had no place in Hitler's perfect Aryan nation. There were enlarged photos of a couple such children, naked and entirely unaware of the fate that lay just before them. The spare and simple evidence of such enormous and systematic cruelty, meted out to the most defenseless of the defenseless, staggered me, and my husband led me out of the place in tears.

Out in the burning sun I thought about how swiftly Americans accept and then normalize the monstrous things that go on now, that have gone on for hundreds of years. We are the world power that Hitler killed to be, and we assume we achieved that power far more justly and humanely. But the banality of evil threatens to undo us precisely because of our freakish, unprecedented stature as a world power. We shake off the details at our own risk, as Lincoln and Jefferson pointed out centuries ago. Remembering them as vividly as I did in Washington is about the best homeland security I could have hoped for.

THEY'RE GOING CRAZY
OUT THERE

2002

It hardly seems possible now, nearly ten years later, that at the moment Los Angeles was setting fire to itself with the tinder of its driest and least-fed souls, I was getting a facial. It was three o'clock in the afternoon, and I was reclined in a chair in an Inglewood salon, my face hot and moist and not feeling very much better than it did when I walked in roughly an hour before; but that's the beauty business, which dictates that you'll look worse before you look transformed. As I finished up, my face glowing an unnatural red, one of the salon owners came into the room and announced a little breathlessly that she'd just heard the verdicts in the Rodney King beating case, and they were all not guilty. We were all immediately incensed—me and the owners, Belinda and Regina—though not shocked. This sort of thing happens routinely and historically enough in black communities so that people are never surprised. When it happens you renew the outrage that is about the only thing black people have passed intact from one generation to the next, outrage that is generally dormant and subcutaneous until it is activated by something like the Rodney King verdicts. The outrage got me out of that chair and moving faster than I otherwise would have—the whole point of a facial, after all, is to relax in the aftermath—my face still flushed and raw, though now instead of annoying it felt appropriate. Belinda and Regina empathized with Rodney King's misfortune and the whole miscarriage of justice; they shook their perfect bobs and clucked their tongues sharply. They had more customers to tend to, but they wished me well.

I went home because I didn't know where else to go, yet. During the short drive I listened to talk radio out of habit and heard, to my surprise, growing pleas for calm. That could only mean that people were getting out of hand somewhere, and it was catching and irrepressible. I felt suddenly energized and maniacally happy at the idea of spontaneity, any spontaneity, overtaking a city like Los Angeles, which in my thirty years here had proven damn near impossible. It's like trying to build muscle on a long, tall frame that refuses to move quickly; the most intense exercises administered to that many square inches just don't take. Something was taking now, and though I figured it wasn't good I couldn't help but marvel anyway. When I got home the phone rang almost as soon as I walked in the door. It was a teacher friend, Ottis, who I had last seen earlier in the afternoon, not long before I went off for a facial. Ottis was a minister and a youngish veteran of the '60s civil rights movement; he had a passion for history, which is the only reason he taught a few times a week, in the adult school. He didn't need the money. He was a staunch social progressive who lectured his class constantly about the evils and futile logic of conservatism. "Girl, can you believe this?" he cried. He was clearly in his element, as energized as me. "They're going *crazy* out there!"

He said he was going over to a rally he'd heard about happening at First A.M.E. Church, near Western Avenue and Adams Boulevard at the northeast border of South Central. I didn't exactly like the idea of going to a church, which I knew would preach pacifism and healing—a word I would grow to hate—more than address specifics of the verdicts and how they might actually be wrong. The problem I had with religion generally is that it accepted everything and never condemned anything as wrong, or it condemned too many things as wrong, and neither view was useful in the modern world as far as I was concerned. But I had to go somewhere, and Ottis was all charged up, and though he was a minister he would hardly stand for platitudes from Rev. Chip Murray, or anybody else. He picked me up and we drove in the bright late-afternoon sun south toward First A.M.E. Going along Crenshaw Boulevard I first noticed a change in the weather; the sun was the same but an unease was rising, like fog off the ocean, from the streets. It was permeable and almost invisible but it was swiftly reordering a landscape I had seen a thousand times before, altering it beyond recognition. The closer Ottis and I got to our destination, the murkier it became, until we came to a dead stop near Western and Adams because so many cars were milling about, trying to park for the rally or trying to get the hell out because the drivers sensed something bad was afoot. For the moment we were all in suspended motion like millions of hapless atoms in a newly frozen ice cube. It felt like the pristine stillness that comes before a nuclear attack or a big earthquake; unease kept gathering like smoke as the sun beamed on. Before I could tell Ottis how anxious I was feeling, he began shouting and pointing: "Look at that!"

People were wandering the streets as if the streets weren't there, filling them up with a certain defiance, shutting them down. A rough-looking man in a blue hooded sweatshirt was coming vaguely toward us, wielding a trash can. He stopped suddenly and tossed the metal can with all his might, like a javelin. That broke the cars out of their lethargy; one blond white woman in a black BMW gunned her motor, backed up with a screech, and took off west down Adams like a bat out of hell. Other people started craning their necks to determine not parking spots but points of escape; any thoughts of solidarity and Rodney King were giving way to instincts of self-preservation, which in L.A. means drive, baby, drive. Ottis and I did, after sizing up the ugly mood, which was expanding before our eyes, and weighing it against going to the rally. The ugly mood won out. Neither of us said so, but we didn't want to be on foot when shit really started happening; today of all days it was probably best to follow the local creed and live out of your car if you had one. I was grateful for ours, though I had mixed feelings about the facial, about the indulgence and oblivion it encouraged. It suddenly seemed impossible to argue social reform when I was spending fifty dollars a month that I didn't really have on the promise of a surface improvement that I didn't need all that much, and wasn't likely to happen anyway. The fire on my face had cooled, the incriminating evidence for the moment gone.

Ottis and I headed west and didn't stop until we hit Brentwood. I don't know why we traveled that far; I suppose we wanted to ensure our escape from the haunted forest of South L.A. and its roiling clouds of discontent to the bright Oz of somewhere else. Those distinctions were usually clear, but not today. Our energy high had broken down to a kind of gray nervousness that lacked the romance of three o'clock. We knew the city was burning, and where. We sat in a Brentwood bar with a smattering of white people who preferred to watch a Lakers game on television than tune in to the news. Ottis and I fairly reared up in indignation, loudly deploring the apathy of *certain people* in this city, and believed our indignation. They looked mildly ashamed but said nothing. We had the floor. To these folks we were not sellouts or deserters but emissaries of conscience, loud but eloquent voices of condemnation and reason; we represented. We couldn't quite face the rally but we could do this, here, all day long. We were good at it. The streets, we learned that day, were not our pulpit. That was the fallen altar for the faithless, the pulpit of an old imagination, the province of pitifully angry people with trash barrels and nowhere to throw them. We had new havens—mahogany bars, spas, salons—in which to forge the future. Transformation was still in our hands, to say nothing of our faces.

Celebrity is unavoidable, especially in Los Angeles. It bears on everything, even intractable matters of race that seem wholly confined to forgotten urban landscapes and to the inner-city industrial complex of nonprofits, community groups, consultants, government programs and the like. Celebrity and race are an uneasy mix, at best. But sometimes the famous slip their usual role of illuminating the ghetto for profit, pathos, or image-pimping and do something entirely different, either through their own efforts or through others' inspired reassessment of them. Sometimes a combination of both. This section records a few of those times.

THE ACCIDENTAL POPULIST

MAGIC JOHNSON GIVES SOME BACK

February 1999

Magic was in the air in a most unlikely place: a community meeting in a drab, school-cafeteria-sized room at the Department of Water and Power, across the street from the Crenshaw mall. The meeting was of an advisory body to the city's Community Redevelopment Agency, one of a dizzying array of such groups that at one point promised to be the missing link between revitalization money and the long-thwarted will of the people. Inasmuch as South Los Angeles looks as frozen out of big-scale development today as it did in '92, when the world witnessed the violent apogee of that thwarted will, these advisory groups had gotten pretty much nowhere, generating press statements, surveys, meetings, public hearings—but little magic. The machinery of community input had been oiled to perfection, yet nothing significant happened on the economic front until Earvin "Magic" Johnson opened his multiplex movie house on the grounds of the mall and folks dared to start talking about the dawn of a new era. (It had to be, if only for the remarkable fact that Cecil Murray and Charles Blake, pastors of L.A.'s two biggest black churches, who were rarely seen in public together, both showed up to give pre-ribbon-cutting invocations.) For the last two years the John-son Development Corp. had worked to cinch a deal that would rebuild the adjacent, ailing Santa Barbara Plaza, but had lately hit a political snag with Councilman Mark Ridley-Thomas that threatened to undo modest steps that nonetheless had not been taken by a development company in the area in decades, and never before by a company that was black-owned. The con-gregants at this meeting filled the room to overflow because they wanted to know what exactly was going on with this deal, this thing that had moved past talk and paper and was solid enough for them to be concerned about its future. The room was as electric with this rare triumph—this arrival of a plausible deal—as it was with rising anxiety that this venture, too, would fail; people buzzed, or leaned against the walls, or at the very least leaned forward in their chairs as they waited for an update.

Ridley-Thomas and various city types took the stage and droned officiously on about scenarios and possible roads and all the angles and deliberate speed being applied to enacting the will of the people. Chairs creaked and the buzz softened to occasional whispers. When the floor was opened to questions, Ridley-Thomas got not a question but a rocket. "I've been out there in the streets, you know, and the brothers out there, they're down for Magic," said the young man in the dark bomber jacket, his voice even but loud, edgy. "And the word is, if this development isn't done by Magic, well . . ." He spread his hands. "There's some talk I heard about burning the place down."

Magic Johnson is trying not to look pleased. He sits forward, shakes his head slowly and tries to muster some gravity to counter the blush of a famous Magic grin that snuck up at the very end of this story, which he's just heard for the first time. He rubs his big hands together like a Boy Scout starting a fire with a stick of wood. He says as solemnly as possible that he doesn't condone violence, doesn't hold with threats, and offers that the young man's passion on his behalf is appreciated but his words were, perhaps, ill-advised. He launches into a heartfelt recitation of his belief that in the end we must all work together, that we're all on the same side and, despite our natural differences, we all want the same things—easy words to embrace coming from a man who, despite his own long-running superstardom with the Lakers basketball club, was at least as famous for his selflessness on court, for expounding on and then demonstrating the virtues of teamwork.

That said, Johnson sits back and lets the smile finish itself. The smile is not vengeful but satisfied; it is a smile of some pure astonishment and a little delight at finding himself at a political impasse at all. Johnson respects obstacles but doesn't give in to them, rather relishes them—the exception being his HIV-positive status, announced to the world in 1991. In the shadow of that greatest of obstacles, all others are merely problems—he would say challenges—that can be surmounted by well-thought-out, well-executed plays. That need to devise new plays is what drives him, what makes Earvin Johnson "Magic" and what has been most responsible for the business empire known as Johnson Enterprises. Some might have figured it was the HIV discovery that threw things into high gear—live a crazy fantasy while you can—but the less dramatic fact is that Johnson has been working toward something of this scope his whole life. As a boy growing up in Lansing, Michigan, he had his own lawn-mowing franchise, and his local heroes were two thriving entrepreneurs named Joel Ferguson and Gregory Eaton; young Earvin cleaned their offices and dreamed of the day he, too, would own nice buildings and delegate labor to his own staff of employees. In addition to a several endorsement deals he had as an athlete, Johnson, with the help of his agent and various business mentors, cut some groundbreaking deals that established him not merely as a pitchman but as a man in charge: co-ownership of a Pepsi distributing plant in Maryland, and establishment of Magic Johnson T's, a T-shirt marketing company that secured licensing deals with the NBA, the NFL, and other professional-sports organizations and was one of the fastest-growing sports-apparel companies in 1990, the year after it was launched. Johnson also had other things going—concert promotions, charitable outfits—years before he took on his riskiest venture, development. This was different, something that harked back to his boyhood imaginings of building a business, from the ground up, that was entirely his own. When the Magic Johnson Theatres multiplex was under construction, he would sit in his car in the dirt-filled parking lot late at night, marveling at what he had wrought.

Since focusing on black economic development, Johnson has reset an agenda that hadn't been set in decades. His growing enterprises here and across the country are forcing discussions about slow growth vs. no growth that had never before been necessary. After putting away the pro-basketball jones for good in 1996, he turned his attentions fully to business ventures, and before anyone really knew what was happening he swooped downcourt and scored a number of deals that alone promise to change the long-neglected face of South L.A.: a $150 million commitment from CalPERS, the state's largest pension fund, for the purchase of Ladera Center and redevelopment of the Santa Barbara Plaza; first-of-a-kind partnerships with Starbucks and TGI Fridays; and, with fellow celebs Jheryl Busby and Janet Jackson, the purchase of Founders National Bank, the sole black-owned bank in the West.

Johnson sees his inner-city developments, the ones charting territory so new there's no real name for it yet, as something much bigger than himself. Not as big as God, but spiritual insofar as business undertakings in minority areas can be, sometimes must be—leaps of faith and all that. "You know, if I'd listened to everybody's advice, there'd still be no movie theaters in the hood," he says almost impatiently. "But if we [black people] don't do it, who's gonna do it? We'll be complaining about the same thing forever. It is my responsibility, not only to teach young people what's possible, but to make older people proud, too. So many people have come up to me and said, 'We're so proud to have this place.'" He suddenly grins full strength, savoring his victory and the fact that he is able to share it with other folk. "I *love* going to my theater on Friday or Saturday. Don't have a problem in the theater with people recognizing me, but when I go to the concession stand—whooo, boy!"

Magic Johnson is giving inner-city redevelopment the one thing it never figured to have: celebrity. It's something he is more than willing to employ for the greater good, though Magic is a bit of a stranger to the man who's always called himself Earvin. By his admission, the two personae have converged at points in the past, though now they're separated for the purposes of work. One is a brand name, the other is the product itself; both are crucial to the success of Johnson Enterprises. "When I walk in the door to do business with people, I'm Magic," Johnson explains. "But when I finish business, they're calling me Earvin."

In the hood, the name Earvin registers blank looks, but "Magic" invokes everything good and heroic and possible: championship basketball, sportsmanship, modesty, belief in God, bold new enterprise, recycling dollars. Though Johnson frequently cites his ties to the Crenshaw district—he and his wife, Cookie, belong to West Angeles Church; he is a regular client of a neighborhood barber—his presence, in the manner of most celebrities, is more broadcast than actual. Yet his business concerns make him real enough to locals, who say that Johnson's abiding interest in bringing retail amenities—lattes, business suits—to the area more than qualifies him as a flesh-and-blood brother. He is closer to the people than traditional black organization heads and politicos, who have proved better at delivering uplifting speeches and doling out awards from behind podiums than at facilitating change.

Johnson's skirmish last summer with 8th District Councilman Mark Ridley-Thomas over the development of the Santa Barbara Plaza perfectly illustrated the point: Ridley-Thomas's chronic resistance to development and his political maneuvering in the plaza deal—threatening to kill it because Johnson backed a stadium bid in Carson instead of his own bid to rebuild the Los Angeles Memorial Coliseum—stood in unflattering contrast to Johnson's just-do-it exhortations. The standoff solidified Johnson's image as a community champion who was being wronged by a bureaucracy that had been indifferent and ineffective for so long that it knew no other way to be. Following critical media coverage and public outcry, Ridley-Thomas grudgingly backed down.

The incident baptized Johnson in fire, and he recalls the wrath of Ridley-Thomas, a longtime friend, soberly but with lingering bewilderment. "I've always supported Mark, and he supported me on the theaters," he says. "But the city took us through a *long* process on this one. Mark took it personal, which is too bad. He called me up at night really upset [after reading about Johnson's position on the Coliseum in an L.A. Business Journal article], threatening to pull the permits on the expansion of the theaters, which was already under way. He was like, 'I'll show you who's in charge around here!'" Johnson shakes his head. "My partners asked me what I wanted to do. I said, 'Man, I'm ready to walk.' We were going to leave the L.A. thing alone. We were getting a lot of deals coming at us; we didn't have to go looking." But then the bad press hit, and Ridley-Thomas was suddenly not so anxious to have Johnson Development Corp. bow out and leave him in public-relations quicksand. JDC still has the project, and though the pace of progress has been snail-like, corporation officials expect the deal to pass the City Council in the next month.

Johnson says that through all the setbacks and political minutiae inherent in development, he tries to maintain a sense of higher purpose instilled in him by mentors like Earl Graves, publisher of *Black Enterprise* magazine, and super entrepreneur Bruce Llewellyn. "Bruce taught me a lot about business," he says. "He once asked me when I was first starting out, 'What do you want to do?' I said, 'I want to be a businessman.' He said, 'No, you've got to be better and bigger than that. You've got to be more than that.'" He pauses, then continues, "The row with Mark was good, in a way. If I'm going to be a player in the community, this taught me a valuable lesson. Politics is politics, to a degree. We're building movie theaters everywhere, like in Harlem, and everybody says, 'I'm the man, you got to come to me first.' If this stuff [in L.A.] bothered me, it's only because Mark and I knew each other. We're okay now—I'll never be against him—but I stood firm and something had to give. At the end of the day, you need the project, you need the jobs. I understand you got to play the game, no problem, but I don't want to be blindsided.

"But I feel good about what happened. The bottom line is, we're not going to turn our backs."

Though he is publicly apolitical, Magic Johnson espouses tenets of individualism that might be called Republican: The government will not save you, he says. Black leadership will not save you. You're the only one who can make a difference. Go for it. But this is more sportspeak than anything, and while it might be incidentally Republican, Johnson does not readily absolve the sins of wholesale urban neglect, unlike agitprop black conservatives such as UC Regent Ward Connerly and talk-radio host Larry Elder. He hopes that what he's doing will set examples for the public sector, the private sector, guys on the street with little money but plenty of vision, because, he stresses, he just can't do it all. "Actually, we need twelve more Magic Johnsons," says local architect and developer Michael Anderson, a veteran of Crenshaw development wars.

"Believe me, he doesn't have to do what he's doing," says Eric Holoman, a personal financial accountant with Bank of America and Johnson's longtime friend. "He could be very comfortable—take his money, invest it quietly, make more money, travel, have fun—but he doesn't. He's furthering a business cause that needs to be furthered. He has a conviction, and that's what matters." Michael Stennis, owner and heir to the Golden Bird fried-chicken restaurant chain, says Johnson's commitment to a cause a that over the years has eaten alive the best of intentions is nothing short of amazing. "Peter Ueberroth of Rebuild L.A. finally quit because he couldn't get big business to come in and stay—Earvin's the only one doing it," he says. "Nobody had to twist his arm. Even black people told him he was stupid to do it, that it would fail, but that didn't deter him. He wanted to do things big."

There's another, simpler explanation for the genesis of Johnson's business passions. As a twenty-year-old star Laker recruit and new arrival to Los Angeles, he struck up a friendship with Joe Smith, then chairman of Elektra-Asylum Records and a Lakers season-ticket holder. Smith, who eventually helped renegotiate Johnson's contract, recalls with a laugh the day he invited Johnson to his lavish Beverly Hills home. "When he saw all this stuff—the wine cellar, the furniture—his eyes got four times the normal size," says Smith, who now works as a music consultant. "He was in awe. He was like, 'How can I get these things?'" Johnson freely admits that his motivation for community improvement is acquisitive—ensuring that folks have a basic right to things, but more important, to as broad a range of things as possible. That's what's missing from the inner city, and that's what makes him perfectly happy to peddle the Magic Johnson name to corporations that would otherwise be perfectly happy to continue setting up shop at points comfortably west and north of the 10 freeway. "The Santa Barbara Plaza is just the beginning," says Johnson. "I want to own the Ladera Center, the Baldwin Hills Crenshaw mall, Fox Hills Mall—I need to own them. Then retailers would trust me, and I could bring in people like Nordstrom, I could bring in the quality we need, that we want, more easily."

Some agitate for social or educational reform; Johnson's push for the economic right of a predominantly black neighborhood to have a Nordstrom's Rack may seem trivial by comparison, but what it represents in the context of class-driven progress in the '90s may turn out to be as significant. Johnson is clearly proud of the fact that his theaters on King Boulevard boast rocking seats, high-tech sound, uniformly polite young employees suited up in vests and bow ties. "We deserve the best," he declares, and it is exactly that encompassing sentiment, that identification with all black people tired of being short-shrifted not just by movie theaters and shopping malls but by public education and job opportunities and criminal-justice injustices and all the rest—that inclusive *we* and *our* that Johnson employs so purposefully and passionately in conversation—that is the biggest reason he has emerged, intentionally or not, as a man of the people.

"Magic, he's a down brother," says Mark Broyard, a musician and a morning regular at the Boulevard Cafe in the Santa Barbara Plaza. "I look around, and I don't see the James Worthy Center or the Michael Jackson Center, or anybody else openly giving their money and putting their names on things. Crenshaw is the hub of black activity, but Mark Ridley-Thomas is doing nothing. Magic's the catalyst for everything that's happening here. When he's finished with this plaza, I hope he starts on the east side of Crenshaw." Smith chuckles at the notion of Johnson, the accidental populist. He lauds the Johnson Enterprises endeavors as more than worthy, but says Johnson has an overarching need to stay in the spotlight—that it was only after Johnson made peace with the fact that the basketball court was permanently behind him that he turned to business full-time. What better way to attract attention than to tap a market that had never been tapped before, to burst onto a scene that was hitherto devoid of heroes? "He needs to be idolized, worshipped, applauded, he really does," says Smith. "Though he'd drop all this business stuff in a minute if he could play for the Lakers now and make $25 million."

At the same time, Smith adds, Johnson was never just about money, or even fame. "He thrives on pressure, on getting out there with the people, getting into the crowd," says Smith. "With most rich guys, it's enough to be rich. Not Magic. He felt cheated because his career was cut short. He had all this energy and nothing to do with it. He was so wired after he quit basketball, he'd show up to anything, supermarket openings. He's like Bob Hope, who would still be performing if he could still stand up."

Although the majority of people have good things to say about Johnson, a relative few have mixed feelings about the hurricane path of his ambitions. These folks say that his company, while extolling the virtue and deserving nature of the minority community, is to some degree guilty of exploiting it. In its eagerness to establish an inner-city monopoly, they say, Johnson Development has put the squeeze on the same hopeful black entrepreneurs it claims it wants to encourage.

Several years ago, Marvin Jackson, president of the homeowners group Crenshaw Neighbors, was shopping an ambitious plan for a $15 million theater and retail development at Manchester and Broadway, a blighted corner that had been further damaged in the riots. Jackson and his team were looking for a joint-venture partner; city officials sent them to Kenneth Lombard, head of Johnson Development Corp. and president of Magic Johnson Theaters, who proved less than encouraging. "He admired our proposal but basically said that this was their market, that it would infringe on Magic's turf," says Janis Paxton-Buckner, a co-author of the proposal who was present at the meeting. "They were telling us this even though they had no plans themselves to build there. City officials, especially Mark Ridley-Thomas, killed the project, but it was Johnson Development that put the nail in the coffin."

Lombard says he rejected Jackson's plan because it didn't fit the development criteria that JDC had recently formulated with CalPERS. "From a theater perspective, we're looking everywhere for sites, and if there's a way for something to come together, we look at it," says Lombard. "This just wasn't workable for us."

Lombard is no stranger to economic sudden death. In the early '90s, he was an executive with Economic Resources Corp., a local nonprofit that operated the Baldwin Theater, the only black-owned first-run movie house in the country. In 1992, at his initiative, ERC formed a historic joint venture with American Multi-Cinema (AMC) to create a new theater chain, called Inner City Cinema, that promised to catalyze the growth of new movie theaters in the post-riot central city. Lombard was named president of the chain. But the Inner City venture dissolved quickly and acrimoniously a year later when AMC sued ERC—its own partners—for misrepresentation and financial misdealings. Lombard was never implicated in the financial misconduct—in fact, the lawsuit says it was Lombard who attempted to bring the whole matter to the ERC board's attention, for which he was subsequently fired by his colleagues. Lombard was down, but not for long: several months after he left the ERC and Inner City Cinema, Magic Johnson announced his intent to build a theater complex on the grounds of the Crenshaw mall—with Lombard as his chief operative. Lombard declines to comment on the details of the lawsuit, which was dismissed in 1994, though it is safe to assume he is more content with the fruits of the second venture than he was with the first.

Questions about the Baldwin Theater's ultimate demise still linger. A prominent Crenshaw businessman tells the story of a grassroots group that was looking to reopen the theater. The group was told by Johnson Development that if it planned to open the Baldwin as a first-run house, it would do so at its own risk.

"There are lots of folks who had an interest in developing, then Magic comes in with a brand name, and bingo, he's a savior," says the businessman, who asked not to be named. But he also acknowledges that a certain amount of cutthroat maneuvering is par for the development course, and that it may be worth the end result. Indeed, in all of the criticism leveled at Johnson, no one—except for some Santa Barbara Plaza tenants who are understandably wary about redevelopment—suggests that Johnson quit what he's doing. "At the end of the day, the Magic theaters are a good thing," says the Crenshaw businessman. "It's nice, it's clean, I go there. This is more of a business thing than a black crabs-in-a-barrel thing. Johnson Development made an investment here, they'll get a return on that investment, and they'll stay. That's what matters."

Still, there is an inherent tension in committing to both social ideology—uplifting black neighborhoods—and the most efficient business practices possible; Johnson Development has found itself caught up more than once in a crossfire. Owners of Eso Won Books, one of the few thriving small businesses in the Crenshaw area, publicly charged the company with hypocrisy after it decided not to grant the bookstore a lease in its newly purchased Ladera Center. Last spring, the theaters were targeted in a protest by a group called Project Islamic HOPE for showing *How To Be a Player*, which the group felt exacerbated black sexual stereotypes. (Theater officials went ahead and showed the film, but have since exercised some quality control, announcing last November that Magic Johnson Theatres would *not* be showing *Belly*, a black gangster saga, because of its "overwhelmingly negative and violent depictions of African-Americans" and its "potential to create disruptive situations for our theaters' patrons and employees.") And some feathers have been permanently ruffled over the strict policy of not allowing caps or gang colors in the theaters, a measure designed to deter would-be troublemakers. "I wear baggy pants, a cap, but I'm a teacher and a fifty-two-year-old grandmother—

how the fuck am I going to be a gang member?" snaps Yvonne Hutchinson, a longtime Leimert Park resident who was rebuffed by security on her first visit to the theaters because she wouldn't take off her cap.

"That's not respectful. You're in the black community opening a business, saying you're for the community, but you have this assumption right off of something very negative. It's a misguided philosophy that plays into the same old stereotypes that all black people are potentially dangerous. Why is it I can go into any theater in Westwood and nobody asks me to take off my cap?" (The theaters have relaxed the rule over the years and now routinely make exceptions for women.)

Others say that Johnson, for all his pro-community speeches, is in fact not investing much of his own money and is merely fronting for the real profiteers—big corporations like Starbucks and Sony. But supporters dismiss such perceptions as so much urban paranoia, the result of years of negligence and fractured promises. "This whole idea that Earvin is not serious, that he's dabbling, really gets under my skin," says his friend Eric Holoman. "In the business world, nobody sinks in all their money on a project. You get partners. Even if he wasn't investing any of his money, he doesn't have to spend his time trying to get other people to invest theirs. Of course there are things at stake—if this thing doesn't work, Earvin loses, too. But if it works, everybody wins."

The notion of black capitalism—wealthy blacks investing in black communities and independently creating a sort of trickle-down economy in the hood—was controversial long before Johnson gave it fresh currency. Though a simple idea advanced by black and white leaders alike, from W.E.B. Du Bois to Richard Nixon, it is criticized as a remedy for urban ills because it implies that society at large is ultimately not responsible for the troubled state of its black citizenry. Neither do all moneyed black folk believe that even massive investment by their ranks in shopping centers and the like will come close to rectifying generations of institutionalized racism and miseducation, as Johnson's confrere Charles Barkley has argued. (Of course, such thinking neatly enables blacks like Barkley to go about buying BMWs with nary a twinge of conscience—conspicuous consumption is, after all, the American way, and black folks in many ways are the most patriotic Americans of all.) Yet Johnson appears to be having some measure of influence: at his urging, Lakers center Shaquille O'Neal recently decided to become a partner in the Carson football-stadium project along with Johnson, Michael Ovitz and a host of other well-heeled celebrities. "When I first met Magic Johnson, before he had even said hi to me, he told me all this fame and getting your picture taken stuff is fine, but you need to start owning things," O'Neal told the *Los Angeles Times*. "As a seventeen- and eighteen-year-old kid, I didn't know what he was talking about at the time, but now I do realize what he was saying."

Johnson's pastor says that his critics, whether they mean to or not, are also holding Johnson disproportionately responsible for "giving back," which has become a buzz phrase among the black middle class but has never been practically understood. "This is not a cross I lay only on the shoulders of the very rich," says Bishop Charles Blake, who worked behind the scenes to help resolve the Santa Barbara Plaza conflict in Johnson's favor. "If I don't do the things with my own money that I should be doing, I shouldn't expect others to carry the rest of the load for me."

Even if Johnson realizes all of his development dreams—even if he does complete the plaza in record time and start on the east side of Crenshaw—it remains to be seen if residents will keep up their end of a tacit bargain and shop in the neighborhood. Middle-class consumers in Central L.A. have grown so accustomed to going elsewhere for quality goods that they might not be persuaded to come back to where they never went in the first place, even if it is in their own backyard. Mall magnate Alexander Haagen, who redeveloped the Baldwin Hills Crenshaw Plaza as a grand urban experiment in 1988, couldn't do it (though locals always complained that his company dropped the ball on leasing tony stores); whether Johnson can is literally the million-dollar question. Macy's recent, very unceremonious departure from the mall doesn't bode well.

Johnson, for his part, is undeterred by the criticism, even downright serene; he's acknowledged the challenge, has done his research, and stands by his actions. "We talk a lot of trash but don't do our homework," he says more than once. "Why are there so many fast-food franchises in black communities? Because people sat down and figured out that's what black people buy. They did their homework." But he knows the grounds of fear, of doubt. He knows that despite the tract-home normalcy represented by his movie house, despite its fiscal success and plenitude of smiling employees, it is not the suburbs, and for all the mighty potential of the urban market, this market, like literary black fiction and intelligent black movies, might be given only one shot. It is therefore critically important that the Magic Johnson Theatres remain, as they have thus far, incident-free, and that requires a delicate balancing act between community accessibility and community censure. So while theater officials denounce the possibly incendiary *Belly* and require men to have caps in hand only, they do vigorous outreach—special rates and events for seniors and kids, hosting the annual Pan African Film Festival—and patrons disgruntled over a late-starting movie or slow concession service are issued apologies and free passes. As anybody who's experienced years of meager-to-no goods and services in black neighborhoods will tell you, this customer-first attitude makes one hell of a difference.

Johnson is certain that he will prevail, that his terms will be accepted and then embraced. He insists there is no one who cares like him, who wants to be there like him. He tells the story of an older man who wrote to him to complain bitterly, like Yvonne Hutchinson, about the no-caps policy at the theater. Then the man came to the theater with his adolescent son, who willingly complied with the rule. "The man wrote me back and said, 'Now I understand, because my son showed me,'" says Johnson. "We're the outlet for people, the place where they don't worry, and have fun. We're their two-hour escape from reality."

Magic Johnson's greatest strength is the fact that he is consistently present. He pays attention; he doesn't ignore or condescend or talk ahead of you. His double-edged charm combines a nearly child-like fascination with the unfamiliar, even the banally unfamiliar—a man who has everything, he will nonetheless study your thirty-dollar wristwatch with real interest—and a grown-up ability to make it all feel familiar and comfortable.

During my first encounter with Johnson, he is getting his feet done. In an upstairs dressing room at Paramount Studios, a woman bends over his plus-size-13s, silently brandishing an array of pedicure instruments one by one. She focuses on her work, moving nothing but her hands, clearly wishing to be as unobtrusive as possible during this interview—she probably wonders, as I do, whether I can conduct a serious interview at all with a barefoot Magic—but Johnson is not quite granting her invisibility. Even as he talks to me he fixes her with a quizzical gaze, studies her clippers and files, mentally notes her progress, lifts a foot and offers another before she has a chance to ask. He acts like he gets this done all the time and like he's never gotten it done before (the pedicure, not the interview).

The second time we meet, Johnson's late-night Fox TV show, *The Magic Hour*, has been unceremoniously canceled less than six weeks after its premiere. He is philosophical about it, but there's a notable condensation of his spirit since I saw him last; he's disappointed. He does not like to fail—it happens rarely—or to be denied a stage. Ill-starred as *The Magic Hour* was, it at least occasionally focused the altruism in people who sneered for a living. During one of the final shows, the red-eyed rapper Coolio stopped Johnson in midsentence to give him a nod for his ongoing development activity in the hood. "Nobody talks about that," Coolio said heatedly. Johnson smiled—a small smile by Magic standards—and shrugged. "Thanks, man," he said. "I just try to keep it real, like you."

For Johnson, keeping it real means keeping it moving. Onward and upward: one of the tenants he's working to secure for the Santa Barbara Plaza is Krispy Kreme Doughnuts. ("You *know* them, don't you?" he tells more than asks me, an eager, faraway look in his eyes, and I nod vigorously, thinking I may have seen Krispy Kreme in a movie.) His record label, Magic Johnson Music, debuted last August. In October, his talent-management and promotions group became a consultant to Mike Tyson and determined to recast his sordid image; Johnson stood at the boxer's side and vowed that when Tyson begins making millions again, he'll make sure he has enough "life skills" to put the money to good use. This Sunday, *Passing Glory*, the first production from Magic Johnson Entertainment, premieres on TNT. It's too obvious, but it bears saying: Johnson could be a politician, one of the old-fashioned variety that kisses babies and flashes the victory sign. Someone recently suggested to him that he run for mayor. He laughs at the thought, but not dismissively; it is another unfamiliar thing to examine, at least for a moment. "Wow, I would love to be that guy," he muses at the prospect of being a leader. "But people would have to decide who that is. I fight our fights for us; I know what it's like to approach a company and get rejected. I'm not scared to invest my money, put it up. God blessed me with a vision. I can see something and make it happen. Everybody—black, white, Chicano, Japanese—has come up and commended me on the job I'm doing in the community. Just today, a white guy told me, 'Congratulations on doing something that nobody's doing,' and he was firm about it. It was nice to hear." He smiles ruefully. "But I'm just a country boy from Lansing. People have also said, 'Boy, you crazy.' "

THE EMPRESS'S NEW CLOTHES

SERENA, TO THE DISMAY OF MANY, MAKES THE SCENE

September 2002

It is both monumentally frustrating and oddly comforting to be reminded that, a year after the terrorist attacks, Americans haven't lost any of the clue-lessness or cultural myopia that shapes our national character and makes us grate—on *nerves*—the globe over. In bad times people understandably cling to the familiar, but it's almost as if we believe that an obsession with the outcome of *American Idol*, coupled with a determined ignorance about our unraveling environmental policies, is not a problem, but just what we need to improve things, to bring down the price of gas, bring up the price of stock, and in general clear the close air. Race has always provided much of this strange comfort; through peacetime and war, Jim Crow or no, it has never failed to reassure people of their respective places in a shaken society. Nor, of course, does it ever fail to reaffirm just how fucked up we still are.

The flap over Serena Williams's new tennis duds at the U.S. Open picks up that double-edged sword where we last left it (let's see: reparations, Donovan Jackson, Allen Iverson . . . well, maybe *left* isn't the right word). When Serena stepped out onto the court to play a round in a short, poured-on black catsuit courtesy of Puma, all hell broke loose. Pundits carped that this was wrong for the sport, wrong for feminism, wrong for youth role-modeling. Far richer was all that *wasn't* said, though it was communicated clearly enough in pho-tos that put Serena's mahogany skin, considerable sinew, blond braids and sculpted butt in everybody's face, right where our deepest fetishisms of race and sex are never supposed to be. The whole package was like a bomb threat that forced everybody to leave the building, though people stood outside at a distance and theorized plenty about what happened—Serena didn't show good sense, she was acting out, she might suffer from low self-esteem (Dr. Joyce Brothers's bird-brained offering). No one spoke even in passing to the possibility of some time-honored ethnic notions being responsible for much of the buzz, except Serena Williams herself, indirectly; when questioned about the outfit, she said with trademark candor: "It really sticks to what type of shape you have. If you don't have a decent shape, this isn't the best outfit to have." Translation: if you can't deal with a typically robust black woman's figure in full relief, you'd better learn how.

Certainly there have been body-baring tennis outfits before, from Suzanne Lenglen's right on up to Anna Kournikova's, but we've had a template (Marilyn Monroe, *Playboy*) for talking about those. We've never had Serena.

So what in the world are we to do with a girl who gets out in front of our fears so often, and who actually has the right to do so because she's number one? Serena as the top female tennis player in the world changes everything. Both she and her sister Venus belong to an unquestionably new breed. Neither woman is the symbol of black resistance that their predecessor Arthur Ashe automatically was; as champions in the Tiger Woods era, they do not protest so much as prescribe. They expect—perhaps naively, though rightfully—to be taken merely as themselves, and to set the trend rather than counter it simply by occupying positions never before occupied by blacks. But they know full well that black girls from Compton don't exactly conjure up images of success in the pro-tennis *monde*, which is still a bastion of the American elite; they know that beads and blond braids and frank self-approval only increase the paradox—this might be Li'l Kim or Foxy Brown, but not the reigning tennis queens whom we imagine, at the very least, as having sprung from college tours and suburban sensibilities. In the last generation we have all firmly separated good blacks from bad with a sort of hip-hop color line, and Serena and Venus routinely defy it: they're hood rats who speak like Valley girls, haute couture enthusiasts who refuse to straighten their hair but see nothing overtly political about it. They have plenty of attitude on the court but none of the sullenness or dreaded chips on the shoulder we associate with black Americans in general and with black athletes in particular; to the contrary, Serena and Venus are among the most emotionally open players on the circuit—giggly when they win, gloomy when they lose, entirely willing to answer questions from the press, even those with clear racial overtones that have *me* wishing they'd scare up some of that Compton trash talk, if only for a minute. But no; when a reporter asked Serena earlier this year if she felt she was worth all the "bank" she was making, Serena said, Yes, of course I do, and moved on.

I would have stopped and lectured the guy, but maybe Serena's unruffled-ness—spiritual and sartorial—works better. Looking good on her own terms is clearly her best revenge, or the best answer to those who may be terminally uneasy about her high profile. The good news is that Serena appears not to give a damn. She's no crusader, but neither is she looking to calm nerves, or to prove that she's really just like Martina Hingis or Monica Seles—she prefers to prove emphatically that she's not. But like a lot of young women still shifting from adolescent to adult, Serena has a lot of little girl left. Her catsuit is in your face, yes, but it also speaks to an eagerness to don that new red Sunday dress and parade it around for public affirmation of what she already knows—it looks cute! When Serena explained to the press that her catsuit "makes me run faster and jump higher and it's really sexy," the superwoman analogy sounded less aggressive than adorable, a refreshing bit of youthful hyperbole in an age when everybody grows up way too fast, and black kids from inner cities are assumed to have no childhoods at all. That Serena was sporting Harry Winston jewels, a tiara, and pink tennis shoes along with the catsuit further evidenced a giddiness that was lost in all the stern musings about the black spandex, that always seems to get lost whenever she's written about in any detail. At least the Williams sisters force the issue in their unstudied way, often tagging their comments about their own appearance with truth-or-dare questions like, Wasn't that fabulous? Don't I look good? Ladies and gentlemen, say *no* at your own risk.

What I will say at the risk of undoing my own undeveloped sense of fabulousness is, I wish *I* looked that good. Ironically, the flip side of the criticism is that some black people fear Serena looks *too* good; after generations of being cast as the other side's sex fantasy, the thinking goes, black women hardly need to aspire to be pinup girls. The catsuit is not so damaging for the gender as it is for the race, something Karen Grigsby Bates and Marcy Deveaux say without saying—it was like reading invisible ink—in a predictably polite *Los Angeles Times* story on the subject. Serena has a great body; Rudolph has a red nose, and it glows. So what else is new? Better to tone it down for the sake of history than to let it shine for that of vanity. Except that, well, Rudolph's nose turned out to have a divine purpose, and while I wouldn't take Serena's catsuit quite that far, I would wager that her steadfast insistence that people accept her dazzle or examine the reasons why they won't will liberate more than a few of us from one of our deadliest comfort zones.

But it will take time. I remember all the grumbling on the golf courses that first attended Tiger Woods's habit of wearing bright red (shirts, not dresses) on Sundays, the subtextual fear that the next thing you know, these folks will turn up in their lime-green suits and alligator shoes and ruin another perfectly good American tradition of understatement. In '03, of course, everybody wanted to be like Tiger; whether anybody will want to be like Serena, who has more edges and appears far less willing to soften them, remains to be seen. Watching a recent CNN story about supermodel Tyra Banks's summer camp for teenagers, I was struck by how truly hypocritical all the Serena controversy was. Tyra was describing how, as lead camp counselor, she consciously stripped off all her surface glamour and put on jeans and sneakers in order to connect with her charges, most of them black, city-raised, and wholly unacquainted with their own attractiveness and personal strengths. Undeniably a bit sappy, but undeniably the sort of effort we applaud for so-called at-risk kids (i.e., kids of color). How, then, could Serena's unequivocal self-invention be anything but progress, especially from a woman who not only is the stuff of stifling fetishes but also is a long way from being the stuff of American beauty standards? The times may be slow to change, but not Serena. Her outfit in the next round of play was, naturally, a serene pink and white. Shocking.

FALLING FOR TIGER WOODS ▬▬▬▬▬

2000

It's been well over a year now since I became a devotee of Tiger Woods. It was instantaneous, highly combustible love, the kind that in a span of a weekend cheerfully made mincemeat of the fact that I'd never watched a golf tournament, set foot on a proper course or swung a club more than twice in succession. I fell for Tiger the same way the tomboyish protagonist of one of my favorite adolescent books, *Tunes for a Small Harmonica*, fell in love with her wispy English teacher, a man she despised until one morning, listening to him read aloud one of his favorite obscure poems, she sat up in her chair and fell in love in the tiny rhythmic pause between one stanza and the next, in the drawing of a breath.

Tiger happened to me like that. I was sitting on a sofa on a Sunday, the last day of the Masters last spring, dragged there by a friend who insisted that black history was being made and I needed to witness it. Somewhere between the tenth and final holes the heavens opened up over my head and the poetry of Tiger fell rapturously into place. I divined the meaning not merely of his pending iconhood, but the things nobody knew or cared to think about: the razored hairs running down the back of his neck, the constraints yet wild possibility of his youth, the touching sureness of his stride as he headed into the terrible unknown. Here were outsized puppy feet at heartbreaking odds with a lovely, perfectly formed face and the guileless eyes of either a saint or a complete madman—God damn if I wasn't going to be the one to find out which thing he was. In a few hours Tiger reconnected me with a heedless kind of faith and a sense of journey I hadn't felt in years; he made a Siddhartha out of me at a time in my life when, despite having potency of almost palpable weight, it couldn't have had less direction.

It's all the more remarkable because the last thing I ever thought would inspire me is golf. The closest I ever got to the sport was during childhood, growing up on a south Los Angeles street that dead-ended into a public course. On hot summer afternoons a group of friends and I would convene at the course fence, collect the balls that had accidentally been hit into our street and shamelessly sell them back to passing golfers for a quarter, after which we'd head to the neighborhood liquor store to spend our loot on ice cream and such. My best friend of the last fifteen years, the one who lured me to his living room last spring for the Masters, is an aficionado who regularly held forth on the subtler glories of golf, but to little avail. I hated golf in the elliptical way I hated asparagus, not because I didn't like the taste, but because the whole thing was so colossally unappealing I could never bring myself to taste it. In short, I didn't see the point of embracing golf—until Tiger Woods, and the Masters.

Tiger made a fool out of me like I hadn't been made since 1984 and Bruce Springsteen's "Born in the U.S.A." tour, when I thrilled to a whole canon of images I had never seen or lived but felt nonetheless—a Jersey boardwalk, a dark road to nowhere, the small-town entropy of dreams. Words failed my enormity of feeling; at Bruce's concert I could only throw up my arms, sway, waggle fingers in delirious assent. Tiger, in a very different but no less significant way, brought me to my feet and made me do the same thing in front of a television. If Bruce illuminated for me the redemptive power of despair—of a life poorly lived, of the chance at another—Tiger illuminated a similar power of confidence, of possibly getting your shit right the first go-round. Last April, at the age of thirty-five, overburdened with caution and a sense that my dubious star had risen and was rising no further, that was a revolutionary thought indeed. Golf was suddenly the most salient of metaphors. Tiger was not only convincing me of my own native ability to tackle the unknowable, he was making history, and in the process agitating a tsunamic wave of sociocultural introspection beneath his golf-spiked puppy feet, introspection of a scale that hadn't been forced upon this politically somnolent country since *Plessy vs. Ferguson*.

Which is not to say that we agreed on everything. Tiger and I had our political differences, which were sharpest at the points where he asserted he saw no skin color, that he felt affronted at being called only black. "Oh, bullshit, Tiger!" I shouted at the television screen as he sat placidly across from Oprah. Have I, who proportionately share the same genetic mix as you, along with scores of other black folks, been a Negro all this time for nothing? We had to talk. Still, I was hopelessly enchanted; Tiger was flawed, but magic, and more magic for being flawed. He couldn't sing, but like Bruce, he had a sheer force of person and could make things happen by lowering his eyes and wielding his golf club/guitar. I resolved to go out and buy all of Tiger's greatest hits. In too many years of romantic misfires and running myself through maturity checkpoints, I had grown to miss hero worship, that eager sense of surrender, the mindless postering of bedroom walls with an adored male image. I started hunting for posters and fantasized about things I would never do, but that revived me merely because I considered them: tattooing a Tiger heart on my arm, stowing away in his private plane.

My boyfriend at the time, a sometime actor and longtime caddy, did not take kindly to my new interest. He was solidly with Tiger throughout the Masters triumph—"Kicked those white boys' asses up and down the fairway!" he exulted—but quickly lost empathy when I began sighing over the latest Nike Tiger ad or gazing at a *Sports Illustrated* photo spread with a charged reverence he thought should be reserved for him. To admire Tiger as a bastion of racial uplift was okay; to consider him as anything beyond was blasphemous and unsettling. There was nothing my boyfriend could do but set about deconstructing a myth I had already made; of course he failed, and we eventually split. He took particular umbrage to the fact that a couple of girlfriends and I drove up to Palm Springs one weekend last fall because

Tiger was playing in a tournament at La Quinta. None of us had ever been to such an event before, but we were willing to do anything (which wound up including changing a flat tire and enduring snubs by tournament officials) for a glimpse of the Man. "Tiger Woods!" my ex sputtered in the end. "He's all right. He's . . . a kid. Nothing special about him."

"Beg your pardon?" I said, not bothering to conceal my sarcasm. "Nothing special?"

"Well. First of all, he looks like a whole lot of people I know. Common. Second of all, he probably won't be around that long. I know golf, and golf goes away from you. You're great one minute, a dog the next. There're a whole lot of guys been through that." He went on to detail how Tiger's ferocious swing would throw out his back, how his quick temper and penchant for winning would always undermine the patience that was much more essential to success than he yet realized. He implied that Tiger was a lot like a million other brothers out there who, however smart and however willing, were destined to lose their way.

Not that I'm trying to establish a pattern, but I've gotten similar Tiger wariness from other black men, men for whom athletes are a no-brainer when it comes to objects of admiration. Nor do they seem to mind when the women they're close to profess an affinity for Michael Jordan, Jerry Rice, Ken Griffey Jr. But they are superstars to the point of seeming most real as video montages and marketing strategies, not people; Tiger is that rare superstar who seems unfinished, emotionally accessible, in part because golf grants him amazing space. He is a cowboy, a range rat. Rather than sharing turf with ten other players or squeezing shoulder to shoulder on a bench, he is always alone with a vast green canvas. When he muffs a putt, he flinches for a gallery of thousands, and the world, to see. At one point in the tournament, flushed from the sun and having to hustle from green to green like so many foxholes, I was crouched directly behind him, right at his pants leg. He stood a couple of inches off, arms folded and lost in thought, tall and deeply brown and borderline skinny and, in the most extraordinary sense of the word, ordinary. My ex was right, but not in the way he thought; I could have swooned.

Close up, Tiger squirmed beneath his famous telegenic cool: he sighed, fidgeted a little, blew his nose, moved to take off his cap but thought the better of it, sighed again. In the dead spaces between strokes he didn't entirely know what to do with himself, and couldn't decide because he didn't know who or what was watching him, so he could only stand looking a little bewildered and overly solemn. The constraints of his altar-boy composure were nearly palpable, and my heart went out to him; despite having obscene amounts of money, Tiger had to be in one hell of a spot. I wanted more than anything to express my sympathy, but golf etiquette forced me into that same damn silence.

A year later Tiger is not as routinely setting the world afire (neither am I, but I'm trying), and the world is growing impatient, sometimes nastily so. Consider: he finishes in the top five in all of the tournaments he plays for the first three months of the year, fourth in the Masters, third in the rigorous British Open, and it is not good enough. A sports analyst on cable television grouses that "Tiger has shown me nothing." Oprah gets him back on the show so that he can publicly assess this slacking off. A recent item in the sports page of the *Los Angeles Times* concludes that Nike made a big mistake in sinking millions into creating a line of Tiger golf wear that is too funky for older people, too conservative for hip-hoppers—Tiger, alas, is essentially a man without a market.

The spotlight swung back to him, briefly, in the recent PGA Championship, in which he led on the first day of play with a record-setting score of sixty-six. But other players quickly moved ahead, then eclipsed him, and though Tiger wound up finishing in the top ten, nobody would describe it as anything but a disappointment. All this doomsday is, of course, nonsense to me. Tiger still claims all the stars in my eyes and most of the space of one wall of my office cubicle. One homemade caption taped above a pensive magazine picture of him reads, OOOOOO BABY!! and elicits raised eyebrows from people unacquainted with my obsession. A glossy autographed picture sent to me from his management firm (but he signed it himself, I'm certain) is still tacked in an exalted place above my computer at home, just above postcard shots of my other muses—James Baldwin, Toni Morrison, Lorraine Hansberry, Oscar Wilde, Anton Chekhov. Bruce I long ago internalized, but that doesn't mean I am not seized with the feral, familiar pangs of what life might be, of what is left, when I hear the opening strains of "Thunder Road." Tiger and I have a long ways yet to travel.

HOMEBOYS IN OUTER SPACE AND OTHER TRANSGRESSIONS

TV IN BLACK AND WHITE

August 1999

Laugh aloud if you must, but the *Los Angeles Times* has speculated on that possibility in its fevered reporting of the fact that network television, as it heads into the last fall season of the millennium, doesn't have a single new show featuring a minority lead character. This has prompted outrage from black people, chiefly the NAACP, which has declared the situation emblematic of a general lack of parity; the association has mounted something of a march on Hollywood and has threatened to sue. (Latino groups have done the NAACP one better—beat it to its traditional punch—by announcing an upcoming "brownout" of prime time.) Such militance in an age of black reticence is both heartening and unnerving. I get the feeling that Kweisi Mfume and the television industry might settle out of court and agree upon a legal recipe for rectitude: no fewer than ten new shows by next year, each of which must feature 3.5 black faces minimum (identical twins, such as Tia and Tamra Mowry, or two child actors under the age of twelve counting as one).

I would like to cast an unpopular vote: I don't want to see any more new black people on TV. With all due respect to Mr. Mfume, enough is enough. With few exceptions, the black television presence has come to mean fetishized ghettoism or insipid vamping on the middle class, buffoonery across the board, nonexistent character development—to the point where the only black programs I watch with any regularity are TV Land reruns of *Sanford and Son* and *The Flip Wilson Show*. They at least represent the high point of what's always been a nadir. In the black-consciousness '70s, the characters of *Sanford and Son* and even *Good Times* were engineered with some dimensions beyond skin-color pathology, which is why they endure as family in America's collective TV memory, occupying as definitive a space as the Cleavers and the

Bunkers. A generation ago, black characters in even the cheesiest shows earnestly aspired to some kind of progressivism—Linc in *The Mod Squad*, the inner-city hoopsters in *The White Shadow*—but in the age of crack cocaine and Def Comedy Jam, blacks are mined almost exclusively for hood sensibilities or comic relief, frequently both. Today, our perspective on the creation and control of images is so out of whack that we embrace tokenism—now called diversity—as empowering: Lisa Nicole Carson, the sassy, wild-haired sidekick of *Ally McBeal*, is heralded as a star in black fan magazines increasingly eager to chronicle stardom.

Carson's prime-time "success" notwithstanding, the fact is that the dregs of talent and resources are being thrown to black audiences like offal was thrown to slaves. Ladies and gentlemen, we have arrived at Chitlin TV, and I, for one, ain't hungry.

The philosophical question is whether it is better to have junk food than to have no food at all. Like radio and film and advertising before it, television is a lapdog of popular culture, and as such has never been a reflection of our best impulses about race, but our basest. It is certainly invested in perpetuating minority images, just not the sort we want to see: *Amos 'n' Andy* and *The Little Rascals* were more than popular in their day, even among blacks, but popularity came at the dear price of dignity and a sense of artistic worth. Buckwheat, Lightnin', Urkel, Martin—we would like to think we are progressive, that we Americans embrace forward motion as a thing beyond absolute necessity, but in the case of bettering black images, we have in fact succumbed to entropy. So what is progress? Given the lowest-common-denominator syndrome, a thousand new black shows in a single season might actually militate against it, as WB and UPN demonstrated with tripe like *Smart Guy* and *Homeboys in Outer Space*. The irony is that only a few short seasons ago, the *L.A. Times* rolled out a story not on the vacuum, but on the impressive volume of black-themed shows debuting on network television—and subsequent vicious reviews and commentaries rendered that volume pretty much beside the point.

Despite blacks' criticism of the current crying lack, the representation we are clamoring for is not merely physical or numerical, and it is rooted in Hollywood's history of keeping blacks underemployed and black images viciously circumscribed. Comedy has always best suited the latter purpose, which explains the rarity of black television dramas—no one wants to view black life in anything but exaggerated terms. Black programs without a comedic core have historically failed: Nat "King" Cole's variety show in the earliest days of television was high-quality and black-headlined, an apparent contradiction to the nervous white sponsors who ultimately refused to support it, despite Cole's enormous popularity as a singer and entertainer. (Flip Wilson succeeded many years later where Cole couldn't, but Wilson was, of course, a standup comic.) Now, with black comics the most visible, venerated and youth-friendly of television performers, we are staring down the barrel of the same problem. Even those few thoughtful black shows that succeed in spite of the odds, that cross over to a wider audience—*Cosby*, for one—do not establish patterns for future successes; Hollywood rushes to knock off *Melrose Place*, but who is really looking to knock off *Cosby*, with the exception of Cosby himself? Black longevity has tended to be personality-driven, not industry-driven or industry-cultivated, perhaps because while few blacks appear before the camera, far fewer appear behind it—as writers, directors, and producers.

In one paradox among many, black performers have always been the backbone of American entertainment, but not its payroll, and while blacks have always argued for more sheer numbers, they have argued louder for better industry regard—not more shows, but the latitude to produce shows, such as *Frank's Place* or *I'll Fly Away*, that don't rely on black shtick. What's at stake here is an essential American freedom, that of self-determination. It's not quite a civil right, but it's bigger, more spiritually encompassing, and therefore harder to attain; nor, in this case, can self-determination be accomplished entirely by the black collective self. We are tired of appearing stupid to ourselves, but the peculiar thing is, has always been, that we can't solve the problem alone.

Some good may issue from this. I'm glad the somnolent NAACP has rediscovered its fighting spirit (though I would be happier if it took up the fight against, say, substandard public education of black children), but it is still stepping rather gingerly around the issue of quality. It gets raised here and there, with *The Secret Diary of Desmond Pfeiffer*, with Eddie Murphy's *The PJs*, but it's often wrong-headed; to miss the satire of *The PJs* is to accept the straight-up jive of *Martin* as irrefutably hip and culturally accurate. And we are loath to implicate ourselves as bricks in the wall: BET congratulated itself recently for launching the nation's first black production studio, but its maiden project is a slew of television movies based on black romance novels. I certainly don't quibble with blacks' right to be as lowbrow as whites or anyone else, but please, let's not describe the peerless Angela Bassett or Loretta Devine knocking about in a soap opera as freedom.

The issue circles back to progress, what it is or isn't, what it's been down-sized into, and whether or not we are all asking too much of television to do its part in shifting the course of history. How can we redirect a corporate behemoth like television when we can't persuade Macy's to stay put in the Crenshaw mall? Black people and television may appear to be at each other's throats at the moment, but they have a far more symbiotic relationship than anyone would care to admit. Networks put out shows and black people watch them, twenty hours more a week than non-black households. Representation, lest any diversity zealots forget, is the result of politics and influence, not numbers.

Having said all that, I have to confess that I'm still a marginally active member of our TV nation. All right, all right—I've watched my share of *Martin* and *Malcolm and Eddy* and *Sister Sister*, when I was actively trying to kill an evening, when I was in a mood to spite myself. Occasionally I laughed, but more often I'd get sour. Who did these television producers take me for? Who did Martin Lawrence take me for? I smelled collusion, and one night I turned abruptly to the A&E channel, where I was equally flatlined by a biography of Jamie Lee Curtis. I was bored, but bored in peace. I was staging a nonviolent demonstration against racial inequity—King would have been proud. There might be some civil rights potential in this stuff after all.

WHITE MAN WITH ATTITUDE ▬▬▬▬▬

HOW RANDY NEWMAN WENT FROM POP MUSIC'S REIGNING SCHLUB TO MOVIE-MUSIC ROYALTY

November 2001

On the morning of September 11, I leave a message on the answering machine of Randy Newman's manager. "Is that second interview we scheduled still on?" Nobody calls back. A thin veil of clouds yawns open to lovely weather, a sparkling blue-and-white mirror image of New York City, mi-

nus the smolder of dead planes and wounded buildings that plays in two-or three-minute intervals on CNN. My younger sister, the lawyer, shows up at the door; she can't go to work because she works downtown and the courts and everything else are closed, and she's already packed her infant son off to daycare. Her nerves are too jangled to sit at home and do nothing. I fix her some grits for breakfast, and together we watch more CNN.

Hearing nothing from the Newman camp, I resolve to keep the appointment for professionalism's sake. My sister in the front seat, I drive to Newman's home in the Palisades on highways and roads made clear and more hospitable by disaster, fear, and orders to stay home. Overhead the sky is brilliant and boundlessly, stupidly optimistic. It strikes me that the morning so far, with its easy juxtapositions of tragedy and homily, of everything going to hell on television and everything coming up roses where I live, would be perfect fodder for a Newman song.

> Look at those mountains,
> Look at those trees,
> Look at that bum over there,
> Man, he's down on his knees . . .

Newman shouts "Hello!" in a startled voice from upstairs before appearing in the foyer in rumpled shirt and shorts. His television in the spacious dining room is tuned to CNN. He looks bewildered, partly by the unfolding news of the world and partly because I've shown up. He doesn't seem to know if I'm supposed to be here any more than I do—his manager is apparently too upset to return calls. "Okay. Where should we talk?" he mutters, rubbing his head of graying curls and glancing about his palatial house like he's never seen it before, as if it doesn't quite agree with him. We settle on his studio in the backyard. He takes his seat behind his desk, next to the Steinway grand that's always within reach during conversation. "I figured this would happen in my lifetime," he says, fingering the keyboard idly, talking and playing nearly to himself. "I just didn't know when. Myself, I'm fine." We discuss what we know at this point about the attack's cause, the logistics, the body count, the futility, and the inevitability of U.S. military strikes, of war. But what unsettles him most are things much smaller. "You know, you see it and it's almost too big to look at," he says of the hijackings. "Then somebody told me that a guy in the plane that crashed near Pittsburgh went to the bathroom and called 9-1-1 and said the plane was being hijacked." He shakes his head. "When you hear an individual story—a guy in the men's room, and then the *plane crashed—it makes it rougher somehow. You hear there's a guy, and it becomes real to you. That he had the bravery to say that. It makes it worse."*

For nearly thirty-five years, Randy Newman has been making records, and 2001 is like any other year. He has no comeback album or down-and-out-in-the-industry stories, thanks to a second career as a successful film composer, and thanks to a pop career that, admired as it was, never really ascended in the first place—to be down and out you must at some point have been high and *in*, and he never was, quite. So the only reason to write about Randy Newman is that he's still Randy Newman, unrealized pop star (the film scoring he calls well-paying grunt work, something to essentially support his studio habit). At fifty-seven he is perhaps more amiable than in the past, but no less a malcontent. Artistically, he's as much an enigma as he was when he officially arrived on the music scene in the early '70s with albums like *Good Old Boys* and *Sail Away*. At a time when pop music was splitting its sensibilities in two, echoing the raw anger of the '60s or offering soothing philosophical counterpoints to it—The Eagles, Carole King, James Taylor—Newman was doing neither. He was following some weird interior compass that often led him back, back to slave times or Reconstruction or an obscure historical event, or to various observations tied to no history at all, all of which violated pop music's ironclad rule about being in the moment.

He violated other rules, too, never directly addressing love and heartache and broken dreams; though he had plenty of discontent, Newman was not a rebel—he was too glum and unsexy for that. He was a kind of accidental analyst and humorist who happened to be under thirty. He was famous, he knew rhythm, even lived it, but he was never what you'd call *hot*. Even all the attention generated by the only two Top 40 singles of his career, "Short People" and "I Love L.A.," focused more on the songs themselves and their questionable sentiments than on the man who thought them up.

It's hard to tell if Newman's okay with this—the first time we talked, I detected in him, at points, a lingering hope that one day he'll be a superstar. But he understands it. "I feel like an outsider. I always have," he told me. "I feel like an outsider in this country. Being Jewish is part of it. Philip Roth had this in a book: the next great Jewish genius after Moses was Irving Berlin. He took all the Christ and blood out of Easter and made it about fashion. He made Christmas about the weather." He laughs, relishing the idea that Irving Berlin pulled a fast one on fundamentalist America. "He wrote about Alabama, and he was never *there*! Sometimes people on the outside who want in so bad look at it differently, look at it harder. I'm very interested in the country, though I don't necessarily feel a part of it."

But Newman's music took alienation to new human depths; the personas in songs like "Half a Man" and "It's Money That I Love" may not have been his, but the feelings were. He wound up striving for a kind of emotional equity that pop music, skewed as it has always been toward love and triumph, never cultivated; in Newman's songs distance and disaffection and ignorance get equal time as significant, even sympathetic, characters in the theater of daily life. Newman credits part of his circumspection to growing up Jewish but atheistic, and another part to his father, Irving, a fiercely intellectual doctor who was attentive and conscientious with patients but spared them no painful truths. "I get my sense of humor from him," says Newman, somewhat reluctantly. "I don't have his consistently bad temper, not to the point of being unreasonable. He treated a lot of famous people. One of them was Oral Roberts, whom he liked very much, though my father actively grumbled about religion. He made fun of it. Once Oral called him in the middle of the night and said he had terrible hemorrhoids. My dad told him, 'Why are you calling me in the middle of the night? Why don't you stick your *other* finger up your ass and heal yourself?' " He howls at the memory.

Dr. Newman was something of a departure from family tradition, which was—surprise—scoring films. Randy's uncle Alfred was pretty much the gold standard for movie music during Hollywood's heyday; he composed for such classics as *All About Eve, Wuthering Heights, The Grapes of Wrath, How Green Was My Valley*—even the trumpet-driven fanfare that accompanies every screen appearance of the 20th Century Fox logo and has become the shorthand theme song of Hollywood itself. Alfred racked up a total of forty-five Academy Award nominations and won nine of them. Another one of Randy's uncles, Lionel, was senior vice president of music at Fox for forty-five years, in addition to conducting for and scoring films; his 1969 effort, *Hello, Dolly!*, nabbed an Oscar. Yet another uncle, Emile, heads music at Samuel Goldwyn, and still another, Robert, is a studio executive. A cousin, Thomas Newman, is the Grammy-winning composer who scored *American Beauty*, among many other films.

The point is that Randy Newman is downright royalty in two of the most influential industries in town, if not the country, and he still manages to be a schlub. Even though he's evolved into a respected film composer in his own right, notably for Disney/Pixar and films like *Toy Story* and the recent Pixar release *Monsters, Inc.*, he complains about the machinations of the business and worries that he might be film-composing himself right out of whatever sociopolitical relevance pop music still affords. "Film people give me adjectives, and I write something," he says, a little wistfully. "I can't write *shit-piss-fuck-fart-damn* for Disney." And what he does write, he believes, often never breaks an audience's consciousness—not even the most evocative and influential of his scores, like *Avalon*, *The Natural*, and his first major assignment, Milos Forman's *Ragtime*, a film that was tailor-made for Newman's fascination with the dark energy of Americana.

"That big pile of movie music," he says, gesturing to carelessly stacked sheafs on top of the Steinway, "like some of it you don't even hear if the air conditioning is on in the movie theater. The time you have to spend doing movie music is not commensurate with the impact that it makes. Sometimes I think, 'Why am I worried so much about whether this is a B-flat or an F?' But I can't help it. I can't help but take it personally when directors say, 'Could you do this or that on the ending?' It hurts my feelings and makes me angry a bit."

Still, the musical purist—and perhaps the fatalist—in him enjoys the challenge of scoring, with its compressed work schedule and solitary studio confinement that can go on for weeks. "I'm really hard on it," he says of his film music. "I mean, I've written in 4/4 my whole life"—he bangs out a sample bar—"but in a movie you can't do that. It's open, but you gotta hit things in a picture, in animated pictures especially." To demonstrate, he plays fitfully, impressionistically, following some imagined action. "What you do is subordinate—it's meant to help the picture. I'll have something I like, but I'll have to truncate it because the picture dictates it."

How does he feel about that mode of working? He sighs and crosses his arms. "There's a song I remember by James Taylor, called 'Bartender's Blues,'" he says, and begins singing in that familiar mocking/mournful voice: 'I need four walls around me to hold me tight, to keep me from drifting away . . .' And I do. I need that discipline from without, and that's the strictest kind, having to write for a picture on deadline." He shrugs. "But I'd write if I didn't have it."

Newman has been nominated for an Oscar fourteen times, meaning he's consistently recognized by the industry for his efforts, but he has yet to win. I suggest the possibility of a Newman backlash, a reluctance to anoint another member of his family, even as the family must be acknowledged. Newman has another idea. "I thought at first there might be a possible bias because I came from pop music," he says. "But I've done enough scoring now where that would have no effect. There's always a reason a score wins—it's a movie they love, or one that wasn't very popular but was a serious effort, like *Postino*. I mean, I do *comedies*. Of the fourteen films I've been nominated for, I'd say I had a real chance of winning maybe only three times."

That doesn't seem to bother Newman at all. Unlike his failure to become a true pop star, not winning an Oscar seems to bolster the peculiar confidence he's always drawn from being an outsider: he might forever yearn for acceptance, but much of his identity rides on not getting it. "The people who really know a lot about film music don't run the Academy," he explains. "There are only a couple of hundred people in the world who really know a good score from a bad one. It's too arcane. It's like cinematography—I get to vote for that, and costume design. That's ridiculous, I mean, look at me. What do I really know about costume design?" He chuckles. A long blue thread that's been hanging unnoticed from his sleeve the entire conversation quivers in assent.

Newman is not nearly as ambivalent about his pop canon as he is about his film one. Musically speaking, he's proudest of his studio albums, and his only regret is that he hasn't made more of them (he's released eleven over his career, versus thirteen film scores in the last twenty years). Yet when asked about the larger meaning of music to him, or to anybody else, he admits an utter lack of faith. "I don't believe music can change anything," he says decisively. "Except fashion. And maybe the way people speak. What Madonna's wearing is a hell of a lot more interesting than anything she says." He doesn't have much good to say about current Top 40. "All harmonic interest has gone out of pop," he declares, "though I don't listen to much of anyone for edification." With typical equanimity he doesn't believe it's all a wasteland, either. He likes early Alanis Morrissette and Everclear and Lauryn Hill because, he says, they have something to say. He especially admires hip-hop wild boy Eminem, whom he calls a great comic artist with a gift for character, like himself. But overall, he doesn't think people are listening much to lyrics—not that they ever really did. "Music's a strange medium for meaning," he muses. "Radio isn't it. There aren't a lot of people who'll listen without eating potato chips. And with my music, to like it, you have to listen to it. It's not something you put on as background music at a party." He grins. "You might if you were a *snob* of some kind."

This has always been true of Newman's music, which leads to a standard question of how it has aged. The answer isn't standard: it hasn't. Randy Newman is exploring the same big-picture themes not just of yesteryear, but of the ages—the various meanings of companionship, abandonment, greed, human bondage, imperialism, patriotism. In cosmic time, barely a minute of Randy Newman has passed; we're still waiting for him to hit a stride or get to a point. This is distinctly different from the career trajectory of most gray-ing rockers: man plays guitar and rails at the world, gets famous, gets drunk/drugged out, gets older and/or has kids, gets reflective and/or more politically conservative, releases an album that is notably softer in tone than anything previous and is deemed "accessible" or "mature."

Randy Newman was always mature, or he was always a punk; in either case, he sings any song from *Land of Dreams* just as believably, or *unbelievably*, as he sang it thirteen years ago. Despite a bout with drugs in the '70s, and a battle with Epstein-Barr syndrome in the '80s, he seems no worse—well, no *different*—for the wear. His wonder and disgust with the world are the same. He has been married twice and has five children, the last two under ten. Not surprisingly, he likes the idea of being the artist as an old man; a guy who never exactly had the world on a string. Age brings him a certain measure of relief. "I thought my last album was good," he says of *Bad Love*, an ostensibly intimate record that critics couldn't resist describing as Randy Newman finally letting his third-person guard down—in other words, maturing. Newman actually agrees, to a point. "*Bad Love* was rock & roll, but it was talking about being older. It wasn't eighteen, or twenty-one, or twenty-seven. It wasn't thirty-five. That may be a bad thing. I don't know." He looks at me and gets inspired. "Writers are allowed to be fifty-seven and do their best work. They're expected to get better or stay as good. I guarantee you that Philip Roth liked his last book. He's not going back to *Portnoy's Complaint* going, 'Ah, *then* I could write.' That's suicide. Music is different, I know. There's a lot of evidence that it's a young person's game. More people have gotten worse than have gotten better."

Newman likes to talk, but he likes to play more. His playing is directly him in a way that his lyrics, unvarnished as they are, are not. As he talks, he often turns to the piano to answer a question or give a fuller picture of himself. "Here, this is what I do," he says at one point, and with his left hand begins vamping a growly bass beat in straight time. He starts humming, and the right hand joins in with a syncopated melody, relaxed but urgent in a bluesy kind of way—this is the hallmark of so many of his mid-tempo songs, from "Short People," "Roll With the Punches," and 'It's Money That I Love" to "You Can Leave Your Hat On." The ballads—if one can call them that—like "Marie," "I Want You To Hurt Like I Do," and even "Sail

Away"—are old-fashioned in a different sort of way, lushly orchestrated or sparely orchestrated but precise as a bolero, as carefully designed as the faster material seems offhanded. This is all illusion, of course; Newman casts everything to very specific effect. But he's also open to change and different interpretations, which may be why many other artists, from Harry Nilsson to Aaron Neville, have covered Newman songs. Tom Jones's version of "You Can Leave Your Hat On," for the movie *The Full Monty*, became a latter-day anthem of sexual liberation, which Newman wholly appreciates but finds amusing.

"I didn't take the guy seriously," he says, referring to the song's protagonist. "He's weak, he's asking the woman to stand on a chair . . ." Newman goes to the keyboard again and sings in a register low enough to be a mumble: " 'Baby, take off your coat . . .' It's really nothing, sort of sleazy. But Joe Cocker did it like this—" He sings the same line again in a much higher key, and it bursts forth, a revelation. "You put it in a higher register, and it changes the whole song. I could have sung it like that, I can sing it up there." He considers his own mild professional envy. "But I don't have the instinct," he finishes. "I meant it to be . . . that. I picked the wrong key. It's not a sexy song."

Humane as his music is at its core, Newman himself has never been characterized as being even remotely warm and fuzzy. Profiles over the years are filled with adjectives such as acerbic, irreverent, intelligent, pointed, satirical, wry. Newman's closest friends admit he's something of a grouch, but with good reason: he grew up shy and insecure about his looks, especially about his crossed eyes that were never quite corrected after several surgeries and which required thick glasses all his life. The self-doubt and introversion proved good for his musical development, not so good for his public image. Not that Newman's admirers ever considered that a problem; Lenny Waronker, his closest friend since childhood and longtime producer, essentially coaxed the young Newman out of his shell into a vaunted career. That was public-relations coup enough. "What it really boils down to, I think, is that I had a much clearer picture of his potential than he did," Waronker said recently. "I think my enthusiasm eventually wore him down, though he fiercely resisted it. Let's face it, you can't shield yourself indefinitely from someone relentlessly reminding you of your greatness. You want to hear it." On a more personal level—a phrase that would doubtless make Newman cringe—Waronker said that his friendship with the singer "helped me to understand so much. I just think that being around [Randy] has made me smarter and better."

That's about as touchy-feely as people get about Newman. Even in Hollywood, a place famous for its gush, Pixar director and frequent co-worker John Lasseter said he chose Newman to score kid-oriented films because "that blend of twisted humor and emotion is really unique." And, he added significantly, "He never speaks down to an audience in either the songs or the score. It's always from an adult point of view." Clearly, Newman's music represents him better than he represents himself. That's his greatest wish, and his greatest fear.

I first heard Randy Newman when a lot of people first heard him, via his radio single "Short People" in 1977, when I was fifteen. I immediately liked the song for all sorts of reasons—its sing-along simple-but-affecting melody, its driving piano, its droll but entirely serious take on the menace of mindless prejudice (Newman says the song was also a conscious musical inversion, and arguably a spiritual perversion, of the Captain and Tennille's "Love Will Keep Us Together"). I also connected Newman immediately to ragtime doyen Scott Joplin, whose work I deeply admired and felt had been grossly misinterpreted by a public that wanted to consume it for its great Negro entertainment value, then discard its complexities and contradictions like bones. Newman was also misunderstood, but he was certainly more in control of his fate and his product than Joplin had been at the turn of last century. "Short People" was at once radical and old-fashioned, flinty social commentary propelled by the cheery bombast of musical theater and American traditions reaching all the way back to Joplin and Stephen Foster. (I remark to Newman that he could have been Joplin's librettist, given the music the tart words and tension it deserved, and he seems genuinely impressed by the thought.) Newman fit my adolescent sensibility of not fitting, but in a good, almost arrogant way—his stuff wasn't quite rock, but it rocked. He knew it, too, even while he hid behind the adenoidal voice, unruly hair, thick glasses, and general loser persona. In another time and place, Randy Newman would have migrated to my clique of oddball friends in high school, and we would all have silently appreciated his smarts and self-deprecation and inability to get dates. He would have been a hero.

Later, in the early '80s, a friend introduced me to the Randy Newman I had always sensed was there but had never met—"Mr. Sheep," "Jolly Coppers on Parade," "Rednecks," "Sail Away," "Louisiana 1927," the nevermore-topical "Political Science." I was astonished to hear a white singer get away with repeatedly using the word "nigger," which since the official death of minstrel shows has been guaranteed to trigger outrage in America of some sort, somewhere. It evidently didn't; I ask Newman why, adding, as a kind of disclaimer, that I love the song "Rednecks" and the whole *Good Old Boys* album. I was especially moved by "Louisiana 1927," a portrait of the devastation wrought by the infamous flood of that year, though I've always known full well that the narrator is a cracker and wouldn't hesitate to shoot me on sight if he thought I was trespassing on his sorry, waterlogged property. Creating such odd, even alarming but resonant emotional tableaux is Newman's gift. "If I were Neil Young or Dylan or someone else, people might have noticed, but there was this enormous apathy," says Newman of the N word. "Mostly they didn't know. In [early-'70s] Boston they were in the middle of all that school busing, and they took it off the air. Actually, I feel nervous every time I say the word, every time I play the song, just like I do with 'Christmas in Capetown.' But it made a point that seemed more in question than it does now. The North doesn't have any more moral superiority in the way it treats blacks. Things weren't great anywhere . . . but this is the really segregated town, L.A. More segregated than Atlanta, or San Francisco."

Newman knows L.A. in a way celebrities who live here generally don't, and he appreciates it — both the subtleties and the abominations — in a way most us of here don't bother to. For Newman it's less a company town and more home, as well as a logical landscape for his creative and political idiosyncrasies: he talks fervently about the color-coded inequities of public schools ("It's *really* sad"), about the north Long Beach/Compton rivalry, about the shifting demographics in South Los Angeles ("*Where* did all the black people go?" he asks me at one point), about his affinity for the Harbor Freeway ("It's one of those obscure roads, but it goes a long way"), and his dislike of Santa Monica Boulevard ("Ugly from start to finish"). Newman was born here but spent the first three years of his life in New Orleans, and vacationed there in the summer until the age of eleven or so. Clearly, the South made an indelible impression; in his critically lauded 1988 album *Land of Dreams*, also unofficially voted The Album Most Likely To Be Autobiographical, Newman details those impressions in songs like "Dixie Flyer" and "New Orleans Wins the War" ("Momma used to wheel me past an ice cream wagon/One side for white and one side for colored/I remember trash cans floating down Canal Street/It rained every day one summer"). In an interview last year, Newman said that, despite its obvious shortcomings, he liked the South, and Southerners, their traditions of civility, the South's — particularly New Orleans's — sense of being a world apart from modern America. "There's just a few things they're bad on, Jews and blacks and gun control," he said. "It's one of those ancient things, but they do go deeper with people than we do in the rest of the country. They always did. They just had it written down on walls: 'No Colored.' 'No Jews.' Boston didn't have it written down. L.A. didn't have to write it down."

Part of the reason I identify so strongly with Newman is that he apparently finds it difficult, or untrustworthy, to be himself in his art. For him it's personal; for me it's that plus something else. Black artists historically have been allowed public identities, never private ones, so that their music is read as a reflection of social or even emotional struggle. The reverse is true for white artists, particularly singer-songwriters: the world proceeds from *them*. But Newman has always found intimacy and soul-baring confining and against instinct, and so has embraced emotional obliqueness and a storyteller role—the de facto black musical tradition—by default. Despite the prevalence of the first person in his songs, he positions himself as the conscientious observer in somebody else's shoes. Newman does this with such sincerity and lack of judgment that his songs emerge as unique in the annals of American song: examinations of broad types—bigots, boozers, imperialists—narrowed into people, played by Randy Newman. Newman is none of these people, and all of them; he is the medium who channels them, gives them heart, or brains, or motive. None of this guarantees you'll like the characters any better, but Newman's job has always been to make things clearer, not more bearable.

"The third-person thing has always been my natural mode of expression, but it's never proved very popular," he muses. "I'm not the 'I' in my songs a lot of times, and if I were, I wouldn't be heroic. I think it's some kind of character flaw, not necessarily an admirable modesty at work. I think it's shyness, and it turned into a style." It's a style that allows him to speak passionately where his shyness would ordinarily prohibit it. "In my songs, characters and people always come first," he says. When they don't, they're not as good. "I don't want to preach, I want the person to make the best case he can make. Like in 'Rednecks,' the guy's making a case, a good case, and yet he's not—" He stops abruptly short of judgment. "Would *you* want to be his neighbor?"

Over the years, people have been tempted to say that Newman champions the underdog or the anti-hero, but like many readings of his music, that's often way too simple (the enduring controversy over "Short People," one of his least thematically complicated songs, makes the point). Newman scoffs at the popular notion of heroes, but admires heroism. He isn't really a pop singer, but he has no quibble with popularity. He may live in his own head but enthuses over the lowest-common-denominator likes of Lionel Richie and ABBA. "I fucking *love* that stuff," he says heatedly. "Of course in ABBA you have the winner taking all, the loser standing small. You have some language difficulties there, but it doesn't matter at all. I don't look for irony." Pause. "Now, I wouldn't want to be listening to it dying in a plane crash."

What Newman actually likes most about pop music—ABBA notwithstanding—is its veneration of male cool, which officially started with Elvis and lives today in hip-hop. "That's certainly the hippest stuff going," he says of hip-hop, a bit admiringly. "It's all part of that. I remember coming out of Marlon Brando movies feeling like"—he squares his shoulders, puts out his chest, grins ear to ear—"you know what I mean? It's a big deal, that feeling. I don't know who's the Brando or the James Dean anymore, but that's the lure of the music. Feeling hip and *tough*.

"But you can't believe your own story," he adds. "That rock-and-roll life. You can't pretend you're tough." I ask Newman what he thinks of the whole rap genre, which may be the current incarnation of cool but has always suffered creatively from its own hollow posturings of thugs, gangsters, and womanizers. Black artists are generally encouraged into such postures and self-referential stereotypes by the music industry, which exacerbates the problem. Newman agrees with that, but resists pessimism. "I assume some of these guys have some interesting stuff going on," he says a bit defensively. "Dr. Dre is making some very good tracks for Eminem. I mean, kids aren't looking to Neil Young anymore, or to me." He brightens, like he's just had a better idea. "I'll tell you a story. I don't know if it's true. I don't stand by it—I'll deny it. A singer has just been on this awards show, and his manager comes backstage, a Jewish guy. This white guy—we'll call him Andy—is back there doing coke and drinking. He's had substance-abuse trouble or something. The manager says, 'Andy, you've worked so hard, why are you doing this?' The guy says, 'Leave me alone, you little Jew bastard, I'm just enjoying myself after I've had this big triumph.' They wander into a room where a bunch of black guys are hanging around. The manager says, 'Come on, Andy, let's go, let's go home, and start over again.' Then the guy starts yelling real loud, *'You Jew prick, you bastard!'* And some of the black guys start saying, 'Yeah, yeah,' getting into it a little. And the manager says, 'Okay, Andy, I'm going.' There's a crowd of black guys gathered around. Then when the manager gets by the last guy, Andy turns to him and said, 'My-y-y niggas.'"

Newman cracks up. "I don't know, that's such a *bad* story. But it's a phenomenal one. They're like egging him on, Andy's high, feeling a part of it—'My niggas.'" He shakes his head in disbelief, or disapproval, or something else.

Randy Newman's wit is formidable and obvious, but after spending time with him, I find myself more impressed with his heart, which is also formidable, though not what he's known for. Newman likes to keep even his most loyal public off-balance, guessing at who he is or what he might mean. But he also frets about being misunderstood. He's come to expect indignation over "Short People" and "Rednecks," but what's thrown him more recently are fans agreeing with the rednecks, singing the refrain proudly ("We're rednecks, rednecks/We don't know our asses from a hole in the ground") at concerts, or taking the simple uplift of "Follow the Flag" solemnly, at face value. Yet Newman will never blame his audience, to whom he's always accorded more integrity and insight than the characters in his songs. "It's difficult," he says, reiterating "Follow the Flag" on the piano and listening closely. "It's not meant to be patriotic, but it's a close call. It's obvious to me, but . . . maybe I didn't do it well enough."

That kind of falling short seems to be the artist's greatest worry; his song "Maybe I'm Doing It Wrong" was also the name of a revue of his music done at the La Jolla Playhouse back in 1982. He regrets "The Blues," a song from his *Trouble in Paradise* album of the following year that mocks a boy who finds solace in playing music; here was the intruding "I" that Newman had dedicated his whole life to avoiding. That didn't mean he didn't participate in the goings-on; he wanted to, and did. He still does. He may never be in charge, but he never stands so far away from the essence of things that he can't feel them. Feeling, he believes, is everything. I remark how I always thought his hit "I Love L.A.," despite its subversiveness and frank criticism of us, was also joyous and deeply felt. "Yeah, it's so chamber of commerce—Imperial Highway!—it's just *funny*," he exclaims. "There's some kind of ignorance L.A. has that I'm *proud* of. The open car and the redhead and the Beach Boys, the night just cooling off after a hot day, you got your arm around somebody." He crosses his arms again and smiles in wordless satisfaction, smiles from the momentary depths of a rock-star dream on a bright and terrible day. "That sounds *really* good to me. I can't think of anything a hell of a lot better than that."

I'm always proud to say that I was born and raised in Los Angeles. The notion of L.A. as home defies expectations and challenges the West Coast uninitiated to picture a place that's specific and lived-in—with named streets and neighborhoods, with sites of historical significance—rather than the old placeholders of Hollywood, palm trees shooting up into orange skies and a flatland of freeways. The details of L.A. are an argument against those lazy generalities that I'm always happy to make. But the other side of that happiness is a frustration with the last big American city of dreams, how it has let black people down. The pieces in this section speaks to the let-downs—mediocrity, isolation, the demographic crush of immigration—and to the dreams that persist in spite of that. For all its failures, L.A. still represents self-creation and reinvention for all, and faith dies harder here than just about anywhere else.

WELCOME TO INGLEWOOD —
LEAVE YOUR ASPIRATIONS BEHIND!

WHY COMING HOME HAS BEEN A LABOR OF TOUGH LOVE

July 2005

Every day, if the weather cooperates and my exercise conscientiousness holds, I go for a walk. I get in my car and drive about a mile north of my house, park on a sleepy side street off Manchester Boulevard and begin an elliptical, four-mile-plus loop around the once-fabulous Great Western Forum in Inglewood.

The walk is an hour long, steadily though not extremely uphill, and has virtually no cross streets to encumber thought or concentration. I also have the company of many other people on this walk; we nod in passing, exchange brief hellos, or if we are plugged into something electronic, vigorously wave to each other in silence. I realized, after about a year of this, that besides trying to shed fifteen pounds with the least amount of sweat, I was also making a kind of daily pilgrimage to one of the touchstone buildings of my childhood. I grew up in L.A. near Century Boulevard and Van Ness Avenue, just east of the Inglewood border, and for everybody in the vicinity, not only was the Forum the home of the beloved Lakers, its vast parking lot was a concrete open field that invited us to race go-carts, ride bikes, rollerskate, skateboard, operate toy cars and airplanes by remote, launch kites in a sky clear of telephone lines and—finally—learn to drive.

The Forum was the beckoning plain and eternal point of exploration that we imagined kids in less urban places—the Valley, Orange County—had in abundance. It was also something else: the lake or swimming hole or fishing pond that our parents, not long out of the poor but warmly recalled South or Midwest, talked about as the refuge they took from hard times or from hard-eyed white folks when *they* were young, a place to go that always felt comfortable and possible and never turned them away. This was what the Forum was to us in the early '70s, a hallowed ground that was both exceptional and humble, public but somehow secret, limitless in the opportunities it gave us to be the standard-issue kids we needed to be, with our kites and planes and presumptions of inheriting the good, post-South life our parents had laid down for us. Things were on the up-and-up. The Forum was the best reflection of Inglewood itself. Inglewood was a small city without great wealth, but in our eyes, it glittered; with its sports palace and spirit of civic accommodation, we knew its fortunes would only increase.

Besides the Forum, Inglewood had Market Street, which my friends and I would visit by bus most Saturdays. Market was the sort of old-fashioned main drag that marked many a city in Southern California, set them apart from amorphous Los Angeles and the even more bewildering, oceanic sprawl of L.A. County. Market was a few minutes west of the Forum and had that same casual magic, and everything we needed in the span of three blocks—two movie theaters, two department stores, drugstore, record shop, knickknack shop, bookstore, several boutiques, snack shop, shoe stores, head shop, jewelry, and gift stores. If you had no money to begin with or went broke before the end of the day, you could simply wander; contemplate buying something on layaway or sneak into another showing of a fifty-cent double feature. There were options.

As it happened, Inglewood was mostly a black city that had rapidly become so after 1965, when the Watts Riots convinced many whites who had for decades dominated metropolitan L.A. west of Main Street that their time was up, or that they could no longer live in the ethnic isolation they'd designed for themselves and taken for granted. Inglewood was about the last white town to fall, mostly because it's as far west and south as you can go before hitting Westchester, Playa del Rey, El Segundo—coastal havens that were, and still are, pretty homogeneous.

I was aware of none of this growing up; to me, Inglewood was simply a place for family, and I assumed it would stay like that. There was no reason for me to think otherwise. When my family took the suburban plunge in 1976 and moved thirty-five miles, from 98th Street to West Covina, we stuck it out in a strange land for less than a year before moving back to the place we always considered home—Inglewood, our suburb of choice all along. We had friends and family who peeled off over the years to Downey, Cerritos, Arleta, even Woodland Hills, Orange County, and then, sometime later, Diamond Bar, Moreno Valley, and Riverside. We nodded congratulations but tacitly declined to visit; *they* would simply have to visit *us*. Inglewood was the center of gravity, the still-evolving frontier of good things and significant change not merely for our family but for the whole black community, and in the biggest sense for every wishful thinker in L.A. determined to flesh out a dream of easier living, because fleshing out any dream seemed so possible here. In Inglewood, that was going nicely because blacks lived here in great numbers, not in the usual cordoned-off inner city or redlined enclave, but in a real town a few miles from the Pacific, the great, golden omega of the Western frontier. We had almost made it.

Inglewood is different today. It is solid and livable, but no longer arcing up or reaching for new possibilities. It seems finished with itself, content with its few successes and general mediocrity, which, while not inspiring, is better than the outright despair that permeates most black neighborhoods still. But it is not so golden anymore, which in some ways feels worse. Mediocrity is a sin of ambition that distresses me because, after being gone for the better part of twenty years, I live in Inglewood again and would like to stay put. My husband and I bought a townhouse in 2001, then a house the following year. The house is wonderful, luminously green, and accented with California-Chinese lanterns that were high style in 1953, when the house and the entire tract were built. My block is well-tended and exudes the heart and optimism I associated with Inglewood in my formative and most patriotic years, when I would have defended the bizarre entirety of Los Angeles against anybody on Earth. A neon spire still winks atop the Academy Theater on Manchester—one of L.A.'s best-preserved movie palaces, now a church—and is one of the first, best things you see when you're in a plane returning home in the dark, a grand old light of red and purple to warm that odd moment between dropping below the marine layer for the last time and touching down, again, at LAX.

Of course, there's the Forum, not as fabulous as it once was, because the Lakers—along with the Kings and the L.A. Sparks—moved east to Staples Center in 1999, but it's still the sprawling gathering place of my youth. Other things, though, have changed in ways I can't quite fathom and don't want to accept. Market Street still has some lovely edifices and a sense of being the heart of town, but overall it has moved backward, receded into a distance; through the years the theaters became porno houses, then nameless storefronts, then sealed tombs; JCPenney collapsed into a swap meet, and the once-elegant Boston Store into a shuttered old jewelry expo. The men's clothing shop, with its flagstone front, and the Big 5 are hanging on beneath a bare forest of new streetlamps and shrubbery the city put up some years ago as part of the $3.6 million Market Street Renaissance. Like so many things, the revitalization effort, started with great fanfare in 2000—with a ground-breaking ceremony starring the local middle school band and speeches by assorted dignitaries—then faltered. It might simply have paused, but a pause of a decade (and getting longer) is too ominous for optimism.

There are fast-food outlets—too many to count—on corners where there used to be full restaurants and services and offices. People look much more wary of each other than they used to; despite the city's middle-class moorings, the stigma of being a black town has, in the pitiless era of hip-hop, grown greater over time, and Inglewood now seems resolved not to challenge that stigma any longer, but to suffer it. Embracing home as I once did has gone from being a cause for joy to being a cross to bear, an unpleasant reality that sets my smile on edge. I love community and always have, but I also moved here to prosper, to look forward. The querulous looks I often get when I tell people I live in Inglewood now anger me. When I drive home and realize I've passed one beauty shop too many and realize those people might be a little bit right, I get angry—mostly at Inglewood. The clean shroud of hope and memories vanishes, and my city stands naked as the promising underachiever who fucked up and could least afford to because everybody was counting so heavily on his success. *What happened to you?* I want to shout out the car window at the offending landscape. *Where did you go?* And sometimes: *Why am I here?*

Yes, I know. What's happened in Inglewood—or hasn't—has happened swiftly to black communities everywhere in the last couple of generations: job loss due to de-industrialization, government disinterest, shrinking tax bases exacerbated by the passage of Proposition 13 in the late '70s, bad schools made worse by resegregation, crack cocaine, upwardly mobile blacks bailing out altogether and moving either back South or anywhere *not* black. The list goes on, and the fallout is undeniable. But in my mind, Inglewood was supposed to be special, different, a charmed L.A. place among L.A. places that could weather all that and come out on the other side.

Only a year ago it gained a kind of prominence it had never had before as the archetypal small town that fought off the evil advances of Wal-Mart, the biggest corporation in the world, hell-bent on building a Supercenter here. Inglewood voters—myself included—defeated a ballot measure that would have allowed Wal-Mart to build on sixty acres of land with virtually no civic oversight or public input. It was David beating back Goliath, self-determination triumphing over corporate master-planning, and worried people in unspoiled small towns across America cheered. The fact that Inglewood was a black and Latino city that Wal-Mart assumed would be a path of least resistance made the victory that much sweeter, and in our rejection of the ballot measure there was affirmation of some sense of self and a collective vision of a future. Even Inglewood's famously fractured City Council joined forces to oppose Wal-Mart to declare that, yes, the city could and would do better; overnight, council members became advocates in a way they never had before.

The sense that real reform and accountability were taking hold in Inglewood from the grassroots up was bolstered by the Coalition for a Better Inglewood, the watchdog development group that materialized to fight off Wal-Mart and encouraged a brand of activism in the city that it hadn't seen in a very long time. True, the coalition is a creation of the Los Angeles Alliance for a New Economy (LAANE), the Santa Monica nonprofit best known for its living-wage and pro-labor (and, lately, anti–Wal-Mart) campaigns in Santa Monica and elsewhere. But just enough Inglewood folk—residents, church leaders, politicos—joined the effort to give it a more local feel.

And yet more than a year afterward, the vision that looked so imminent is looking, well, fuzzy. The coalition has shifted from being philosophically against Wal-Mart to being willing to negotiate a community-benefits agreement that would include affordable health insurance, guarantees of overtime pay, and other union-like conditions that Wal-Mart is famous for not granting any of its employees anywhere on the planet. A bold tactical move, perhaps, but one mapped out by LAANE strategists looking to up the ante in their long-term struggle against Wal-Mart and looking to make Inglewood their test case. Benefits agreements negotiated between big developers and communities are generally positive things—the developers of Staples Center have one with the city of L.A.—but the one now being floated by LAANE on Inglewood's behalf raises some thorny questions about outsiders calling the shots; after all, the voters who nixed the Wal-Mart initiative last year might very well have been nixing the idea of Wal-Mart in Inglewood at all (*I*, for one, was).

Meanwhile, the combination of political will and capital interest that has revitalized other small cities, such as Culver City, Alhambra, Pasadena, El Segundo, Long Beach, South Pasadena, and Santa Monica, can't get any traction here. Inglewood has some encouraging signs—in the last four years, major retailers like Target, Home Depot, Costco, Bally's Fitness, and Staples have all sprung up like mushrooms around the proposed Wal-Mart site on

Century Boulevard. As every commercial developer and real-estate agent knows, stores beget more stores, and the mile of Century between Prairie and Crenshaw (what the mayor likes to call "The Marketplace") is beginning to look like a miniature city of commerce, all sandstone buildings and oversize parking lots; Marshall's and Red Lobster and Chili's are slated to come next.

All of this is reassuring to a point, progress even, but it is not enough. Stores are fine, but these stores could be anywhere; they are generic rather than specific, pleasant accouterments that tend to obscure the main story rather than illuminate it. Not that I don't appreciate having a Jamba Juice or a Bally's nearby, but if big-box convenience was all I wanted, I would have moved to Diamond Bar long ago. What I want, what I came back for and what Inglewood represented to me, is a place with inimitable character and ambition made of more lasting stuff, a place that can *survive* Staples—or Wal-Mart, if it comes to that. A place that will always be a point of return.

I am not living this uneasy feeling alone. My friend John has been fuming about the unspectacular failure of Inglewood for years. He doesn't live here but is a longtime developer who deeply believes that urban African-American communities—what's left of them—can and must thrive, and that middle-class communities like Inglewood can and must lead the way, but is equally convinced that Inglewood won't thrive, because its political leadership is simply not up to the task and never has been. (Because of his ongoing business interests in Inglewood, John did not want to use his real name.)

It galls him to no end that the window of opportunity for twenty-five years of black leadership to leave a lasting and positive legacy in Inglewood is closing. We have been here all along but have failed to make this place ours, on our own terms, to lay a base of black prosperity and fortitude that future generations can build on, or at least leave a mark that they will not forget easily or eradicate completely. We have lived here, he says, but not made a history.

Though he's overstating things a bit, it's clear to anybody living here any length of time that the people in City Hall most obviously responsible for Inglewood's future are not doing their jobs. Elected officials, planners, redevelopment types, consultants, assistants, hired guns—collectively, they're all getting paid to carry out a vision that they haven't bothered to formulate.

"You know something? If these people were running a Fortune 500 company, they'd be goddamn *fired*," John says. His anger is righteous and not uncomplicated or uncompromised in itself. But somebody must hold Inglewood, and other places before it, accountable, rather than just write it off as yet another black neighborhood to bite the dust. Somebody has to act like it matters, make the wholly preventable demise of a middle-class town like Inglewood out to be a tragedy of epic proportions, a tragedy that even now, in the tenth or eleventh hour, has a chance to go another way.

The city has its believers, certainly, though even they can't help but qualify their belief. Don Eislund, former president of Inglewood Park Cemetery, one of the city's flagship businesses, says progress will go swiftly once two things happen: the airport settles on a modernization plan, and the Inglewood council members get on the same page about development and the general direction of the city.

"We need a unified front," says Eislund. "There are so many things out there that could be done, so much state and federal funding we could tap into. We need to be proactive, not reactive. Right now we're being reactive."

Richard McNish, who heads Inglewood's economic-development department and is widely admired around City Hall, thinks the city might finally be winning the bruising battle of image. "In black and brown communities, lower property-tax rates and higher density gives you *higher* spending power," he says. "Business is finally catching up to the realization that we folks got money. Inglewood is a marketplace, not a charity case."

The city's truest believer, however, may be Diane Zembrano. Every small town's got at least one. Zembrano is a full-time Inglewood activist and civic booster who never misses a council or school-board meeting and is probably the only person in town who read the seventy-page Wal-Mart initiative cover to cover; she dismisses the stunted Market Street revitalization project as "trees and bricks—a waste" and laments the fact that no real community voice has been part of any redevelopment plan so far. Inglewood did hold several neighborhood forums last fall to gather citizen input for its Economic Development Strategic Plan, essentially a fast-track effort toward a working general plan, which the city hasn't had in decades. Zembrano went to one of the strategic-plan meetings and was unimpressed.

"The consultants told people what they were going to do, rather than take the people's pulse," she says. The big shocker, she says, came when she "suggested a bookstore and was basically told, 'People in Inglewood don't read.' " Zembrano, who moved to Inglewood from Texas in 1956, would ideally like to see the city returned to a modest glory that she, like me, remembers from childhood. "We should be refurbishing those red-carpet movie palaces we used to have down on Market," she says, almost wistfully. "We don't value what we've got."

Another city official, who asked to remain anonymous, agrees. For all its attributes, she says, Inglewood's biggest problem is that its leaders constantly sell it short, and the Market Street Renaissance is a case in point.

"I didn't support the project because it was too paltry," says the official disdainfully. "It was cosmetic. I pushed for something like the Grove or Old Town Pasadena, but that's not the plan that was put forward."

Of course, the fact that Inglewood hasn't *had* an official plan in years made it a vacuum that tended to attract projects of the most dubious merit; a City Hall source said somebody once proposed a fish farm on Century Boulevard, a suggestion that ultimately didn't fly but that tied up the property for a couple of years anyway. "We seem to let developers get what they want," says the official. "Why not hold out for something better?"

John says that, demographically, developers see black communities as having spending power but also trending down in terms of income and education, and that's the precipice it's on. It's market research that laps into racial bias, making cause and effect hard to quantify. But the proof is in the continued absence of things like bookstores, or in Trader Joe's once telling Inglewood Councilman Ralph Franklin that there's no "market" in Inglewood even though black people regularly swarm the nearest store in Westchester. Franklin says that Trader Joe's has recently changed its tune and *is* considering coming to town.

Every morning during my Forum ritual, I get hopeful, even arrogant, and every time I drive back south to my house, past the shiny Costco and Smart & Final to a suddenly dead zone of doughnut shops and meager or empty storefronts, I darken. I reluctantly remember that the good times of the '60s and '70s, despite the influx of blacks, occurred when chiefly whites still governed Inglewood. Things were comparatively better economically then than now, but still. This is a town that first planted its flag as the Centinela Adobe in 1834, incorporated in 1908, and by the '20s was the fastest-growing city in the United States, as well as the world leader in the production of chinchillas. In the 1950s, as aerospace in South Bay boomed, a team of military engineers developed the nation's first Intercontinental Ballistic Missile—the Atlas—in Inglewood.

Like most small towns with any history in Southern California, the city was, of course, notoriously segregated—an investigation of an incident of police brutality in the '20s rather accidentally revealed that several high-ranking members of the Inglewood police force belonged to the Ku Klux Klan. But that was then, and though the racist legacy lingers in very real ways, I'm convinced that black folks can do more to build on the blithe, little-town-that-could ambition that Inglewood once stood for. I lapse into bitter suspicions about the wherewithal of my own people. I confess to friends that it was my Jewish husband who ultimately had to persuade me to move here, because I knew far better than he what lay west of Crenshaw, on the other side of the stately pines that line the boulevard medians: *niggers,* poor folk, apartment dwellers, drug runners, and gangbangers, all festering for years in the infamous square mile of Inglewood known as the Bottoms. I chastised myself for thoughts like this, for buying into what I call vicious stereotypes, and pushed them aside. But at moments I couldn't help it. I worried in advance about a sinkhole that would drag down not only property values, but also my lifelong hopes for finding the Great Community and my place in it. This wasn't just about being a homeowner, it was about history, about an exodus and a triumphant return, and I had to judge Inglewood harshly because I couldn't bear not to be right about that.

The problem was never with *all* of Inglewood. Like every black neighborhood in L.A., it has its gradations. I liked the condo complex on Manchester where I used to live, though it was gated and security-guarded and closer to the north end of town, which borders bona fide upper-middle-class Ladera Heights, Windsor Hills, and View Park. South Inglewood is closer to South L.A. and is a much more tenuous matter. It has considerable business activity—the Century Boulevard stores, the Hollywood Park Casino, and the just-sold racetrack—but it also has considerable issues. Century Boulevard running west toward the airport is a wasteland of fast food, knockoff 99 Cents Only Stores, auto-repair lots, adult bookstores, and squat motels, hardly the welcome-to-L.A. yellow brick road that tourists might expect. South Inglewood figures largely into the city's image problem, which Hollywood cemented years ago in movies like *The Grand Canyon* (in which Kevin Kline gets a flat tire on the way home from the Forum and almost pays for it with his life) and *Pulp Fiction* (in which Eric Stoltz's dope dealer snaps at wary customer John Travolta in a fit of drug-addled pique: "What do I look like, a nigger? Where are we, *Inglewood?*").

Not to be snobbish, but Inglewood is not like Compton, Watts, Crenshaw, South-Central, or even gold-standard Ladera Heights. It has a small central government, a decent household income of $50,000 and excellent real-estate value, all in nine square miles. The problem is that the people in charge of Inglewood either don't really believe that or don't know how to use that information to Inglewood's benefit. After the election last year, Wal-Mart promptly bought the sixty acres at 90th and Prairie—the biggest parcel of viable commercial real estate in the county—where it intended to build its Supercenter. Now Inglewood doesn't own the property and, absent a battle to fight, doesn't seem to know what to do about it next. In the meantime, Wal-Mart is almost certainly preparing to relaunch efforts to build a store on its sixty acres, though how and when is unclear. The city was so eager to get a Red Lobster restaurant onboard at Century east of Prairie Boulevard, it sold seventeen acres that it *did* own to mall mogul Alexander Haagen for five dollars a square foot—about a quarter of what it was worth.

Councilman Franklin actually argues for selling Inglewood cheap, at least in this case: the south side of Century abuts the worst part of the Bottoms, he says, and needs this kind of development—any development, really. The problem is that Haagen could build the Red Lobster, or not. In fact, all the new chain stores that have gone up bought or leased land on the 240 acres that constitute Hollywood Park, known chiefly for its racetrack. Hollywood Park was recently bought by Bay Meadows Land Co., a development company that hopes to revitalize a horseracing business that proliferating Indian gaming and casinos have undercut; evidently the casino that's been operating at Hollywood Park since 1994 hasn't been enough. Some see the potential demise of iconic Hollywood Park as yet another blow to the city's identity. Mayor Dorn, however, is fairly itching for the track to go; he's said that those acres can be much better used by putting up luxury hotels, restaurants, more retail. He says Hollywood Park's closure would clear the way for Inglewood to finally realize its potential as a major entertainment and shopping attraction in Southern California. Yet Inglewood has played spectator to all this change, mostly standing by, watching, waiting, and cutting a ribbon or two.

To make matters worse, the city's redevelopment agency hasn't done things here where and when it actually could, à la Market Street. When the Lakers fled, the Forum was bought by Faithful Central Bible Church in a historic deal in which African-Americans acquired a major concert venue for the first time. Faithful Central had ambitions of building a luxury hotel on the grounds of the Forum, but nothing has happened so far. There is a $40 million plan on the table to improve Century Boulevard with new streetscapes, public-works improvements, and other amenities meant to catalyze development, but it's been on the table for almost three years now because it hasn't nailed down funding. Imperial Partners, a black-owned development company that also has a project slated for Watts, is hoping to build a tourist-minded hotel and entertainment complex at Century and Prairie Avenue, but it hasn't yet acquired all of the land it needs and things are moving slowly.

Complicating progress is Inglewood's tortured relationship with the airport, a logical source of funding for any number of Inglewood projects—such as street improvements or hotels—simply because of its proximity to LAX. The proximity is that much more significant in light of impending airport expansion, but Inglewood's response so far has been to file a lawsuit over the current proposal. Not that that makes much difference; beyond getting millions in federal grant money to sound-insulate houses—virtually all of Inglewood lies in the flight path—the city has never figured out when or how to maximize the airport connection. My developer friend John says it's yet another vacuum created by Inglewood leadership's lack of will to take the longest view possible, construct a vision, break it down into pieces, and then *do* it. "We don't know how to do deals," he says. "There's this welfare mentality where we always look for public money—subsidies, grants, noise-mitigation money. *That* we understand. But when it comes to doing something of our own and making deals to benefit *us*, especially long-term, we don't know how to do it."

What makes Inglewood appealing, what still stimulates the imagination, is not development at all, but neighborhoods like mine where people still care for their houses as if they were the Taj Mahal. What makes this city is all those provincial-sounding tree streets off big thoroughfares like Manchester—Oak, Ash, Fir, Cedar, Spruce. They defy disappointment with their harmonious rows of low pastel stucco and high Spanish tile, wrought-iron gates, wide plate-glass windows, and generous porches that recall the South and—like the South, I suppose—fly the occasional American flag. Outside this tableau, things are markedly different, or they're not different enough. Like many black neighborhoods, Inglewood suffers from low expectations that have fostered a somewhat indiscriminate development philosophy I call "anything is better than a hole in the ground." There's a reason for that; neglect and decay are fearsome-looking to black people, cancer cells that evidence a familiar sickness—graffiti, vandalism—that has permanently hollowed out black sections of big cities everywhere. It's always better to be doing something instead of nothing, fixing those broken windows instead of standing idle. But this approach often forces us into bizarre positions, like treating a new Fatburger or Krispy Kreme as if it's the Taj Mahal instead of the blight it would be in a different context, a different mindset, or a different place.

Inglewood's longtime mayor, Roosevelt Dorn, has proudly called himself pro-business since he took office in 1997, and if your ideal of business stops at retail, it's true. Dorn can't get enough of retail. He loves Century Boulevard and all that building activity and all those big stores that refused to come in the past that have since come, and that now generate millions in sales-tax revenue every year. To him, it's part of realizing a new kind of social justice with all deliberate speed, a long-deferred acknowledgment that Inglewood is as worthy of a Target as the next town.

A former juvenile-court judge known for his own way of doing things, Dorn supported Wal-Mart last year—the only member of the Inglewood City Council to do so—but being on the wrong side of public opinion hardly seems to have given him pause. He sees Wal-Mart, the minimum-wage, no-health-care, biggest-retail outfit in the world, not as his city's ultimate degradation but as its ultimate validation—all those jobs for youth, all that sales-tax revenue. (Full disclosure: last year Dorn sued my father, Larry Aubry, and his paper, the *Los Angeles Sentinel*, for defamation when my father wrote a column claiming that Dorn had taken several thousand dollars in contributions from Wal-Mart. A judge threw out the case last fall.) A few nuances notwithstanding, the mayor is clearly in the anything's-better-than-a-hole-in-the-ground camp, though he is also quick to complain that Inglewood is unfairly maligned and underestimated.

"The image of Inglewood is *not* Inglewood," he tells me indignantly. "This is a very desirable place to live. The property value is skyrocketing. Our elementary schools are really coming up, and we're working on the middle and high schools. Crime is the lowest it's been in thirty years. We have received a bad rep, and we do not deserve it."

What Dorn doesn't seem to realize is that part of Inglewood's bad rep is his own; famous for his autocratic governing style and penchant for praying before council meetings (he's also a minister), Dorn in many ways typifies the ego-driven, myopic leadership that is holding Inglewood back. (Dorn resigned as mayor in January 2010 after being charged with inappropriate use of public funds.)

Dorn, for his part, maintains that he is Inglewood's ultimate business partner and flag-waver, and it's up to other city officials and civic leaders to follow suit. He boasts that all sorts of developers are interested in coming to an L.A.-area town that's full of "prime property"—Wal-Mart is only one—and well they should be. Dorn agrees that the airport connection must be better exploited, but says much will depend on what position L.A.'s mayor,

Antonio Villaraigosa, takes on expansion, and what his Airport Commission will look like. But make no mistake, Inglewood is growing.

"As we speak," Dorn says confidently, as he says everything, "the renaissance is clearly on the move."

I used to meet John sometimes for coffee and our many heated chats at a place called the Howling Monk Jazz and Coffee Bar. It was on a big corner at the north end of Market Street, the still-alive part of downtown that I would frequent because of the Big 5 sporting-goods store, a decent photo place run by Koreans, and the Monk. The Monk was big and airy, accented with bamboo blinds and filled to its high ceiling with jazz music and the wonderfully pressing, perpetual smell of gourmet coffee brewing somewhere behind the counter. A water fountain burbled outside on a small plaza, where people lounged or read on wooden park benches. The Monk's owner, Kenneth Moore, would often join us, at least in conversation. Moore is the aging hippie of the Black Panther set—fiftyish, bushy beard, partial to wearing cotton button-down shirts and suede loafers that look infinitely more hip than the endless reinterpretations put out by the Gap and Banana Republic. He is thoughtful and reflective, but with a robust sense of humor that he's needed to get him through the ordeal of losing his business.

The Monk closed more than two years ago, after Inglewood convinced Moore that he was just what they needed to help bring Market Street back to life as part of the millennium revitalization program. After some thinking, Moore took them up on it; like others, he harbored a dream of doing well for himself and doing some good in the community he's lived in for the past thirty years. He had quit his cozy accounting job at Paramount Studios to start a line of specialty coffee, and now he had a chance to go for broke with a restaurant where he could wed coffee to his other great passion, live jazz.

Moore says he was sold on the whole package—coffee, jazz, community enrichment, black culture, music, revitalization, and empowerment. And Inglewood had actually shown him plans for what was officially called the Market Street Renaissance, the first time Moore had ever seen any kind of vision of Inglewood committed to paper. "They painted such a beautiful picture," he says, slightly incredulously. "They had this brochure of Market that really looked like the Third Street Promenade (in Santa Monica)—theaters, restaurants. And they said it would be a priority for the city."

But it wasn't. Part of it was timing—the Howling Monk opened barely three months after 9/11, when small businesses in big cities that relied on tourism started to seriously feel the pinch. Part of it was simply that Moore, by his own admission, was a novice restaurateur who realized too late in the game that he was woefully undercapitalized. But Inglewood also failed him, big time. The shrubs and streetlamps came, but no more businesses; it was like setting a table for dinner guests who never arrived. The big boxes on Century Boulevard started going up in earnest, entirely overshadowing Market Street as a development priority and a sales-tax base. Moore got behind on his city-sponsored business loan and couldn't get his phone calls to City Hall returned. At the Monk's farewell concert, where the walls shivered with deliriously improvisational jazz and throngs of supporters who lived well beyond Inglewood, nobody from City Hall showed up. That haunts Moore the most.

"When I opened, they were all there for the photo ops," he says. "In the end, with very few exceptions, they all stayed away."

They all stayed away from taking any blame, too; Jesse Lewis, Inglewood's community-development director, took the wide historical angle and cited bad economic conditions and "retail leakage"—Inglewood residents going out of town to buy Gucci loafers they can't get here—as the culprits responsible for Market's decline. He also waxed hopeful about a Market comeback as a mecca of sit-down restaurants, clubs, and cultural attractions, though he was vague about a timeline: "As you get into the next fifteen years," he says, "that's what we want to do."

After that, I started frequenting another place not far from there, A Cultural Affair Coffeehouse on La Brea. It's on the northern, moneyed edge of town, the pocket with the greatest concentration of longtime white residents and fairly recent arrivals looking for the best real-estate value for their money in a market still going mad. They are a generation removed from those who resisted flight forty years ago and never left.

This part of La Brea is pedestrian friendly and the most picturesque business scene in Inglewood: besides the coffeehouse, there's a seafood restaurant, a Cajun bistro, a hip boutique, and an equally hip shoe store and shoe-repair place that's worth wandering into for the antique décor alone—a passion of the owner. There are the ubiquitous beauty salons too, but North La Brea feels on the verge in a way that Market Street, and even Century Boulevard, do not. It is homegrown but high-aspiring, a smallish place with big ideas just as Inglewood itself used to be. Like the Monk, A Cultural Affair strives to be more than a coffeehouse. It sells African goods and has hosted a street bazaar, film screenings, spoken-word nights, and special events. Like the Monk, it wants to be a successful business and something more.

Co-owner Margo LaDrew is a pragmatic visionary, someone who has great faith in La Brea but almost no faith that Inglewood shares the feeling. Like others, she indicts not just Inglewood for this, but black communities everywhere that find it so impossible to make things good right where they are—in other words, to *be* a community in the fundamental Webster's sense of the word.

"This is a black place with no cultural anything, no vision for itself as destination, and a pathological inability to finish anything it starts," says LaDrew, taking a break on a hot afternoon. LaDrew is tall and striking, with a husky voice and a dark ponytail pulled straight back on her head. She knows Moore and empathizes with his struggle. "The city left him out to rot on Market," she says flatly. "They did things backward." But for her, as is true for a lot of us around here, hope creeps eternal. It's the earthquake theory of life—every time something doesn't happen increases the likelihood of it happening the next time. Inglewood *could* shake things up, could do the right thing. "If the city could just focus people coming here, point out where they can go with signs or something . . ." LaDrew looks out of her window at the other shops as she speaks, imagining. "A couple of crosswalks, maybe. Traffic lights. That'd be great."

LaDrew doesn't ask for much. None of us do, even John, who rages on only because he thinks the community's got nothing to lose; the moment he sees evidence of a vision, even a modest one, I know he'll stop. He will be as eager to praise Inglewood as he has been to bury it. Most people in Inglewood are careful to do neither, like my neighbors who gather at block-club meetings each month. After roll call and an abbreviated social hour, the host goes through agenda items: dues, plans for a party, money collected for somebody down the street who had a death in the family. Then new business: a low-grade supermarket coming to Crenshaw—all right, a ghetto supermarket—taking over the lease of an established one that left unceremoniously, without so much as a thank you. A gas station that's gotten dangerous at night. A long-abandoned building on Imperial that's become a nuisance, but the owner, who lives somewhere on the Westside, won't sell it or tear it down.

Here is where we could take a position, put our foot down, offer a plan: instead, I feel the bright living room start to button up, a chill wind gusting through, and then somebody mumbles that we have to keep that stuff over *there* in the Bottoms from coming over *here*. Property values and all. Nods, murmurs, a few grave looks, as if we're Roman senators voting on what to do about a colony giving us more trouble than it's worth. I understand trying to keep these lines in the sand; I'm a homeowner, too, and everything that means.

But the truth is that we *all* live in the sand. We all have one eye fondly on the neighborhood and the other looking somewhere else; it's like eating in a good restaurant but sitting near the door so that if some untoward shit breaks out you can leave fast, get out. I don't want to live that way, not here. But after the block club finds its upbeat groove, after the sign-off and the happy rush to the refreshment table, I see in people's eyes the shadow of a confession: if I could leave, I would. The corollary to that is: if things were where I want them to be, I wouldn't want to leave at all. I think we have to make Inglewood a place you can't leave, because, frankly, we're out of places to run to. And anyway, in Inglewood I prefer to walk.

Today I walked around the Forum again, past that sixty-acre lot that might get even bigger with the racetrack likely to get razed a few years down the road. Or if Wal-Mart rises again, or that hotel in the sky Dorn talks about comes down to Earth. Or maybe, against all expectations—high, low, ridiculous, nonexistent—the biggest hole in the ground to date will end up being my next big field of dreams. That's the utterly unexpected California, and the Inglewood, that I still live for.

RAGS TO RICHARD

April 2000

The beauty and bane of Los Angeles, still, is that so much of it has to be introduced to the world, again and again. Few know its soul; more believe it has no soul at all. The city doesn't mind these misperceptions; sometimes it relishes them, takes them as protection from the harsh historical and sociological elements that over generations have leveled sections of grand places like Chicago and New York into flat planes of urban redundancy. Despite its ungainly size,

L.A. is still in its big-town infancy—and it may turn out that it will always remain there, a perpetual teenager. A gawky, sharp-elbowed agglomeration of neighborhoods that haven't yet found each other and never really intend to. Then there are those neighborhoods that everybody is busy leaving alone. Neighborhoods that are on their own, slowly set adrift by sprawl and changing tastes, by specific racial fears that over time soften into the view that the place suffers from a general and unredeemable unfashionableness. The most these islands can hope for is to be admired from a distance, which is lately the fate of little Leimert Park.

This is more than ironic, because Leimert itself was once secessionist, a high-end corner of L.A. carved out by developers within the Crenshaw district (which in turn was carved out of the much bigger, more amorphous South Central). Constructed in the 1920s as a white, upwardly mobile bedroom community with an urban resort feeling like neighboring Hancock Park, Leimert by the '60s was increasingly black, still upwardly mobile, very urban, and, while hardly a resort, a relative oasis consistent with the dream locale first imagined by developer Walter Leimert. Through the '70s and '80s, the neighborhood solidified a reputation as the end of the rainbow for L.A.'s moneyed blacks who still had some social conscience and sense of history left in the nearly numb body politic; they had a vague but growing certainty that the place should and must remain a haven for the upwardly mobile, yes, but also for the upwardly thinking. (Of course, many Leimert Park residents in the '70s who had been there a while realized during that time that they couldn't possibly make the next suburban move out to the San Fernando Valley and get comparable housing, so they stayed. Remaining in Leimert was often less about taking a stand or claiming community and more about acknowledging that one couldn't move to, say, Woodland Hills without paying substantially more money and getting substantially less house, though that was compensated well enough by the presence of predominantly white neighbors. The hard fiscal truths and dashed hopes for social mobility that keep black folks where they live are not the stuff of pride and uplift, but in the end they're as good a catalyst as any for urban revival, maybe the only catalyst.)

It was in the middle of this kind of dubious but distinct renaissance that Richard Fulton opened his coffeehouse on 43rd Place, across from Leimert Park Village's miniscule park. In the decade before, Leimert's official commercial district—all three blocks of it—had found new purpose as an encouraging mass of black-owned businesses selling or housing black arts and culture opened their doors. Tiny Degnan Boulevard, the village's main thoroughfare, became home to a dance studio, theater, gallery, African fabric store, artist's studio, museum of black and African historical artifacts, tailor shop, jewelry shop, black bookstore, and a storefront jazz and performance space ambitiously called The World Stage. Richard's coffeehouse, Fifth Street Dick's Coffee Company, was just around the corner from all this. It was named not for where it was, but for where he had been: 5th Street, a street that runs through the heart of downtown's skid row.

A Seattle native, Richard had spent nearly five years on and around skid row as a homeless, hopeless drunk, though in his most lucid moments he said he always fantasized about owning a place dedicated to sublime coffee and superior jazz, two of his favorite things besides the bottle. When he finally got sober, he made good on that dream in Leimert Park, which at that point in its renaissance was the only place in the city that made sense for what Dick had in mind. Richard acquired a high-ceilinged, narrow space reminiscent of a Southern shotgun shack and painted white clouds the length of the ceiling—a tramp's-eye view of the world, he told me, his paean to the sky that during his time on the streets both condemned him as a man without a roof and filled him with a sense of unlimited possibility. In those moments he had felt surges of joy and made him feel, low as he'd fallen, that opening a jazz coffeehouse was the most modest and doable of things. He eventually got picked up off the streets by an Alcoholics Anonymous wagon, encouraged back to life, then to living. In 1991 he had no money, connections, business history, or local history of any kind in Leimert, but he launched Fifth Street anyway.

Of course, it wasn't going to be that easy: two weeks into business, the riots hit. Richard and his fellow merchants on 43rd and surrounding blocks joined together with garden hoses to beat back the flames and the restive feeling that ravaged other corners, some of them mere yards from Fifth Street's. But the village was unscathed, and that was miracle enough. After a baptism amid, but not in, the fire, Richard knew he was in Leimert for the long haul.

The jazz aficionados in L.A. and places well beyond instantly praised Dick's as a well-timed addition to serious jazz venues that, like blues venues, were steadily shrinking in number. The locals loved Dick's more because it provided something Leimert needed to really qualify as a neighborhood undergoing a renaissance despite a tenuous after-dark reputation—a spot willing to stay open late at night, all night on Friday and Saturday during marathon live sets that turned out to be an integral part of formerly homeless Dick's jazz and coffeehouse dreams. He assumed people would not only come, they would stay. At Dick's, you bought strong brew and sweets downstairs and went upstairs to settle in and hear music; between performances, Dick filled the air in and around the place with jazz blaring from big speakers put out on the sidewalk. The speakers faced the park and played music loud enough to shiver the wood walls in the coffeehouse, loud enough to make the chess players sitting near his place on the park's grassy edge lean in, as though in a stiff wind, to hear each other talk. Nobody really minded; we preferred an exaggerated presence to the resounding absences that had plagued Leimert and the whole Crenshaw neighborhood for too long.

Richard was Leimert's unofficial mayor of the new age and its goodwill ambassador, his comeback story the perfect analogue to the area's own re-emergence as the locus of the highest, and humblest, aspirations of L.A.'s scattered black populace that, maybe for the last time this millennium, believed in the magic of a single purpose. Here on the small mountaintop of Leimert was the democratic demography blacks had lost—a community of artists, thinkers, researchers, itinerant protesters, and rabble rousers, educated fools, uneducated sages, vendors a shade above street hustlers, activists forged in the crucible of prison time, assorted community prophets never comfortably out of destitution. Many things that normally squared off against each other lived easily here, if in small numbers, and Dick lived easiest of all.

He liked seeing me. I had been among the first to take note of his arrival with a story for the *Los Angeles Times* that was among the first features I ever did as a professional journalist. Richard was gratified, though he had much more interest in the very small publication I had written for before getting the *Times* gig, the monthly called *Accent L.A.* that I helped run out of a mid-city apartment with a good friend, a veteran *Times* reporter himself who over twenty years had grown tired of his employer's breezy neglect of any news in the inner city that wasn't about mayhem or ethnic festivals. *Accent* was meant to be an alternative to all that. Richard's story had appeared in one of our last editions in '92; we petered out after five years of never having enough staff or steady ad money, though the serious goal of being a monthly kept us going, made us feel pleasantly beholden to something bigger, more demanding and more enriching than our modest journalistic enterprise. After *Accent* folded and I was installed across town at the *Times*—it was the mayhem of the riots, ironically, that finally woke the sleeping giant and helped put *Accent* out of business—I'd frequently stop by Dick's. I had notepads on the driver's seat and stiff new business cards that proclaimed my step up. Dick took one with a mix of admiration and amusement, and greeted me with: "Hey girl, when's that *Accent* coming back? Sure do miss it. We need it now more than ever!"

I understood. He was not expressing criticism for what I did, but wistfulness about where I did it. I agreed with him. Working the Crenshaw district for the *Times*, I was fulfilling my calling half right, which was probably a higher proportion than could be claimed by most black people who liked to consider themselves in the struggle. But it often felt like little consolation. A bigger *Accent* would have been a far greater coup than the nod I got from the *Times*, which had only expanded its post-riot coverage of the city in a fit of conscience, or rare embarrassment. (The expansion didn't last: three years later, the section I was recruited to write for died, and coverage of Crenshaw and South Central collapsed back to its original proportions, or actually something less than that. Richard hardly remarked on it.)

Richard may have been Leimert's mayor, but he was no diplomat. He freely criticized the area councilman, a black man famous for his pomp and for preaching the sanctity of community post-'92 while wholly thwarting the will of the people. Richard aggravated some of his own neighbors along 43rd Place by running AA meetings out of a building directly behind the coffeehouse. Some people privately thought that invited an element Leimert could ill afford to have, given all the unrepentant crack addicts in the area who gravitated to the park the way addicts do. Richard, visionary and recovering substance abuser, paid such middle-class concern no attention at all. But he did so with his ready, almost beatific smile, gravelly tenor, and graying corkscrew dreadlocks that were at pleasing odds with a frank and constant wonder at his own good fortune. Now if *Accent L.A.* had only come back to chronicle things, if he could have left copies of it every week at the door for his fitfully enlightened, long-suffering patrons of good news, his dream world would have been as real as he ever dared to hope. The renaissance would be complete.

It wasn't to be. Close to the turn of the millennium, in the years after the *Times* reneged on itself, Richard got sick with throat cancer. It came on incomprehensibly, as life-threatening conditions always do: one week he was all smiles and plentiful dreads, the next he was dulled and shriveling and leaning on the arm of his employee, Silvia, who quickly and gamely became his nursemaid. They were an odd couple—Silvia tight-lipped and impassive where Richard was eager to share. But she worked as hard as he did and, at midlife, had the same improbable youthfulness. She wore graying dreads, too, but tinted a hot pink; at the coffeehouse she wore a cap, coveralls, sneakers, and piles of silver and stone bracelets that clinked musically as she went about filling orders, the jewelry singing an optimism that Silvia found hard to put to words but needed to put out. When her boss got sick, she began tending to him and his vision without missing a beat or betraying any grief. People who knew her and walked 43rd every day reported Richard's illness to me well before I saw him in that condition, but I was still not prepared for the day in early spring when I did see him, out in Leimert's tiny, street-bordered island park. It had recently undergone some improvements and was being dedicated by the same imperious councilman Richard had no use for. (The councilman chose his appearances in Leimert very carefully, which was strange considering that he lived right in the neighborhood, blocks from the park itself.) But Richard was determined to show up; this was his place, even though the city had planted saplings that wouldn't become real park trees for years, even if the weathered edifice in the middle of the fountain had been repainted and not replaced. Even if things were papered over and patched up, then effusively heralded in a ceremony as a new beginning, like always.

Richard and Silvia were sitting at a table, and Richard was leaning forward like one of the park's regular chess players. His big eyes listed in the bright sun, a surgical mask was tied over his mouth. Silvia sat next to him picking through medical supplies, arranging them like silverware. Friends approached them in a way that was utterly casual and utterly defiant of the fact that something was very wrong; they said their hellos in low, easing tones, not waiting or expecting Richard to answer, smiling and clapping him on his thinning shoulder before moving off, but slowly, as if not quite knowing where to go or what to do next. I got up some courage and went over, got up some more and bent down to greet him; I would have kept my distance but didn't know how. He heard me say something to Silvia and lifted his head, as if from sleep. Feeling caught and not a little stupid, I said, "You okay? Things okay? The place looks good," waving back at Fifth Street's. He studied me with tiring but familiar eyes and nodded, shrugged, then raised one skinny fist in a salute—which I took to mean, *Everything's like it's supposed to be.* Fight the power. Life is good by definition, baby, and this councilman's still an asshole even if I can't say it right now. Maybe that's best. I raised a fist back, and laughed.

The cancer was a recurrence that Richard didn't want to treat with chemo or radiation because, he said, he'd rather die than go through that shit again. He wore the mask that day because his tongue had been pushed forward by the cancer and wouldn't stay in his mouth. I saw this for myself a few weeks later at the convalescent home. I hardly wanted to go, but my father, who tends to the dying with the unassuming but unerring resolve of family used to watching the demise of other family, went once a week or more. The home was in Hawthorne, a nondescript town several miles southwest of Leimert: a blander, better-natured version of South Central and a grubby adjunct of the significantly white South Bay. Hawthorne had old coffee shops not yet old enough to be hip or vintage, big auto lots; it was a place with no real foothold anywhere and the last place around L.A. I could have imagined Richard living, even in sickness. My father mentioned one of his visits there to me in a pointed kind of way. I in turn mentioned it to my writer friend Eric, who was quiet for a minute thinking about Hawthorne before saying, "That's fucked up about Dick. Man. That's really, really not right."

It was early April, corning up on another anniversary of the unrest and fires. Skies were clear but the weather was only vaguely warm; winter was gone but spring was still new and uncertain, a baby determined each day to stand upright and each day falling down a little less. Even the nascent warmth succumbing to a chilly coastal wind at sunset encouraged the young season rather than made it lose heart, as it had a month earlier. Hope was in the air, again. Richard's mother had come down from Seattle to help Silvia with things. Feeling the need to do something definitive, Leimert Park merchants gathered together one Sunday, one of the last days Richard could walk (though he had stopped talking for some time), to pay their respects, for lack of a better phrase to describe the final public celebration of a life before it actually ended. In one of the idle storefronts on Degnan, Richard's neighbors put out rows of folding chairs and a makeshift altar built out of kente cloth, candles, drums, and coffee mugs. Richard stood by with his hands in his pockets, a gaunt figure, but his eyes were as luminous as I'd ever seen them, eyes that took on all the weight of words and feeling that other parts of him could no longer support or express. He wrote out his thanks, which after the ceremony somebody read aloud, and he listened with a kind of amazement. When it was over, he looked done. That had been his last appearance and his last official act as the unofficial mayor of Leimert, steward of its very potent but fractured ambitions. And then he was in the pasture of Hawthorne.

I decided to go see Richard there, and Eric resolved to go with me. We would prop each other up. We both had the same overanxiety about death, but also the same writerly fascination with its powers of ultimate transformation and release. Neither of us said so, but ailing Dick had become nothing less than a mystic in our eyes. That we were both raised nominally Catholic comforted us not at all. Yes, we had to go see Dick, but we had to go *see*; we announced the first thing aloud and let the second alone.

The home was modest but surprisingly pleasant, a rambling single-story building with lots of plate glass and pastel floor tile common to office buildings built in the South Bay in the 1960s. Richard lay in a room full of sunlight and music; a portable stereo on a nightstand played jazz loud and nonstop, as it did at his place in the park. This was his place now. Eric quickly took a chair at the foot of the bed—he had realized too late that he desperately didn't want to be there, so he sat nearly frozen, afraid that any extraneous movement could make him bolt. I had no choice but to do better, so I sat next to Dick in his hospital gown, patted his shoulder bone, and trying to convince myself that a smile was still appropriate under the circumstances. The only thing left now was Richard's eyes, more enormous than they'd been at the Degnan ceremony and too worn to be sad or distraught or anything else. He stared up at me from his big pillow like a child, not with the wonder of that day but with something entirely new. I nodded in acknowledgment of this new thing, whatever it was. I took one of his hands and stopped down to kiss his forehead; it was moist. He shifted and blinked slowly, slipped his hand out of mine and with great effort, curled his fingers into a fist. A fist! I was astonished. I made one back. Richard's big eyes sparkled, and I was sure he would have laughed had he not been attached to a profusion of tubes and breathing aids that circled him like tentacles. From his position at the foot of the bed, Eric nodded in a kind of relief. I stood up and squeezed Richard's shoulders hard. Eric stood too. "See you Dick," he said clearly. "See you, man." Everybody swears the last thing Dick said, such as it was, were the words on a note he scrawled to the nurse, to visitors, to anyone within reach of his precious stereo: *Turn the music up.*

Fifth Street Dick's is shuttered. It was closed after many public and passionate vows to keep it going at any cost. The cost was evidently too great; words fall away. Fifth Street may be merely asleep, as I liked to believe that *Accent L.A.* was merely asleep after months and then years of not publishing, an imperishable idea only waiting for the right moment to assume a new and more relevant life. The dark of Fifth Street Dick's speaks also to how it, and we, will rise again, and how we may live no more. How the sky that Richard loved so much will always grant us room to go up, and how, in its suffocating vastness and heartless mystery, it never takes any notice of us at all.

THE EASTSIDE BOYS

My father's trumpet came out on Saturday at dusk after he finished the lawn work—along with the wooden music stand holding finger-worn sheets of Bach, Mozart, and Miles Davis's "Sketches of Spain." He always bowed his head and ruffled the keys before playing. Sometimes his music sounded tired, like he got some days, but mostly it was golden: "The Shadow of Your Smile" and Bach's "Ode to Joy" phrased in low, guttural notes that he seemed to be playing only for himself. I stood away from the music, behind the wrought-iron porch railing in silent admiration of my father's faith. Larry Aubry's life work was built on the notion that things would change for the better. But it appeared to me, even at the age of six, that the battle for true social equality, as much as it shaped my own view of the world, might ultimately be lost. So what, I wondered, sustained his faith? What were his songs made of?

My father, who is now retired, has been a jazz musician, a postal worker, a county probation officer, and a human-relations consultant. But he was, and still is, an Eastside Boy. Not a formal organization, though fully deserving of its uppercase spelling, the Eastside Boys are a loose contingency of men who were part of the first critical mass of black people to integrate metropolitan L.A. They grew up in the '30s and '40s in the five-square-mile area bounded roughly by Main Street on the west, Long Beach Avenue on the east, Slauson Avenue on the south, and Washington Boulevard on the north. Hemmed in by de facto segregation, with Slauson as the Mason-Dixon line, few blacks lived west of Main. Everybody left the Eastside when they could, as soon as they could, starting in the early '50s; it was an outward flow that in retrospect was a hemorrhage, an exodus by black people from a place that both built them and bound them. It's an old story to all of us now: the sudden fury of flight and the broken economy left in its wake, like debris scattered in the aftermath of a storm.

Still, out in the new territory of the Westside and South Bay, of Crenshaw and Ladera Heights and Baldwin Hills, a lot of promise was realized in the form of college educations and fruitful careers—more opportunities for the Boys and their children. The Boys gave to one another, and there was nothing especially noble or self-sacrificing about it. But they now find themselves where they never expected to be, in the role of heroes and gatekeepers, living connections to the last era of bountiful times for black people. They are the flash points of a social upheaval that cast off segregation and laid a new course. They are not entirely sure they have traveled it well, but they continue their work at scholarship foundations and law offices and high schools, and they continue to meet with the easy regularity of their youth. In these and a thousand other ways, they keep alive their traditions of togetherness, which institutionalized racism made both ordinary and imperative—and which, ironically, post–civil rights Los Angeles has made nearly impossible to maintain.

I wonder what traditions I can create, whether theirs have passed me by. Recently I have been consumed with my own past. I flash on happier moments in high school, when I was incurably optimistic. There was nothing to me that couldn't be perfectly placed in the magnanimous geography of the future, which seemed to be forging itself out of days that oozed along with typical Southern California languor. Promise was as close as I ever got to religion, this private, heady faith in things unseen. But the business of believing, of going forward, has proven to be a peculiar process, often no process at all. Belief has thinned over time, worn clean through in spots. It's illusory; some days, hope that was once as sturdy as a tree trunk has shrunk into a reed, thin enough to encircle with one hand. In the worst moments, my despair—that my achievements won't match the depth of my parents', that my generation's sense of purpose will never cohere, that I will always flounder in isolation—feels like a permanent condition of being black, of being always behind, like someone who longs to prosper but has only a hundred dollars a month. So I am anxious to know if I have failed the Boys, or if they have failed me, or if questions like these are my overindulging in personal crises, an emotional luxury the Boys couldn't afford but that they have afforded me. Maybe I, like them, am charged to move on no matter what, despite having a tenuous grasp on the good life I am heir to (apartment, running car, diplomas, singlehood, chronic debt). Except that I don't exactly know how to move, or where. So in the midst of my despair, I decided to seek the Eastside Boys out. None offered up any definitive answers. Yet I was struck at how easily they assumed the depth of my faith, when I so often could not. In spite of a city so changed from what they knew, so disparate and willfully disconnected, they never assumed my spirit was broken—because neither was theirs. Not yet. I took their assumptions like a gift. In my talks with them, between their words and attentiveness and willingness to hope, I could make out the strains of my own particular music again. I could pick up my own instrument and play it.

My father seethes for a moment over something I've just told him: that the production designers of the film *Devil in a Blue Dress* said they had to scour libraries to turn up what few photographs existed of black L.A. in the '40s. "Oh, bull——," my father snaps. He is sitting in the living room of my parents' Inglewood home. "There's tons of people with all kinds of documentation who live right here." It's hard to interview my sixty-three-year-old father. He wants to help. He wants me to see the Eastside Boys project through, though he never quite says any of this. I sit still on the sofa, as still as when I used to listen to his music. Only then he didn't know I was there. He shifts uncomfortably in his seat.

"I didn't have any friends," my father says when I ask about relationships other than family. His fingers drum the arm rests of the rocker. He talks in the jazz speak of his generation, his voice low, his phrases as fitful as a scat singer's. "I don't have many friends now. I hardly socialize." That's true. Despite the breadth of the Eastside, I don't recall my father bringing home acquaintances. Our visitors were family, uncles and cousins and grandparents. Wasn't Hal Miller a friend? Daddy doesn't answer. He says instead that he met Hal at Carver Junior High, where they both played in the school band. Daddy then went on to Fremont High, at San Pedro and 76th streets, in the late '40s, one of a handful of black students when the school was just starting to integrate. (Hal was one of the few black students who attended Los Angeles High at Olympic and Rimpau boulevards.) Daddy was only thirteen when he started high school. He stuck close by his nephew Paul, who was only a little older but much taller and more imposing. "We went to school every day and got the hell out," Daddy says. "It was horrible." He laughs shortly.

Daddy, though, has been a regular at Hal's law office in Leimert Park for years. Now he goes there almost daily, sometimes with his brother. My Uncle Thomas suffered a series of strokes and can't really speak anymore, but he likes places where he can sit and follow talk about things he knows and remembers. Eastside things.

Daddy has warmed up a little. He acknowledges that "my whole thing was the Eastside"—family, friends, professional concerns. He started going to annual Eastside reunions at Hal's house in the early '70s; he goes into his bedroom to retrieve a picture Hal took at one of these events. Daddy is unsmiling, cool, wearing a burnished leather coat and goatee. He never missed one of those parties. Veering close to sentiment, he backpedals. The Eastside, he says, really belongs to Hal. "It's an era that meant something to him," he says. "Not just the past, of course, but the present. The Eastside is his whole deal."

I let these contradictions fall and settle on the two of us like rain. I sympathize deeply with my father's reluctance to give voice to something that might be blown off its tenuous course by words. I, too, fear language's power to magnify as well as diminish everything in its path. I ask him again, my eyes fixed on a blank notebook page, what the Eastside meant. He figures we're finished recording. "To me, it's more a matter of . . . It's a good feeling for me. It's a linkage to a past. It's the sort of environment where it's devoid of judgment. It doesn't matter who you are. Judges to janitors."

Damn right, says Hal Miller, there was no caste system. Hal's voice is brusque and, despite his having been born in L.A., Southern-flavored. "Everybody knew everybody and they lived together—doctors, lawyers, butchers, domestic workers. There was no crime. You didn't have no chance to commit a crime. The old ladies would be sitting out all day on the porches snapping string beans in a pot, yelling at each other across the street, telling each other the news. Shoot, if you did something bad in school, the message would beat you home. You'd get a whipping at school and another one would be waiting for you when you walked in the door." I smile—how many times have I heard this from older people? But Halvor Thomas Miller II is talking business. He's an attorney, and he delivers his story of his beloved Eastside like a brief. In many respects he is like my father: clipped, authoritative, and devoted to family. He's not sure how to treat me, like a daughter or a journalist. He gives up on the question for the moment and looks out the car window.

I am rolling down Eastside streets with Hal on an overcast morning. He's agreed to be my tour guide. He's tried to be offhand about it, about the whole prospect of this story, but he's taking this task as seriously as he takes his role of unofficial flame keeper of the Eastside Boys. Hal's mother was born in Oklahoma in 1904. His uncle, Loren Miller, owned the newspaper the *California Eagle* and was a celebrated attorney who helped win the 1948 Supreme Court case *Shelley vs. Kramer* that struck down restrictive housing covenants and enabled blacks to integrate. A local elementary school is named for him. His cousin, Leon Washington, launched the city's other black paper, *the Los*

Angeles Sentinel. Hal's Leimert Park law office is a pit stop for any number of Eastsiders. Mornings find a clutch of Boys drifting in and out, shooting the breeze to the tunes of straight-ahead jazz that plays constantly over Hal's sound system. Although Hal still practices law, his great passion is organizing Eastside functions. During one of our conversations he picked up a ringing phone and waited barely five seconds before snapping, "No, I can't talk now about that—I'm doing the Eastside." A paper banner advertising last year's Eastside reunion is taped to the wall of Hal's front office, more prominently displayed than the photographs of W.E.B. Du Bois, Martin Luther King Jr., and other black leaders. In the early '70s, Hal started having annual Eastside parties in his Southwest L.A. home. They would start in the afternoon, and by four the next morning the house was overflowing and people were still coming, about five hundred in all. These get-togethers were strictly male affairs, informal fraternities in the tradition of '40s social clubs such as the Cosmos and the Blue Devils. Several times, men showed up with their wives or girlfriends, then pleaded ignorance when Hal informed them the party was not coed; he says that a "No Women Allowed" sign hung prominently for twenty years. The women were sent home. "Completely sexist," my father says amiably, not exactly by way of condemnation.

The crowds got so out of hand that, in 1994, Hal decided to go public with his party and organized a massive event—women included—that he dubbed the Eastside Boys Reunion (the sanctity of Eastside maleness maintained in the title). Hal and his committee planned on booking a hotel ballroom before realizing that the Convention Center was the only place large enough to accommodate everybody. It wasn't easy to get, but Eastside Boy Tom Bradley intervened.

Hal frowns and scratches a thick, combed-back shock of hair. Sitting in my Mustang with his knees drawn up to his chest, he watches the passing streets intently. Suddenly he is leaning out the window, cranking one arm like a traffic cop as he points out places I have to see: the old streetcar barn at 53rd and Avalon; a bowling alley christened by Joe Louis; the Masonic Temple; the site of the jumping Bucket o' Blood club at 51st and Ascot, which was also the end of the B-car line. We flash by row after row of neat, squared-off houses with lawns in front, and though some lots have clearly suffered from age, most are well-preserved. I narrow my eyes and can see their original colors, glistening rose and robin's-egg blue and ochre, on a sunny day some sixty years ago. Small businesses still dot the comers of the residential landscape, Laundromats, and liquor stores, and such. We peel slowly away from the houses until we are riding south along Central and the commercial district, or what is left of it. Hal makes me brake for the Blodgett building at 23rd, the SuperRanch market at 48th, Williams Cleaners at 51st. He speaks proudly about each, though his speeches could be eulogies. He wants to stop near the old Dunbar Hotel at 42nd Street, to pull behind a building in an alley. A small alarm in my stomach goes off: this is a bad neighborhood. I angrily push the thought aside and concentrate on trying to see what Hal sees. Hal is out of the car and pressed against a wire fence. A knot of Latino construction workers behind the fence eyes him with mild curiosity. "We used to sit right here in the alley and listen to the music," says Hal, when it was the Downbeat Club. Hal takes his elbows off the fence and squints through his glasses at the brick facade. Duke Ellington's uncle lived nearby. Duke and Johnny Hodges would practice in his garage for hours and then come here to play. "When we were little boys, we'd meet the musicians when they took their dope breaks out here. Man, Central was nothing but clubs—the Downbeat, Club Alabam, the Plantation. It was a mecca for servicemen during World War II."

We go south on Central to 51st Street, Hal's old street, and he straightens up and grabs the car door handle like we're about to go over the edge of a waterfall on a logjammer ride. He barks at me to pull over to a stop, and as soon as I hit the brakes he's out of the car and striding up to a building where a group of teenage volunteers is cleaning up graffiti. This is the old fire station where Hal and his friends would wait for the firefighters to go home, then jump out of windows onto trampolines used for rescue practice. Hal's best friend was a white boy named Spencer Moxley; fully a third of 51st Street was white in the 1930s and early '40s. One day a gang of black boys jumped Spencer and beat him up; Hal tried vainly to intervene. "My mother sat me down that day and explained to me about racial bigotry," he recalls. "That's when I first became aware of it." In his eagerness to get a look at the station, Hal missed the "Wet Paint" sign on the wall, and now his palms are streaked white. He mutters "damn!" under his breath and frantically tries to wipe the paint off on the grass. I suppress a laugh; for a few moments, he is ten again.

I am driving through the Eastside and thinking the obvious: Avalon Boulevard ain't what it used to be. The street has a funereal air. Between the empty lots and shuttered storefronts are small businesses with weathered signs hand-lettered in Spanish, fast-food joints, tiny churches, nearly invisible motels. People do not walk so much as stand, look pointedly around, and then hustle off to some hastily recalled destination. At 46th Street, faded red printing on a stucco façade had for decades announced the location of

Corky's. Inside, patrons sit elbow to elbow at the bar, and the jukebox blares Chaka Khan, B. B. King, the Ink Spots, the Temps. It's an old-time tavern filled with black folks who moved out of the Eastside long ago but return here for a beer and a game of dominoes. "They come in the afternoon and leave before dark," explains Corky Gaines, who inherited the bar and a handful of other businesses from his father in 1958. This is not my world; I rarely drink, and I see the inside of bars even less. I sit close to Corky, who presides over the scene like a latter-day Santa, down to the ample girth, bushy beard, and twinkly good humor. Corky's a die-hard Eastsider. He was born here and is one of very few Boys who have remained. He and his wife, Awanda, have a house on 43rd Street, not far from the bar. Three years ago, their sixteen-year-old son, Cory, a bright and promising student at Jefferson High, was shot and killed barely a block from home. He and Awanda buried him and stayed on.

"It could have happened anywhere," Corky says. He tells me this at home, in his den where it's quiet, surrounded by framed photos of a smiling Cory. I don't know what to say, so I drink the lemonade he's given me. Awanda is from Pennsylvania. She realized long ago that Corky wasn't going anywhere. Their house is both cozy and expansive, once a daily hangout for their son and his friends. But it is also hemmed in, staked out by iron bars that run along the perimeter of the spruced-up lawn. Awanda sighs. "It's just too bad," she says with a catch in her voice, "that kids now don't see what the Eastsiders had." Until he retired from the post office last year, Corky came to the bar every day at 4 p.m., when he got off. After retiring, he decided to lease the bar to a woman named Ruth Jackson, a former bartender who, like Corky, is a lifelong Eastsider. Now a sign outside the building simply says "The Bar," but the regulars still come. And Corky still goes by to talk with them. He insists he is not looking to pull up roots. "Never will," he says. "My wife and I will never sell the property. Not going nowhere."

Once Walter Gordon Jr. figures out what I'm doing ("What's your name?" he barks on the phone, "Aubry? Oh yes. I know of a lot of them"), he agrees to tell me the history of the Eastside. He sounds more than pleased. L.A.'s black history is a specialty of his. Walter is eighty-nine and still busy practicing criminal law. He dresses in suits and thick-soled brogues and stoops a bit. His wife, Clara, ushers me into a sitting room and tells me to wait, please. Their Leimert Park home is neat and quiet, except for the occasional yap of a Pomeranian. Walter comes in and shakes my hand; I feel as though we've made a pact of some kind. He settles into his armchair, eyeing me expectantly. "Aren't you going to use a tape recorder?" It's less a question than a demand.

"Well, no, but I have a notebook." It suddenly seems terribly inadequate. "I'm interested in your overall impression of things, not necessarily every detail." Walter doesn't cotton to this, I can tell. He wants me to get every word and preserve it. How else can young people learn? He launches into an intricately detailed history of blacks in the city that, despite its plain delivery, unfolds like a fairy tale.

In the beginning, Negro activity was concentrated downtown, around 2nd and Los Angeles streets. That was about 1920. Black folks worked as redcaps and porters for the Southern Pacific Railroad, which originated at 5th and Central; the black thoroughfare was a single block of Central Avenue between the railroad and 6th Street. That thoroughfare began creeping south; it went as far as 9th, then 12th, 18th and, by the 1920s, 25th Street. Walter's father had a real-estate office at 25th and Central and, despite pressure from the real-estate board not to sell to blacks, was kept busy.

Walter got to know the neighborhood helping his father show places to prospective buyers and renters, including black celebrities who, despite their stardom, couldn't live in white areas. Walter also had a paper route that required him to pick up black newspapers such as the *Chicago Defender* at the train station and deliver them to sites along Central Avenue. Gordon remembers the people who started giving black L.A. some definition, some muscle: J. W. Coleman, owner of the city's largest black employment agency ("A giant of a man, six-foot-seven, with a misshapen forehead"); YMCA director T. A. Green; the Blodgett who started the city's first black-owned savings and loan at the eponymous building at 25th and Central. I think of my whirlwind tour with Hal, that breathless attempt to revisit what never existed for me. As a young man, Walter was a member of the L.A. Forum, a black civic organization that met every Sunday in an office at 8th and Wall Street. Black and white attorneys from all over town met to discuss discrimination. Led by the imposing Coleman, the Forum exerted pressure on whites to modify the restrictive business covenants that circumscribed life in L.A.

Block by block, year by year, blacks expanded their boundaries southward along Central. When Walter returned to L.A. from law school in 1936, Central was just beginning to hit its stride as a hub of black business and a mecca for jazz. It would be the best of times for the Eastside Boys. Segregation was still virulent, ubiquitous, but its heavy hand had also compressed the brightest hopes and aspirations of black people into a potent square of time and space made all the stronger because of the strictures placed on it; life, as the laws of physics dictate, found a way. And there was the hope, passed from one generation to the next, that the barriers of segregation would finally come down, but that none of the institutions built in its face—Jefferson High and Central Avenue—would come down with it. Walter looks up from showing me piles of photos. The hour is growing late, and I am a little fatigued from trying to absorb everything. He shakes his head slightly. "Is this what you want?" he asks, gesturing toward the pictures. He studies me through his thick glasses. "I have a feeling that I'm not giving you what you're looking for—what you want." I leave the Gordon house feeling vaguely guilty. Driving away, I think Walter is right. I listen avidly to the stories of how wonderful everything was, and I want to hear about the tragic moment when someone, or something, took it all away. There is no such moment. The Eastside Boys were part of the driving social forces that blew their history to the wind. There are no heroes or anti-heroes. The Boys may live now with their point of origin in their sights, but they do not go back. Their heroism lies in not going back, in recognizing the truth and going forward. That is what I want for myself.

"Come in, come on in," Billy Benfield exclaims before I can get my name out. Billy lives on a street that slopes up to affluent Baldwin Hills—a pipe dream in Eastside days. His apartment is old and rambling, with a palm-tree shaded balcony that affords a grand view of the Crenshaw district. He unlatches the screen door, takes my hand and pumps it. He laughs and gives me a hug; his gaiety is infectious. While I sit and listen to scratchy jazz playing on the radio, he brings out the photo albums and scrapbooks detailing his glory days as a track star at Jefferson High. Jeff was the Eastside high school, known for its champion athletes and innovative jazz instruction (thanks to music teacher Samuel Brown, the school produced such luminaries as Dexter Gordon, O. C. Smith, Ernie Andrews, Frank Morgan, and Teddy Edwards). Along with church, school was the most important social center of the Eastside; if you brought somebody home to meet your folks, they immediately wanted to know your affiliation to those two institutions. ("And if they didn't belong to no church," remarked Hal, "then the old folks would say, 'Well, you better just go on and take this boy back to where you found 'im.'") Eastsiders did go to other schools besides Jeff—L.A., Polytechnic, Jordan, Fremont—but they were outside the proper boundaries, virgin Westside turf. Eastside boys know Billy Benfield, or know what he did. "Oh, Billy," said Corky when I mentioned him. "Yeah, he ran track." The school had championship track teams for twenty years beginning in the '30s, and Billy was a distance runner on Jefferson's city championship team of 1939. High school sports were regularly covered by the *Sentinel* and the *Eagle*, but that year was magic. "I got my picture in the *L.A. Times*," says Billy, pointing to the yellowed clipping with unabashed pride. "Can you imagine?"

That Billy grew up poor on the Eastside seems to have fueled rather than dimmed his natural optimism. He and his mother rented an apartment at Stanford and 32nd Street for five dollars a month. His mother worked days as a domestic. Billy sold papers along Central Avenue or carried grocery bags to people's cars for spare change. He was broke a lot. He sometimes ate dinner at the homes of such prominent Eastside gentry as the Houstons; Norman Houston founded the Golden State Mutual life insurance business (now at Western and Adams). "The Eastside Boys had a real cohesive thing, but we figured that's how it was everywhere," says Billy with a shrug. Jefferson and the track team were Billy's finest hour. He has since worked as an electrician, pipe fitter, and real-estate maintenance inspector, retiring seven years ago from the city Housing Department. His beat covered much of his old neighborhood. Next to the Eastside, Billy is happiest talking about his thirty-nine-year-old son, Benet, and his grandson. Billy's been divorced a long time and went through several periods when he didn't have much money. "We'd get a loaf of bread some afternoons and sneak in a football game at the Coliseum, UCLA games. He didn't mind. We got closer. Later on, when he grew up, he took me to the ball games."

Billy has high hopes for a new hot-sauce business that he started last year with Benet. The Eastside Boys have helped get it off the ground; at the 1994 reunion, they bought cases of the stuff to put on the three hundred tables. Billy can't understand why I'm not married, a bright, promising girl, with the blood of the Eastside running in my veins. Why, he says, men out there must be crazy.

He walks me to the door. I take a mental picture of him in his baseball cap, blue corduroy shorts, and sneakers. Billy is still turning the Eastside over in his mind. "We didn't realize what we had at the time, so we didn't know what we would miss. I take my son through the Eastside sometimes," he says, "but all I can do is tell him about it."

The electronic board at the Convention Center flashes a greeting to the incoming line of cars: WELCOME TO THE EASTSIDE BOYS REUNION. The night is mild enough for strapless gowns and not quite chilly enough for the fur wraps that are nonetheless in abundance. The sea of couples—about 3,500 in all—surges toward the ballroom. I feel distinctly underdressed in my Lycra dance-club getup. This is an Oscar gala with no awards. Looking a little bewildered to find himself decked out like a kid at a high school prom, Hal hovers near the door, grasping hands and dispensing hugs. "You see," he tells me at one point in the evening, as Eastside Boys-turned-jazz singers Ernie Andrews and O. C. Smith wail a tune onstage, "we couldn't get media coverage for this, not these days. All these black people out, but no violence, no shooting." He laughs, a little bitterly. "You would think that in itself is a story."

I sit at the table reserved for my parents, sister, brother, and me. The room is United Nations–conference scale, too big to see all four comers from our table. A large video monitor hangs from the ceiling, but its scope is woefully inadequate. Daddy spies a friend across the room and goes to intercept him. On the way he is besieged by scores of people he hasn't seen in ten or twenty years; I hear Daddy's animated voice clearly above the din and know he isn't coming back. That's all right. No one is really staying put anyway, just resting their feet at whatever table is on the way to another table and another set of friends. Like the rest of the younger people here tonight, I watch and marvel at an event that I—that we—almost certainly will never host. Daddy reappears occasionally with a friend in tow, a little breathless and smiling. "Hey, hey, hey, check this out," he says, shaking his finger continually at the person behind him. "Did you meet this guy? Do you remember him? You probably were too little, but, man, he was around all the time at the house. Yeah, yeah, he used to . . ." I smile with my hands in my lap, nodding, not really remembering at all but wanting to sustain the evening however I can. Daddy, satisfied, talks on and claps a hand to the man's shoulder. His hands rake the air with the same expressiveness they had when he played the horn.

I think back to 1970, when I was eight and he ran for state assembly, putting bright orange posters of himself up all around South-Central; a rare instance, the only one I can recall, of Daddy doing anything resembling self-promotion. It was a handsome picture, depicting him with thick wavy hair and moustache, tie knotted firmly in place. His smile was small and uneasy, and I don't recall his laughing around friends then, even his most ardent supporters, nearly as much as he's laughing now. There was no need to reflect then; there was still the belief that black neighborhoods would survive the loss of neighbors. I begin walking what seems like a mile to the dance floor. I get waylaid myself, by Corky and Awanda. I know Billy's in the room somewhere, talking up his sauce that's on every table. Other people I meet listen closely to my name, then grab my wrist if they recognize it. "I'm so glad you came," they rasp in my ear. I try jitterbugging, with somewhat awkward results—"Soul Train" this ain't—but I am happy taking part. These are not dances I know. But my feet and I have much to claim. I think about Hal's pronouncement: things will get better. I can shift the current of history with a flap of my wings. I can deepen its tone with my instrument. If I walk away from L.A., move off to another frontier and take up another tradition, my passage from place to place will be well marked.

Hal thinks I'll stay on. He says L.A. is just a place where people stay put. Clearly he's going nowhere; L.A. holds the dreams that are left. "Natives don't leave," he says. "For a lot of us, this is the end of the line. This is nirvana."

My father calls me one morning not long after the reunion. He talks fast, a wind storm blowing by many subjects: politics, the state of education, my Uncle Edris's health. One other thing. "How's that story coming?" he asks.

"Which one?"

"The Eastside deal. Have you turned it in yet?"

Daddy's been checking on this story like a sick child, like something entrusted to him. I choose my words carefully for the prognosis. "Not exactly. I'm still working on it. It's a challenge. It's long. Longer than most pieces I write. Different." "Uh-huh." I hear papers rustling. "Well, you know, Hal's been asking about it. He wants to know. That's really his deal. Of course, you know that."

THE KING OF COMPTON

MAYOR OMAR BRADLEY AND HIS REIGN OF CHAOS

April 2001

I don't come here. As I drive through Compton on my way to meet Mayor Omar Bradley, past faded but neat rambling houses and islands of large shade trees, I realize that in all the years I've been informally covering black Los Angeles, I've been strenuously avoiding all things Compton. Los Angeles is full of small towns that feel distinctly apart from it—Inglewood, West Holly-wood, Beverly Hills—but still connected to it, within sight of it. Not Comp-ton. It feels adrift, unseen, its sun and sidewalks and empty spaces hardened by time and indifference. Which is not to say it looks bad. With its tidy lawns and general quiet, it would probably be a disappointment to ardent gangsta-rap fans who imagine it as a kind of ground zero of ghetto. But Compton is not so much debauched as it is detached, which I don't remember until I see it, again, myself.

I'm feeling better—well, less guilty—when I reach the Roscoe's Chicken and Waffles on Central Avenue. During the drive I thought about all the things I've read and heard about Compton and about Bradley, most of them on the outer edge of bizarre—the state takeover of the city's mismanaged school district, the City Council's dissolution of the police force and award of a no-bid trash contract to a man who once testified that he'd passed bribes to council members, the mayor's tendency toward cronyism, autocracy, and occasional public rages, including an altercation with a political rival outside the council chambers because, according to the next day's *L.A. Times*, the man had "drawn his finger across his throat in a threatening gesture." In my car, I heroically decide that I will set things straight where they have always been out of focus, misunderstood; I will give Compton the empathy and the gravitas it has always needed.

But Bradley has no use for my assessment, or anybody else's, and he never stops letting me know that. His aide, Melvin Stokes, meets me first, with scrupulous politeness, and shows me to a table with assurances that his boss will be arriving momentarily. Bradley does, and appears just as obliging until I begin asking about some of his more questionable actions as mayor. Then all hell, which as it turns out is never far from the surface, breaks loose. Ap-parently, he's only met with me to tell me how utterly useless it will be to meet with me at all. He snarls a lot of things through his teeth and uses obscenities freely. He declares that I'm a victim of racism and don't know it, that I'm a hapless agent of the "white-devil media." When I ask him to clarify that, he says something about black people being blindly loyal to Bill Clinton and concludes, darkly, "The oppressed begin to love the oppressor." He gets most riled when I ask him about an incident a few years ago in which he charged, shirtless, into a Compton fire station after fire academy officials rejected a personal check he wrote to pay for his son's tuition. "The white-devil mother-fuckers didn't mention the fact that I was not talking to Compton firefight-ers," he fumes. "If you threaten me, I'll respond to that." He grumbles some more about people making careers out of opposing him and says, "I wish they'd get out of the fucking *life*."

Thick with muscle and broad-shouldered, Bradley is given to a swagger that seems to have been in place long before he became mayor and that is evident even when he's sitting down. He also has the unnerving habit of telling you exactly what you might be thinking about him before you've completely thought it: "You think because I'm a big nigger with a bald head, I'm a bad guy," he begins, looking me in the eye. "I've had twenty-one years of education. I have a master's degree. Why am I treated this way? Because I am a *black man*." This is a challenge only the most foolhardy would accept, and he knows it. Insinuations of racism (if you're white) or ethnic disloyalty (if you're black) are like bomb threats—you always have to clear the building, take them seriously, even if you believe in your gut they are pure bunk. In the space of this necessary and/or cowardly hesitation, Bradley thrives.

In a final effort to engage him in something resembling a civil conversation, I unwittingly address him by his first name and get a stern rebuke from Stokes, a bulky man with deceptively sleepy eyes. He has been nearly motionless up to this point, nursing a lemonade, but he jerks at the word "Omar" like it's scalding water. "Now come on, Miss Aubry, he's the *mayor*," snaps Stokes. "You don't call him that. You give him the proper respect." If respect means hightailing it out of there not fifteen minutes into the interview, that's fine by me. I will leave Compton where I've always left it: alone. Then Bradley abruptly changes tactics. As if I've passed some great test, he stands up and declares that he's now going to take me around town and show me the real Compton, the one I have never seen and the evil media deliberately will not see.

There hasn't been a time in Omar Bradley's eight years as mayor when he hasn't been regarded by large groups of people as mercurial, controversial, or potentially dangerous. Those I interviewed were therefore either very willing to talk about him or irritated with the whole proposition. "Why write about Omar Bradley?" groused one source who generally lobbies me to do the most positive and heartening stories possible on local black figures. "You go ahead and do what you have to do," he went on without waiting for an answer, "but you might risk getting a reputation of always bringing black people down. Don't misunderstand, I completely agree with the complaints about him. A no-brainer. But what does this story accomplish? Haven't we heard *enough* about Negroes like him?"

"Everybody's got an Omar story," said Ellis Cooke, a behind-the-scenes reformer and about as low-key and reasoned a character as you'll find in town. "The complaints about him are valid, but there are other things that don't get aired. We have an archaic tax system that needs changing. We need to figure out why we don't spend money locally. We lack a history of responsibility— we've been discouraged from it," he said, citing Tulsa, Oklahoma, and other places where black autonomy was systematically destroyed. "We simply don't see ourselves as being good or practiced in running cities. We don't have criteria for evaluating an effective leader. That's why I wouldn't waste time talking about Omar."

What they were saying, in part, is that the mere act of holding Bradley up to the light of examination dooms all of us in the black community. We are all implicated in his psychological thuggery, his smarts and iconoclasm and grand intentions gone wildly askew. Viewed from various angles, he is everything unfinished about us: our nebulous leadership, our prosperous but inert middle class, our lower class that's had nothing to lose for a long time, and most of all, our need to be heard. Actually, I found the collective concern about him encouraging, proof that there *is* a black community out there, even if it exists at this point only in some nethersphere of the subconscious or the unspoken or the long dead. Bradley, oddly enough, shows us our heart.

It must also be said that the city of Compton is *not* Omar Bradley. A modest backwater Southern California town lying hopefully in the shadow of South Bay affluence and suburban detachment, it burst into the national consciousness with the swift ascendancy of gangsta rap and its images of black poverty gone dour, brooding, nihilistic, and—just to drive the point of irony home—ruthlessly material. This hard new casting of Compton was both an instant success and a civic poison. Economic development and commercial interest in the city, already in a long and slow decline, collapsed. South Bay proper and its vague promise of a better and brighter community quietly erased its portion of Compton Boulevard from county maps and street guides—suspect by association. So it was that Compton got put on the map in one way and taken off in another—neither way was good—and Omar Bradley inherited the city's dubious new prominence and its even more dubious new mystique when he was elected mayor in 1993, a peak year for gangsta rap and a scant year after the '92 civil unrest. How much Bradley has tried to counter the city's lawless, badass image with appeals to community and calls to progress and how much he simply glories in that image and uses it to his personal arm-twisting advantage have been hotly discussed ever since.

And in this election season, the discussion is at full boil. Bradley is seeking a third term as mayor and a chance to prove his political hardiness amid accusations of everything from dirty campaign tricks to murder for hire. Among his challengers are Eric Perrodin, deputy district attorney, brother of deposed police captain Percy Perrodin, and the object of Bradley's wrath as the man who allegedly made that "threatening gesture"; school-board member Saul Lankster, a longtime Compton operative who was once convicted of a felony (later set aside by a judge) and who is locally famous for his Martin Luther King Jr. impression; and Basil Kimbrew, an even more notorious Compton operative who is best known for testifying in federal court that he accepted bribes on behalf of former Councilwoman Patricia Moore (she was convicted, he wasn't) and apparently the only mayoral candidate who admits to making public appearances wearing a bulletproof vest. The *L.A. Times* recently likened the race to a "situation comedy," which, however objectively justifiable, stings—Compton as the latest WB coon show—and gives sudden credence to Bradley's frequent contention that the white media have more than a little devil in them.

The mayor doesn't give me a choice about whether I'm going on his impromptu tour or not, which I'm not sure is a compliment—does he extend this invitation to everybody?—or more browbeating. I go. Maybe, just maybe, the browbeating is performance, and he keeps his natural sense and good deeds in the glove compartment. And, as I've told myself once today, in Compton one has to see things for oneself. The only thing Bradley seems to keep in the glove compartment is tapes. To a soundtrack of ballads by '70s soul crooners—the Moments, the Dramatics, the Chi-Lites—he wheels around Compton for over two hours, breaking frequently into song and becoming almost chivalrous at our many stops, insisting that I wait for him or Stokes to open my door. He points out medians sprouting African palm trees, and newly built Rite Aids and fast-food joints where there used to be fallow lots. He shouts "hey, brother" or "hey, sister" to friends and citizens in passing cars or on street corners, and shakes their hands in the stores we stop to inspect. At one store, shoppers are so randomly solicitous and complimentary of the mayor that, on our way out, I joke that the whole scene could have been staged. Bradley and Stokes stop dead in their tracks and stare at me like bad fish bait. "What do you mean?" Stokes asks, and I know the only way to extricate myself from the hell that threatens is to say, vehemently and innocently, "Nothing." The mayor, mollified, next shows me his "masterpiece," the Renaissance Plaza at Central and Rosecrans, which boasts a Food 4 Less and is the city's most substantial shopping mall. The plaza is also the site of a recently unveiled monument honoring Cesar Chavez and Martin Luther King — Bradley's tribute to the possibilities of black-Latino brotherhood — though the words most prominently displayed on it are not King's or Chavez's, but his own.

In the car, with Stokes in the backseat and me semicrouched in the front, Bradley is almost happy. His clear pride in the improvements in Compton's landscape is touching; as he talks about them I can practically see his chest swell. In these moments he displays a charisma that is not at all moody or outlaw, but child-like — he's gotten an A on his paper, and he's standing in front of the class showing it off. Even as I sit tensed beside him, half expecting a volley of bullets from one of the many enemies he's mentioned for my benefit, I get caught up in a puerile thrill of victory. "Unemployment has fallen 9 percent," Bradley fairly shouts, while Stokes murmurs something like an "amen" in the back. "People don't want to talk about all this, about the new Pizza Huts, the McDonald's . . ." I don't know if McDonald's ever felt like triumph, but it does now. We stop at Bradley's family home on Compton's west side, where I'm introduced to his father, a fragile-looking but still handsome man wearing blue jeans and house slippers, a shock of white hair and a ready if somewhat vague smile. Family in Compton has always meant a lot more than blood; Melvin Stokes came to live here when his parents died.

We drive through Richland Farms, the city's most well-heeled neighborhood, described by narrow sidewalks and lush, interlocking trees that make it look improbably rural. For all the vilification of Bradley as little more than a street hood, the mayor has big dreams of transforming Compton into a Ladera-style lure for the departed black middle class. He points out the park and tennis courts where Venus and Serena Williams discovered their genius, and where he predicts more tennis players will do the same. He talks about building new luxury houses of stucco, two stories, with sliding glass doors. He talks about the city's recent purchase of a building he plans to turn into a health spa, about the hundreds of kids he's gotten involved in Pop Warner football leagues, about establishing a black Hollywood hall of fame near Compton's downtown. He talks about all this with as much fervor as he talks about getting ex-gang members and dope addicts and dealers off the streets and into programs like Operation Redirection, a brainchild of his that offers job training through rehabilitating old city-owned houses. Improve lives and improve unsightly housing stock at the same time — this is the kind of efficiency Bradley loves. That it's his idea makes him love it that much more. "Build a better world," he says sagely, "and the world will travel."

He tries to charm me with such oblique aphorisms, and I'm more than charmed at junctures not by his deftness but by something quite opposite, his total artlessness. I'm seduced not by the pinstriped suit or the menacing air but by the kid who gives himself an A and can't get over it. But my guard is immovably up; this is an overgrown kid who doesn't know his own strength.

Amid all the signs of progress and the music that serves as its score, Bradley's mood lightens considerably, and he starts touching my hand to emphasize points. One point in particular is how far Compton has yet to go, how substandard the standard remains and how that must change. "I don't have time to fight," he says, impatience creeping back into his voice. "I don't have time. I've got so much to do and so little time to do it. I can't let things look any different than they look where *you* live." He doesn't know where I live, though he knows it's not in Compton. He points to another spot where a tree and grass grow where once had been only broken pavement. "For years we thought it was supposed to be dirt or asphalt. People said, 'They're black, that's how it's supposed to be. They don't like cleanliness, proficiency, efficiency.'" He lapses into a bitter silence.

Pretty much everybody in Compton started out with high hopes for Omar Bradley's mayoralty, even those who have become his most vocal critics. Bradley seemed a thing apart from a tired black political establishment that had the progressive rhetoric down but had stood by and done nothing as South-Central and Compton and Watts slipped into economic and spiritual entropy through the 1970s and '80s. By the '90s, which saw an explosion of Latino immigration and a nervous new emphasis on multiculturalism and pie-sharing and all of us getting along, it was no longer even politically expedient for black politicians to speak directly to the problems of black people.

Bradley would have none of this kind of retreating; throughout his years in public office, beginning with a term as councilman, he championed the causes of strong black men and black self-sufficiency loudly and often. He has ties to the Nation of Islam and recalls a meeting with Louis Farrakhan during his college days as a turning point in his life. Unlike other black politicians who were all too eager to distance themselves from the mean streets they represented, he was a local boy who knew every odd corner of his city and seemed proud of it. He went to Compton Centennial High School, played football and later returned as a coach. Growing up near Piru Street in the

'70s, he witnessed the inception of the Bloods gang there, and though he was never a member himself, his familiarity with the life informed his blunt, cock-of-the-walk style. Whatever their misgivings about that, many people saw Bradley as a fighter in a world of apologists, a bit crazy by necessity, rather like irascible and indomitable L.A. City Councilman Nate Holden. (And as with Holden, his local legend is such that everybody in town refers to him simply by his first name. Omar, like Cher or Puffy, says it all.)

"When I first met with Omar I was 100 percent in his corner," says the Reverend B. T. Newman, a member of Pastors for Compton, a group of ministers and concerned citizens that opposes Bradley's reelection. "He was a bright, upcoming, sharp young black man. I even supported him for mayor against the wishes of my own flock." Bradley had stirred the wrath of many church types when, as a councilman, he championed a casino initiative on the grounds that Compton sorely needed the business. He declared then that he might be voted out for it, "but I didn't run to become a popular person, I ran to make a difference." Longtime resident and civic booster Mollie Bell has her concerns but says that, overall, she likes Bradley's stubbornness and all the things he has stood up for over the years. "The Million Man March, allowing Farrakhan to speak in Compton, coming to a vigil held for crack babies, questioning the relationship between the CIA and the distribution of crack cocaine," says Bell. "The mayor is not politically correct, but he's right there. These are our communities. He has a love of African-American people."

Yet Bradley has been held responsible for the city's social and political isolation. Where Compton should naturally embody local black concerns, it has repelled them. Former Congressman Merv Dymally says he "could never do anything with Compton." An L.A. activist says he never takes his causes there, because it is too likely they will be hijacked or distorted. A veteran political consultant who has worked nearly every other town in Southern California flatly refuses to run campaigns in Compton. The Reverend William Johnson, also of Pastors for Compton, says Bradley has never quite decided which elements of the city and which elements of himself—toughness or expansiveness, hard truth or pliant hope—he wants to represent politically. It is a public-identity crisis unique to modern black figures, but with Bradley it has meant that one day he quotes Shakespeare and scripture, the next day Malcolm X and *Mein Kampf*. "He doesn't know whether he's a Christian or a Muslim, a gangbanger or a good guy," Johnson says dryly. "He has many forms, many guises. He can be civil and absolutely threatening. He's a Christian and a Muslim and a thug all at once."

Other observers say it is paranoia that is most responsible for Bradley's ham-fisted governing style and his reputation as a possible good guy who went bad a long time ago; that the big, unwieldy ideas and altruistic impulses have been undermined by an even bigger suspicion that people are out to get him or wrest control out from under his comfortable seat at City Hall. Bradley has been able to do pretty much what he wants as mayor because he's had a three-member voting bloc in place on the City Council, and the few members who have tried to challenge it over the years have been either ignored or treated with open hostility. For this he has been likened to Hitler, Idi Amin, "Papa Doc" Duvalier, and other despots. "It's his way or no way," says Percy Perrodin, of the erstwhile Compton Police Department. "Complete and total control."

Civic affairs in Compton have always been personal in a small-town kind of way, but the Bradley years have taken such intimacy to startling new levels. A sample: his aunt Delores Zurita is on the city council; his sister Carol Bradley Jordan is on the school board; a nephew, Jamal Bradley, works as his personal aide (and was recently hired at Centennial High as a football coach); Lynwood mayor Paul Richards, a Bradley ally, recently became a housing developer in Compton, with exclusive rights to lucrative projects; Richards also ran a successful campaign for freshman Compton City Councilman Amen Rahh, a member of Bradley's voting bloc (and an administrator at Compton College). Bradley himself works full-time for the Lynwood school district and, by the way, has publicly announced his interest in becoming the superintendent of Compton's schools. And so on and so forth.

Bradley also has a history of problem solving through purging. Last summer, at the height of his clashes with the police department, which culminated in its vote of no confidence in the mayor, he issued an informal gag order to municipal employees, warning that if they spoke out against Compton or its leadership they risked being fired. Later in the year, shortly after treasurer Douglas Sanders stomped out of a council meeting when Bradley prevented him from giving a routine report on city finances, the council contemplated the possibility of changing the treasurer's post from an elected position, which it has been for a hundred years, to an appointed one. Bradley has also been contemplating dissolving the fire and water departments.

Far less genteel are various allegations of intimidation. Last week, Councilwoman Yvonne Arceneaux reported a threat of bodily harm to the FBI. Veteran activist Lorraine Cervantes, who supported Bradley in his first run for mayor and has since supported recall efforts, claims that she, too, has been subject to threats, and responded to one with a flat challenge: "I said, 'You'd better kill me, because that's the only way I'm going away.'" Relative newcomer Father Stan Bosch, who pastors Our Lady of Victory and Sacred Heart Catholic churches, has experienced three church break-ins since he became involved with Pastors for Compton, though he has no evidence they were connected to his political activism. Bosch, who is white but speaks Spanish and leads parishes that are virtually all Latino, has also been accused by the Bradley camp at various times of being a racial instigator, a Nazi, and a local head of the Mexican Mafia. And in one of the more interesting bits of campaign news, Eric Perrodin lodged letters of protest with the city and the Sheriff's Department after he was told that Bradley and a few other officials tried to raid his personnel files in hopes of uncovering some dirt. Bradley, through a spokesman, says that not only was he not involved in the incident, but "I can assure you that on the date in question, I was not in City Hall." It's life as usual in Compton, with a few minor adjustments. "We're walking precincts for Eric this weekend," says Perrodin's brother Percy. "I'll be armed."

There are facts, and there are rumors, and there are wild hybrids that flourish year-round in Compton's climate. The darkest rumor, which I'd heard from half a dozen sources before candidate Basil Kimbrew started holding feverish press conferences about it, implicates Bradley in the mysterious death of Gary Beverly, a fellow Lynwood school administrator and all-around popular guy who was inexplicably shot last summer on the 91 freeway as he was driving home from work. Bradley beefed up his own security after the incident, telling the press that he feared those shots may have been intended for him. The Sheriff's Department, which took over the investigation that originated with the Compton police, has not named any suspects, nor released any findings to date. Through a spokesman, Bradley characterizes Beverly as more than a colleague and says, "It is upsetting that another elected official would go on the record in an attempt to slander my name and outstanding record of accomplishments by indicating that I had something to do with the murder of my dear friend Gary Beverly."

At the end of the tour, well after nightfall, Bradley walks me back to my car in Roscoe's parking lot. As I fish for my keys, he becomes serious again—puts his dark glasses on, plants his feet apart—and asks what I think of him now. I say, honestly, that I don't know.

In an instant the chivalry vanishes, and the cold fury of our first moments returns. I am keenly aware of him standing between me and my car. I try to think of an answer.

"Say it," he says through his teeth. "The people *love* me." Though I'm tired and more than anxious to go home, something in me balks at his naked insistence that I say what he wants to hear. Fortunately, Bradley decides to elaborate. He talks about how he's had to go into his own pockets to bury children whose families didn't have the means or the will to do it themselves. He tells a story about a man who approached him to tell him his daughter had been killed by violence and how he, Bradley, felt responsible for that death as mayor of Compton. As he talks, his lip quivers and he looks distraught, an imposing figure suddenly too small for his fierce pinstriped suit. The moment passes, and he sighs. Before moving away from the car, he insists on giving me a hug. I'm going to be married in a few weeks; I've mentioned that at some point because it seemed like a safe, albeit throwaway, topic of conversation.

"Have a wonderful marriage," he says softly. "Good luck. I mean that."

Omar Bradley's bunkering down has had special impetus in the last decade or so, as the ethnic balance in Compton has tipped steadily away from an African-American plurality. A city that went breathlessly from white to black in the '60s is now going as breathlessly from black to Latino, from roughly 40 percent in 1990 to well over 60 percent in 2000. Bradley has witnessed much of this great demographic sea change from the mayor's office, and though he likes to say he embraces all people—he cites the monument as proof—the demonstrated truth is that he is hardly ready to concede power to anyone, and Latinos are merely another personal encroachment that must be kept at bay.

But now Bradley may have his hands full with Pastors for Compton, a coalition that has brought together all of Compton's dissatisfied but disparate parties—clergy, activists, disgruntled ex-employees of the city, business own-ers, plain citizens, and Latinos who are finally clamoring for inclusion. Its goal is simple: civic accountability. "We want to take Compton back," says Father Stan Bosch, his voice hoarse after a Sunday mass preached before a crowd that spilled out the side doors onto the verandas of Our Lady of Vic-tory. "Omar has no counselors. He says, 'This is *my* meeting, these are *my* chambers.' It's not about him, it's about the people—it shouldn't be about us and our egos. If it is that kind of leadership, I think it's evil."

The coalition's first act was to present the city with a short but pointed list of concerns: the whereabouts of federal housing moneys routed to Comp-ton, the state of the $8 million the city was supposed to save by liquidating the police department, the viability of plans to sell off the water utility, the general unavailability of city budget and other public information on any given day. The group met with Compton City Manager John Johnson and felt encouraged, but a scheduled follow-up meeting never happened. They were disappointed, but hardly surprised: during the first and only meeting with Johnson, the mayor broke in unannounced and launched into what the pastors uniformly describe as a twenty-minute rant. "I don't know *what* he was talking about," says the Reverend Richard Sanders of Mt. Pilgrim Baptist Church.

Thereafter, as Pastors for Compton has grown more public and more persistent, the group says, Bradley has grown more blatant in his opposition and more blatantly quid pro quo. Several of the group's founding clergy claim that he's threatened to strangle their nonprofit housing projects—hold up city moneys—unless and until they turn off the heat. Sanders, still looking slightly bewildered at the memory, says that during a recent meeting with the mayor he was told: "There are projects you want to do. I promise you, these things will not get done as long as you're in the coalition. I'll just give the money to someone else who is not my enemy. Why should I help, when you're doing everything you can to kill me?" The Reverend William Johnson was so taken aback by Bradley's approaching him at a local fast-food outlet to convey the message personally that he circulated an open letter describing how "His Honor told me in no uncertain terms that if I want a favor in Compton or need any money for my projects, he and he alone has control over city funds. It seems we do not have a democracy in Compton, but a dictatorship."

Bradley, through a spokesman, categorically denies obstructing funds, and adds, "Thus far, the ministers of this coalition have been focused on creating division within the community rather than working with the city to improve the quality of life for all interested parties." The ministers are not deterred, but invigorated. "We're not going to back down," says Bosch, whose affable smile and level voice don't hint at a steeliness he developed as an Industrial Areas Foundation community organizer and during stints in other tough spots, such as East L.A. and Mexico. "We have everything at stake and nothing to lose. The time is ripe to shine a light where there's been so much darkness."

Bosch is the combustive spark that Latino activism has been waiting many years for, ever since Bradley was elected mayor and very publicly reneged on a promise to appoint Compton's first Latino councilman to his vacant seat. (He claimed at the time that he didn't have the votes to do what he'd initially agreed to do.) Bosch entered the fray last year, when Ed Aguirre, then a Compton police detective, asked the priest to march with him and hundreds of others to City Hall to protest the increasing hostility the mayor seemed to be directing at the department and his unwillingness to put its fate to a public vote. When Bradley and most of the City Council left the meeting in a huff, Bosch stayed to interpret a question-and-answer session between the hordes of Latino protesters and Yvonne Arceneaux, a black woman and the sole council member who generally does *not* agree with Bradley. "I translated, she listened," says Bosch. "And that's *all* they wanted. Miss Arceneaux said that she had no real power, but it was the first time *they* felt some kind of power." Compton just may show the rest of urban L.A. how to do what nobody's been able to figure out yet: organize and sustain a real black-Latino coalition that, as one observer cuttingly put it, "does more than stage an ethnic festival where everybody gets together once a year and eats tacos and fatback."

While Bosch's reformist zeal has found plenty of amens among his fellow Compton clergy, most of them have in fact supported Bradley in the past. "I didn't want to be in a coalition if it was going to attack Omar," says Sanders. "I have never degraded or defamed him. I have never supported him for mayor, but I've always supported him as mayor. I think he's a brilliant young man, borderline genius, but he doesn't have the temperament or maturity to serve the people. It is Omar's response to all this that has appalled me and made me realize how he really is."

Like many others, Sanders is curiously able to separate the man from his misdeeds, the promise of the past from the gross disappointments of the present. Compton is family, after all, and Bradley its wayward son. "I still consider him a friend, even though I oppose him," says Newman. And Sanders's good impressions linger: he recalls a visit the mayor paid to his office a few years ago to enlist support for a proposal for a swank new housing tract. "I was truly impressed with his passion," says Sanders, "how he grabbed a pad of paper and a pen and sketched out his ideas right in front of me." Bradley later branded Sanders an enemy, even though he had pledged support for the mayor's project in exchange for the mayor's support of a pet project of his own. The future of both is murky. Sanders says the lesson in all this is that "You can have great passion, and be sincerely wrong."

I see Omar Bradley a second time because I really have no choice: over the weekend, I discover that I've left my appointment book in his car. When I walk into his rather lushly appointed office in City Hall, Bradley looks self-satisfied, as if he knew perfectly well from our first contentious moment that I'd end up here. The man who would be king, again, reclines in a big swivel chair behind a wooden desk the size of a dining-room table. On the walls are framed photos of his heroes—Malcolm, Martin—and the office decor includes kente cloth, African sculpture, a Kwanzaa candelabra. Away from the streets that he invokes so often, Bradley is quiescent, thoughtful. He still wants to know what I think of him. Figuring I have nothing to lose, I tell him that he righteously scared me during our first meeting, that he appeared to be very much the gangster everybody said he was.

He looks not angry this time, but a bit sheepish. He talks evenly at first, detailing his experiences in school, an influential teacher, his embittering epiphany that education for black students in Compton during the '70s was a joke. As a football player at Centennial, Bradley says, he played vicious defense against the South Bay white teams, "because we were getting even for the fact that we had no books, and our library was a hellhole." He talks about how he read Malcolm X's autobiography at age nine, Eldridge Cleaver at eleven, *Mein Kampf* at eighteen, later the *Rubaiyat* and Mao Tse-Tung. This is as much equanimity as the mayor has shown, perhaps as much as he can muster, but the heat and anger are already roiling under his words like lava. He erupts, recalling how, as a student at Cal State Long Beach, he challenged another student to tell him about the origin of bagpipes. "They're *African*," he fumes. "You need me to tell you that, so you can overcome that fucking bullshit . . . Education is a blade. Don't tell me, sister, that I talk too much because of your limited exposure."

His fondest theme, in the end, seems to be not African heritage or education or his own regard of himself as a kind of anointed civic savior, but football. When he talks about football, he seems to be remembering the most things and the best things in the fewest moments. He looks both animated and content. "I once ran sixty-five yards and caught a guy on the one-yard line," he says. "I hurt my knee. I put him out for five weeks. That's what I do. I enjoyed hitting people, though I wasn't a great athlete. I'd wait all game for a clean shot, then go kill 'em. I got a killer instinct."

He narrows his eyes and smiles a wide, closed-mouth smile. "From the sound of me, I seem bigger than I am. My coach once told a recruiter, 'He's not that big. But if I tell him to run through that wall, he'll run through it.'"

WEARING THE SHIRT

September 2006

My neighbor is selling his house. I'm taking the news of his selling hard, with a low flame of panic and a sense of loss that's settling in too early, like old age. This goes well beyond the loss of a friend I had just begun to make on my morning rounds with the dog. This is not about me. Inglewood needs him.

Shelton is young, in his thirties. He is black, like the majority of residents here in this city-conceived-as-suburb that borders both hard-luck South Central and the beachy, quintessentially California enclaves of South Bay. Shelton and his wife moved to Inglewood less than two years ago; their block is long and lovely, the one I never tire of walking. It's gently uphill from my own block in an area of Inglewood called Century Heights, which is one those L.A. real-estate monikers that, in this case, makes sense. Century Heights has many things real-estate agents eagerly describe as "charming": sculpted lawns that occasionally burst into bonsai or tropical themes, homey 1950s architecture, ample backyards. It's the essence of civility and middle-class pride of ownership that has prevailed in Inglewood for decades, ever since its inception in the early 1900s as a bedroom community strictly for whites; it retained that exclusiveness later when it became a residential outpost for the aerospace industry that boomed in the South Bay after World War II. When the racial convenants dissolved in the late '40s, white flight steadily followed, but the blacks who moved in kept the idyllic look of Inglewood going, to prove to that they had inherited something wonderful worth keeping rather than something tainted that had to be given up.

They were half successful. Century Heights has endured, but its endurance now looks like something of a paradox. Over the years, Inglewood schools have deteriorated. Commercial development is spotty and mostly uninspired; gang activity has grown. It is these elements, not Shelton devoutly watering his lawn every day, that frame Inglewood for the rest of the world, and that have framed it for some time. Century Heights has suffered from the general downward drift of black America into a vexing stagnation that encroaches upon our middle class and its expectations for modest but endless improvements. The fact is, the prevailing black reality does not sit well in any kind of "heights," and Shelton and his wife finally decided it was sitting too close for comfort. On his block, along with the manicured lawns, he said he routinely saw young black men rolling up in trucks. Sometimes they sat idling in the middle of the street, playing music or hanging out. They did nothing wrong, he said. Nothing illegal. They were cooperative, even polite, parked their trucks properly on the curb when asked. Most of them seemed to have jobs.

But Shelton couldn't help but conclude, somewhat reluctantly, that these consistent congregations of black men meant nothing good or promising or stabilizing for our neighborhood, or for our people. He and his wife were worried about not what it meant, but what it *could* mean. Shelton knew better than most; he'd grown up in South Central, like me, in a much more precarious part of town than Century Heights. He confessed that these guys themselves didn't threaten him nearly as much as they collectively threatened an expectation of blessed predictability and a black social order finally free from the worry of gangs, bad schools, all of it. Driving home at night, he wanted to turn the comer onto his street and not tense up over what he might find, not rage against some blemish that, in the middle of Century Heights' singular loveliness, looked uglier and more cancerous than it probably was. No, he couldn't take that chance. Too, he was sick of his own paranoia and wanted to be rid of it, to not live it anymore: he wanted to consider himself and his fellow lawn-waterers and dog-walkers as the controlling force in the neighborhood, not fear. But he says he's not there yet—we're not there yet—and he can't wait to be. So he's moving. He says it'll be somewhere between Inglewood and the San Fernando Valley.

I tell him that sounds awfully pricey; the always-crazed L.A. housing market has reached a fever pitch, and houses are selling for well over half a million in Inglewood. What comparable place could he and his wife possibly get north of here? Shelton sighs, nods hard. Then he shrugs. Such is the price of non-progress. I'm distraught, but I understand. People in California are used to moving to different terrain, spreading out, moving on: roots and conscience have little to do with it. You set your sights on a place first and figure out money and logistics later. That's California privilege, a vestige of the distinctly Western, covered-wagon privilege of mobility and open land as a tabula rasa that, once you reach the destination, is yours to shape into whatever modest paradise you want. Black people especially are not going to give that up.

At the same time, black Angelenos are giving way. The Latino demographic revolution that has been going on for at least fifteen years in traditional black strongholds like Inglewood and South Central and Compton is nearly complete. Immigration is a high tide that is washing away the sands of community that black people were always a bit wary of calling home, especially as their own Southern immigrant ideals ebbed further into the past. Now that a new people have moved in and are fleshing out new ideals of their own, unfulfilled black dreams feel ever more displaced, uncertain. I felt the displacement acutely during the spring of 2006, when the immigration rights movement swept the nation and L.A. in particular. I went to one of the massive downtown marches out of curiosity and a sense that history might be in the making; I wound up in the middle of the most impressive voluntary show of humanity that I had ever seen on L.A. streets. Here was a congregation that left no doubt as to who lives here, and what sentiments prevail in the places they live. I was inspired, but I felt entirely outside of the whole thing. I was unnecessary.

I spent most of the time pressed against an enormous, slow-moving river of mostly Latino marchers, marveling as much at what wasn't there as what was. The marchers exuded a calm and almost wordless self-assurance that I had never seen at black demonstrations: though fueled by indignation about immigration laws, this event was almost anger-free. People carried the American flag but no animus toward what it represented. In fact, they carried something opposite, a small piece of paradise carved out of imagination and experience; they were riding that covered wagon that was not yet at its destination but that was traveling more miles every year. They were waving the American flag not as a perpetual grievance, as I was used to seeing it waved, but as a banner of their own truth and a clear marker of a journey that was too far under way to reverse course or stop now. If the immigration laws didn't change, it wouldn't matter; the journey would go on, and they would continue to claim home, mile by mile.

Those marchers who wrapped themselves in Old Glory did so sincerely, not ironically. To be ironic would be to desecrate the can-do credo of American opportunity that the marchers held dear and that they had made their own, poor working conditions and low wages notwithstanding. Even the most xenophobic and isolationist citizens among us, even the black middle class who are watching the ground vanish under their feet, whether they try to hold that ground or relinquish it to its fate as whites did before them, can't fault that idealism. We don't want to. What's more inarguably American than hard work? By that measure, Latinos have more than earned their membership in the club.

But that's the rub—"earning" the right to be a U.S. citizen, and more profoundly, an American. Paying your dues, logging your hours. It's a curious, wholly capitalistic approach to belonging that works splendidly for Latinos and other immigrants, but that has never worked for us. Sure, slave labor is what got this country built in its first two hundred years or so; you can't get more industrious than that. But it was racism, not a reputation for industry, that followed black folk after slavery's end, and it's because of this racism that black employment has never been as noble or resonant a cause as that of the immigrant worker—in fact, it's become its permanent antithesis. A long-orphaned cause still looking for someone or something to take it up. Blacks who've more than earned their Americanness are still trying to make that point today, but I realized in the crush of that downtown march that there is literally no place for us to make that point in this movement. Not now. It will have to be made elsewhere, among ourselves, in last-chance neighborhoods like mine and Shelton's. It will not be Shelton's much longer.

I drove home from downtown along a South Central main drag that was quieter and emptier than I'd ever seen it. The protests still played out a few miles to the south, and the small Latino-owned businesses were shuttered as if on a holiday. Their patrons had also gone missing, Mexican families who generated not only sales but sidewalk life for the whole area. Blacks milled about in this sudden and profound vacuum with their eyes fixed on a middle distance, looking as if they were waking up and realizing something for the first time. They looked churlish, not pleased.

On an impulse, I turned off Broadway and headed east to Central Avenue. Central is the fabled thoroughfare of black Los Angeles past, a one-time mecca of commerce, civic activity. and entertainment that flourished in what can almost un-ironically be called the golden era of segregation. Every big city had a mecca, and every big city started losing it in the 1950s; the loss of Central Avenue in the last big American city that was built on the triumphs of making the improbable happen was particularly painful to African-Americans who'd come from the South and Midwest to stake their last claims of a good life here. At 42nd Street I came upon the Dunbar, the hotel that was almost synonymous with a jazz club next door and that was once the boulevard's crown jewel. The sight of it startled me, partly because the Dunbar is refurbished among so many buildings that aren't, but mostly because

I saw that day with great clarity that it doesn't belong. It's a period piece, a museum. In the new Latino reality, and in this advanced age of multicultural-ism, the Dunbar could be read as either a symbol of diversity or of defiance. Or both. On that day the glass looked decidedly half-empty.

I turned onto 40th Place and went a couple of short blocks to the Ralph Bunche house. This is the childhood home of one of Central Avenue's finest, the United Nations diplomat and Nobel Peace Prize laureate who was the first black to win the prize, in 1950. Bunche's house has also been preserved, museum-ized, a jaunty yellow California bungalow that actually looks like many other well-kept places on the block, iron window bars notwithstand-ing. The biggest difference is that inside it is empty, though brilliant: sunlight streams uninterrupted through front bay windows, along scrubbed wood floors, floods an airy parlor that doubles as a den.

I had gone to the Bunche home earlier in the year to observe a group of students from the Ralph Bunche Youth Leadership Academy, which mostly draws on students at Jefferson High School, a short walk from the home. Jefferson is Ralph Bunche's alma mater and the former premier high school in the Central Avenue community; the foyer is still lined with photos of celeb-rity grads like Bunche and movie queen Dorothy Dandridge. All the students gathered on the lawn at the Bunche house on the day I visited, ready and eager in their blue Bunche academy T-shirts, were Latino. I was told by the black director of the program that African-Americans have been members of past classes, just not this one. He paused, then admitted that it had been getting tougher to recruit black students; part of the problem was their shrinking numbers at Jefferson, part of it was declining commitment—they had other things to do, or they didn't quite see the point, or they wanted it to be some-thing that paid. Mostly they were not impelled by the same assumptions of self-improvement and upward mobility that Bunche and his generation had sixty years ago, even in the thick of segregation. The same faith that, to some degree, impelled the Latino students this day. I decided that I was glad some-body was wearing the shirt; the globalist in Bunche would have approved, in theory if not in his heart. He would have had no choice.

My neighbor Shelton does. We all do. Choice is a direct and desired legacy of post-segregationism, and living where you want to is an inalienable Cali-fornia right, and yet I wonder what Bunche would have to say about Shelton's impending move. Perhaps the greatest irony in all this is that Shelton agrees with me that he *should* stay. He knows Central Avenue is gone, but like many of us, he believes in keeping its spirit alive. He knows perfectly well that what Inglewood needs to thrive is what every place needs, a critical mass of concerned citizens who stand their ground geographically, metaphorically, who set agendas and can permanently tip neighborhoods from questionable to livable. But this is hard to do when the tipping is strenuous work and when there are other, easier options. It's even harder if you're black and, like everyone else, conditioned to believe that a critical mass of blacks—certainly if they're young and unoccupied, but even if they water lawns and walk dogs—will run down neighborhoods rather than raise them up.

Shelton and his wife are gone. A single Latino man bought their place, with its cheery yellow paint and emerald lawn and wind chimes hanging on the front porch. I still walk the dog daily, but have glimpsed the man only once. His shoes sit on the welcome mat.

The lawn has not stayed as green over the months, but I can see it's taken care of, watched over enough. By October, paper Halloween decorations appear on the door. I'm encouraged even though the house remains silent, disengaged, not Shelton. I'm glad somebody is wearing the shirt.

LOST SOUL ▬▬▬▬▬▬▬▬▬

A LAMENT FOR BLACK LOS ANGELES

December 1998

Los Angeles is wonderful. Nowhere in the United States is the Negro so well and beautifully housed, nor the average efficiency and intelligence in the colored population so high . . . Out here in this matchless Southern California there would seem to be no limit to your opportunities, your possibilities.
—W.E.B. DU BOIS, 1913

[Black neighborhoods] are a kind of forgotten archipelago in the garish basin of the region. —ROBERT KIRSCH, 1965

As a kid growing up in the west end of what would come to be known as South-Central Los Angeles, my world was limned in black. The prevalence of black people in my neighborhood was not, as it tends to be today, a cause for alarm or a sign of inevitable social decay. Blackness simply encompassed everything—best friends, spring carnivals at the local Catholic school, the butcher at the meat counter, the summer playground director with watchful eyes and a whistle slung around her neck. I was raised in the very justified belief that blacks were as self-sustaining as anyone, that whatever could not be had within a three-mile radius of my house was some extravagance probably not worth too much thought anyway. My world was ordered and comfortable, though varied enough in its self-containment never to make me feel contained: I played jacks on the sidewalk, shot basketball in the backyard, went to the playground when I was bored, spent long afternoons in one of several neighborhood libraries.

I think the perspective of my neighborhood started changing with the proliferation of indoor malls in the mid-'70s, when I was in junior high school. Malls were located in almost exclusively suburban areas that were almost exclusively populated by whites, and my friends and I had to plan daylong bus trips to get to them. I liked going out to Del Amo or Fox Hills, but was vaguely resentful that I had to invest so much time and cover so much ground just to acquire a hot dog on a stick. But everybody in the neighborhood talked rapturously about the malls, about the things that could be had there, and I swiftly came to understand that these things could not be had *here*, that they might never be had here, and what was once a world of plenty seemed more and more like a place of deprivation—still home and the locus of family, but a point that would stay fixed and musty as the world around it changed with abandon.

As it turns out, if black neighborhoods in L.A. had simply remained the same, it would have been a vast improvement over what actually did happen: a steady decline that left areas like my old neighborhood pockmarked with empty lots and façades where sturdy businesses used to be. The neighborhood feels not lived in, but lived out. When I drive through the commercial districts there and elsewhere in Central L.A., everything feels impermanent, poised for flight, like a diner sitting at a restaurant eating a meal but strategically positioned near the back door, ready to beat it at the first sign of trouble. Yet the greatest loss has not been that of stores or businesses, but of people; the greatest catastrophe has been the exodus from a place where I once assumed everybody wanted to stay, a thinning of the bones in our body politic that do not seem to be significantly reforming in all those places we went—Palmdale, Moreno Valley, Riverside. Weakened by this, by rapidly changing demographics, and by chronically discordant leadership, the city's black neighborhoods are struggling to define, or redefine, an identity as the millennium draws to a close. Yet with our mass no longer critical—was it ever?—and not likely ever to be again, I wonder how, or if, black L.A. will survive.

The seven-square-mile Crenshaw district is the only predominantly black area of Los Angeles left, and the strongest argument against cultural annihilation. The storefront churches, screen-door restaurants, and itinerant nightclubs may be weary, but they're still standing, and the area is the base of operations for a hefty percentage of black businesses and institutions: the African American Cultural Center, the Southern Christian Leadership Conference, Baldwin Hills Crenshaw Plaza, Founders National Bank, the Museum in Black, the Black Employees' Association, Fifth Street Dick's Jazz Coffeehouse.

Yet for all its activity, Crenshaw has the feel of an island, a bunker. Lifetime resident and activist Valerie Shaw notes that the city's entire black infrastructure now lies between the 10 freeway, Florence Avenue, Western Avenue, and La Cienega Boulevard. "There is a tremendous sense of loss in the black community—a loss of political status, loss of neighborhoods, loss of history," she says. "What people are dealing with is the breaking of a continuum."

As old-line black neighborhoods such as Watts, Compton, Inglewood, and most recently, South and Central Los Angeles recede in the face of black flight and burgeoning Latino and other ethnic populations, maintaining a black presence becomes an ever greater logistical and spiritual challenge. Area schools with black administrations are finding themselves with increasingly non-black student bodies, and pressing new issues such as bilingual education; on any given summer afternoon a Central L.A. park hosts far more soccer games than half-court basketball matches; a mostly black Hyde Park block club regularly walks the neighborhood with fliers in Spanish to bolster attendance at its monthly meetings. The black side of town is no longer a given; as a recent United Way study observed, in flat but ominous bureaucratese, "What we commonly knew of the black community over the last 20 to 30 years was geographically presented, based on a cluster of neighborhoods with a concentrated majority of the city's black population . . . However, the notion of a geographically determined black community is no longer correct or viable."

We may not have the numbers, but viability is another question. "Ain't nothing gonna happen until we start being a community," says Helen Colman, a Crenshaw resident who jump-started a block club on 71st Street after the 1992 riots and still acts as adviser. Colman talks proudly about what the ethnically mixed club instituted: tree planting, an annual block-club party, a neighborhood cleanup project called Operation Clean Sweep. Lying just south of the railroad tracks and just west of a ragged stretch of Crenshaw Boulevard, 71st Street was at that precarious point where a neighborhood can slide into intractable decay. Colman was determined it wouldn't. "People have started fixing up their homes, improved and painted, and are feeling a lot better about things," she says.

The black people on the block tend to have been here a long time. Current block club captain De De Anderson moved to 71st in 1969; her neighbor Henry Carter came the year before. Both have watched black families move out, either to suburbs or back south to their points of origin. Carter, a native of Louisiana, once watched three black families move out and five Latino families move in almost simultaneously. He concludes that "things have generally gone down" in the last thirty years, though not necessarily because of Latinos. "It isn't getting any better, what with this gang thing and this dope selling," he says, surveying the street from his wrap-around front porch. The houses are spare, but neat and quiet; the blare and bustle of Crenshaw seem much farther away than a block and a half. "But I been here too long. I'm going to tough it out."

Neither does Colman plan on looking elsewhere to lay down roots already dug. Besides the block club, there's her church, St. John of God, a Catholic church at Crenshaw and 60th Street that was once one of L.A.'s biggest black parishes, a meeting-up place for its Southern-bred contingent. The last black priest, Father Charles Burns, left in '94; the Eucharist is now given first in Spanish. That's okay by Colman. "I'm glad for the mass at all," she says. "You learn to adjust, or you leave. That's it. Stay and improve. We're all in the hood together."

A growing amorphousness is the greatest part of our poverty, but it is a part nobody discusses because, by definition, it is nothing you can see. In these politically blinkered times people are eager to put faith in the best appearances, and among black people that best-foot-forward thing is very nearly a historical directive. Black newspapers have always followed that directive, but in L.A., facing the demographic desiccation of their readership, such optimism seems hoary, not so much necessary as desperate and out of step.

This is the furious confluence of events the black press seems willing to ignore: beginning in the late '40s, with the official outlawing of restrictive-housing covenants, blacks began steadily moving out of the Eastside and other areas of L.A. to which they had been consigned. In the '60s, that moving out intensified as local industry dried up and the Watts Riots exploded a long-simmering urban discontent. In the '70s, the industrial base continued its long, slow collapse, and the anti-public-spending movement, rooted in the passage of Proposition 13, took hold. By the '80s, big government was out, urban neglect was in, the much-ballyhooed black middle class was in full retreat and a tremendous wave of new immigration was under way. Many of the black folk left in South L.A. lacked what sociologists call an "option to exit"—they couldn't afford to go anywhere else. Add to that the twin scourges of the crack-cocaine trade and the meteoric rise of deadly gangbanging, and black optimism began to sound like an oxymoron.

The black newspaper may also be in danger of becoming an oxymoron, though that is not apparent in a glance at the *L.A. Watts Times*. If the black community's solvency could be measured by the paper's recent fortunes, that solvency would seem reasonably assured. Last fall, the *Times* moved from cramped, creaky accommodations along the edge of Baldwin Hills to a Wilshire-corridor penthouse that boasts vault-like quiet, soothing pastel décor, and a grand view of the city through a bank of conference-room windows. The new quarters look and feel worlds away from the hardscrabble neighborhood for which the paper is named and from which it took its political impetus after the devastating riots of 1965. The move is ostensibly a good omen—a social climb, something the rival *Sentinel*, the city's oldest black newspaper, might even feature on its society page. But it is also a put-on good face that barely masks deeper problems that have been driving the wild black population flux for the last twenty years or so.

The *Times*'s new digs are in an area that is predominantly Asian and Latino, but associate editor Melanie Polk says that hasn't changed her goal of serving the black community. For Polk, that community is wherever it happens to be; for the purpose of the paper, Watts has long been less a physical place than a touchstone of local black struggle. "It's not so much that we're located in Watts anymore, but that we grew from the ashes of 'Burn, baby, burn,'" explains Polk, whose parents purchased the *Times* in 1975. "The whole point was always to get information and resources to African Americans they otherwise couldn't get."

But many neighborhoods where the *Times* distributes are now at least as Latino as they are black. That has prompted a few tentative experiments in recent years—a column offering tips on Spanish pronunciation and the rudiments of Latino history, very occasional front-page stories on Latino immigration and its effect on politics and culture. These may not seem like big developments, but they are territorial and ideological concessions that black papers elsewhere in the country have not had to consider making. (The *Sentinel*, for its part, has not made them.) Many people see such concessions as compromising whatever coherent black identity is left in L.A., although no one is clear on how to preserve it. The *Times* regularly discusses changing its name and scrapping "Watts" altogether, though Polk is wary of such a move. "We have an established rep that we're very proud of. We have national advertisers for whom the name change would be radical," she says. "We don't want an appearance that we're turning our back on our roots or our mission."

It is jarring to realize that blacks may be holding on by the breadth of a name. The irony is that despite shrinking numbers, black people live very vividly, albeit sordidly, in L.A.'s popular imagination—gangsta rap and Rodney King have come to define the city as much as the Beach Boys defined the Southern California zeitgeist (whitegeist, really) of the '60s. But where the Beach Boys extolled L.A. at its most blue-sky idyllic, King and the boyz reflect the dregs of its failed promise. Black neighborhoods in the '90s are a painful symbol of everything that has gone wrong—despite the fact that Crenshaw is also home to the largest collection of affluent black neighborhoods in the West. This dichotomy testifies uneasily to the fact that while many blacks have prospered, many more have not, that the entrenchment of the more fortunate hasn't mitigated the slide of the less so. And so the Crenshaw district stands divided, with the modernized Baldwin Hills Crenshaw Plaza serving as a kind of Berlin Wall where the two populations occasionally intersect in a food court or shoe store, but later retreat to their respective north-south camps.

The fruits of the great black Southern and Midwestern migration that peaked in the '30s and '40s, driven by a common desire to escape segregation for good and lay claim to California living, have been strange indeed. Black flight from increased crime and sharply decreased job opportunities has scattered the original settlers, to say nothing of their collective dream; blacks have diffused while the problems of decay have congealed into a crisis that too few people anywhere are regularly addressing. Hell, Crenshaw is still anxiously trying to involve the moneyed "hill" people—homeowners in Baldwin and Windsor Hills, View Park, Ladera Heights and Leimert Park—in their own economy.

But then it's no secret that black Angelenos, like Angelenos at large, have generally been less concerned with activism than with securing the inalienable right to live in really nice places. In her recently anthologized piece on black L.A. history, "A City Called Heaven," writer Susan Anderson points out that in the 1940s, Los Angeles was the nation's leading center for legal challenges to restrictive housing covenants. Black leadership here has always kept to very middle-class concerns, and Anderson suggests that the venerable Tom Bradley and his ilk largely forsook the issues of poverty and inequitable wealth distribution for gains in political representation and increased social mobility. Leadership got what it wanted, at a cost. "Poverty as an issue for modern black leadership," Anderson writes, "has been utterly without glamour." It is particularly without glamour—indeed, it is almost an affront—to those whose greatest aspiration is to live north of Slauson Avenue, in the heavenly reaches of upper Ladera.

Self-made activist Najee Ali, whose guiding lights include Geronimo Pratt and Kwame Ture, says the first step toward black recovery is a very public exercise in self-esteem. He is trying to persuade people to officially recognize Crenshaw as a black economic, social, and cultural hub that is worth sustaining for future generations. For the last year Ali has spearheaded a campaign to have Leimert Park Village (with its crown jewel, Degnan Boulevard) renamed African American Village. It is the latest in a fitful series of such campaigns that had an apotheosis with the renaming of Santa Barbara Avenue as Martin Luther King Jr. Boulevard in 1982. Following the '92 riots, a few Crenshaw activists began calling for a designation of the whole Crenshaw district as African Village, à la Chinatown and Little Tokyo, though the idea never gained popular momentum. Whether it will now, with the black population at its most fragmented and least civically active, seems doubtful; the King Boulevard campaign, even with Bradley in office, a favorable political climate, and mainstream support, took many years to push through. (Conversely, it took astoundingly little time for the city of Redondo Beach to rechristen its stretch of Compton Avenue, which runs west from Crenshaw to the beach, Marine Avenue in 1990. The good citizens there apparently felt a complex coming on and administered some first aid before their humbler South Bay brethren—Inglewood, Hawthorne, Compton—even knew that a problem existed. Those of us who found ourselves driving south down Crenshaw, probably headed to the Del Amo mall, realized at some point past Artesia that Compton Avenue had neatly vanished, and felt a chill. What's next?)

Ali, thirty-four, is an ex-convict and gang member who knows something about turf battles, and he hopes to lend this one a tough edge. "We're trying to establish territory, draw a line in the sand," he says. But his African American Village campaign is really not as militant as it sounds; it is a manifestation of a larger wish to persuade Crenshaw's middle class to stay, please. History is against it. L.A.'s black population, like most other immigrant populations throughout the city, has been kinetic: as it prospers, it moves. The difference with blacks is that moving has rotted out a social infrastructure and replaced it with nothing. Ali says it is therefore absolutely necessary to preserve the infrastructure that is left. He argues—as if there really is an argument—that people must see that "Crenshaw is our last frontier, our last stand. There's not a place like this anywhere in L.A. It has to hold. We have to convince homeowners not to do black flight, by any means necessary. We can't hold them legally, but we can shame them into staying."

That sounds improbable, more so because Ali has assigned himself many other crusades. In fact, he assigns one almost weekly. His Project Islamic HOPE, which started out with the single mandate of feeding the homeless, functions today as a kind of clearinghouse for a growing number of black-related causes, from petitioning for justice for nine-year-old rape-murder victim Sherrice Iverson to shutting down a proposed Crenshaw porn shop to protesting black sexual stereotypes in films like *How To Be a Player*, which Ali believes are partially responsible for the high rate of black teen pregnancy, HIV, and AIDS. These are issues that sizable black organizations can't or won't address; I admire Ali's willingness to stick his fingers into as many holes in the dike as possible, but I wonder if he is overreaching or spreading himself too thin to be taken seriously on any point on this crisis continuum.

Ali says no. He sees all his efforts as spokes on a single wheel—the preservation and reinforcement of the black community. This is the wheel on which everything turns, or doesn't. "I'm hitting the panic button," he says. "*We're* part of the reason the demographics are shifting—by moving out and not staying, by not investing in each other and selling to each other. I would love to have a wife and kids, to kick back and watch TV, but I don't have a choice but to be out there and agitate. If you're not part of the solution, you're part of the problem."

He says that a big part of the problem is how black agendas have lately gone out of political fashion and been supplanted by happy-faced missives to build multicultural alliances. In a country pluralistic since its inception, multiculturalism is a given, but Ali argues that the multiculti push now is in fact a dangerously easy way of moving black concerns to the bottom of the list of social priorities. Over the last generation, "black" has lost currency to the point where black politicians and other leaders, mindful of cultivating broader constituent and financial bases, hesitate to characterize *anything* as exclusively black. The term casts a pall, dredging up accusations of reverse racism and cozy victimhood where it used to call the founding ideals of American democracy into question. "Our interests are being compromised by politicians who buy into this market concept of multiculturalism," Ali says angrily. "It's being rammed down our throats." The greatest tragedy, he says, is that black folks have been willing to play the game. "There's so much apathy. I stood up last year at the Malcolm X festival to say a few words, and when I said, 'All power to the people,' everybody looked at me like I was crazy. It distresses me."

Distress is no place to linger; instead, lead from where you are. So believes John Bryant, another young steward of inner-city change. Bryant is the thirty-two-year-old president, founder, and feverish brain behind Operation HOPE, a post-riot nonprofit aimed at revitalizing neighborhoods in Crenshaw and well beyond. Although he is a friend and mentor of Ali, he dismisses the back-to-black-L.A. movement as diversionary and nostalgic—a memento at best, an impediment to real progress at worst. "Okay, so we have self-esteem problems!" he barks. "We act like we just heard about it on the eleven o'clock news!" Like Ali, Bryant believes in a black agenda but, unlike Ali, believes that agenda has no choice but to broaden if it is to stay relevant and keep its eyes on the prize that matters most now: economic empowerment. Operation HOPE in the last six years has launched a variety of community services—a banking and home lending center, a small-business assistance program. Last spring Bryant grand-opened an Operation HOPE banking center in Maywood, a small outpost of a city in southeast L.A. County that is virtually all Latino.

"I'm not black for a living," Bryant says brusquely. "I don't want to be a black community leader, I want to be an excellent leader." That doesn't mean he sells himself out. "Hell, I'm *black*, and if I wasn't first and foremost about black people, I'd have to have my head examined. Operation HOPE was clearly directed at blacks. But we also very quickly made it clear that it was about demographics. In the last stage of his life Martin Luther King was focused on a campaign for poor people—didn't matter what the paint job was. King realized that economic equity was the real force behind social equality. It was always less about race than class."

Bryant sits in his glass-walled office in the downtown high-rise that houses the Bryant Group, the financial consulting firm that is his day job. He often shuttles between this world and close-but-so-far-away South-Central several times a day, and says it is that kind of fluidity, rather than hewing to ground already lost, that will save black people. Migration may be a cultural tragedy, but it is also a fact of life that is accorded too much moral weight. "The [black] community is not eroding, it's dispersing—into Rialto, Carson, Malibu," says Bryant. "Let the process drive itself. Get involved with the results. It's not about Latino or black or anything. I'm so tired of that black B-boy mentality of 'look at me, I'm important, give me attention.' The more powerful thing is subtlety. We need to start finding ways to collaborate. I'd rather have 10 percent of something than 100 percent of nothing."

Every other year, Bryant leads a group of corporate and banking heavies on a bus tour through Central Los Angeles to show them the wondrous economic opportunities that lie waiting to be exploited. Like a carnival barker, he cheerily—at points, too cheerily—hypes all that he sees. ("Look at these beautiful homes on your left, ladies and gentlemen! Nobody hanging out on the street corner, no guns in sight! Surprised?") During the last spring tour, which set off from Crenshaw and wound up in Maywood, the differences between largely black communities and largely Latino ones became startlingly clear. Crenshaw, Baldwin Hills, and much of South L.A. featured lovely, well-tended houses but neglected commercial strips; Huntington Park and Maywood had modest to run-down residential districts but boulevards, like Pacific Avenue, that were thriving with business and pedestrian traffic in the middle of a weekday afternoon. The bus tour started out from La Brea Avenue with much fanfare, but Pacific felt like its pièce de résistance, offering both the thrust of the future and prod of the past. As we rolled slowly down the boulevard with throngs of people on either side, my seat mate, a fellow black reporter and Crenshaw resident, turned to me and said wonderingly, enviously, as if it had just occurred to him: "*This* is the problem. *We* don't shop where we live anymore."

More to the point, we don't *live* where we live anymore; even where we are present, it tends to be in the flesh only. We have grown to believe too much in the larger-than-life status conferred upon us by the varied engineers of pop culture—film producers too enamored of ghetto stories, record executives who revere hip-hop and its unlimited power of product placement—who hardly have our social survival in mind. It has become perfectly okay to invoke the virtues of black people without being anywhere near them. Recently it was reported that Assemblyman Kevin Murray does not live in the Crenshaw neighborhood that he represents, and where he grew up. Doctored addresses are hardly new to politics, but Murray touts the place so eloquently and speaks so forcefully on behalf of L.A.'s black community that his absence from that community is a specific kind of betrayal. Not that one must necessarily live in a place to work for its benefit, but the fact is that, these days, very few black folks who *don't* live in the hood have its future at heart.

Which is not to say that there aren't black phenomena that need to be relegated to the past; there are. One is the willful, often hostile inertia of black politicians and civil servants who ignore the needs of Latino constituents, at everyone's peril. Constance Rice, former attorney for the NAACP Legal Defense Fund, recalls angrily accusing Compton school district officials of the same dereliction of public duty that got white governing bodies slapped with civil rights lawsuits. "I told them, 'If these Latinos were you, you'd be screaming for blood,'" says Rice, who, for the record, maintains a pro-black stance, and believes that many issues are culture-specific and not easily remedied by the platitudes of multiculturalism.

"No question, more and more blacks are becoming a victim population, becoming internally disconnected from each other," says Genethia Hayes, director of the L.A. chapter of the Southern Christian Leadership Conference. "But we can't talk about personal responsibility merely—there's no good health care, day care, there's insurance redlining. Don't *tell* me all black people have to do is get out there and open a store."

Just beneath the conversation of many African-Americans is a frustration at never reaching, as a group, a level playing field, whose existence has lately become America's fondest social myth. "Blacks have been sold down the river. They never got what we were promised," says Teryl Watkins of the Watts Labor Community Action Committee, an organization that has seen its core constituency rapidly shift from black to brown. "We are survivors, but at some point . . . we want to get past that struggle just to keep up a basic standard of living. We're tired, dulled, still in the middle of a rip-off. Shoot, I *want* my forty acres and a laptop."

Covert resentment does not play out only in politics. I have a neighbor who startled me one morning by suddenly announcing over coffee that she was "sick of the Mexicans," who had exhausted her sympathy for everything from leaf-blower rights to bilingual education, who in the grand scheme of things, when one examined how poorly black folks were still faring, had no right to complain at all. I have another black friend who applied for a position with a black-run outfit but was pessimistic about getting the job because the employers, who dealt chiefly with families in Central L.A., preferred someone bilingual. My friend was not angry, not yet, but wistful and despondent because she had been looking for work for years, had been on county aid, and had now finally found a job for which she thought she was qualified—almost. Once a student of marked optimism, she had been left behind by a world that had changed during her long absence from the work force. "I hope I get it," was the last thing she told me, but her voice already sounded far away, like a drifter who must move on not because he wants to, but in order to keep moving at all.

South L.A.'s black population is still considerable, although the dwindling evidence of it can't help but feel disquieting. With the exception of Crenshaw Boulevard, thoroughfares like Central, Western, Avalon, and Main are most notable for the proliferation of Spanish-language Pentecostal churches and ubiquitous *Virgens* painted on edifices ranging from the side walls of liquor stores to car washes. The largest and oldest hardware store on Central Avenue, owned for generations by a Jewish family that refused to leave after two large-scale riots, has been sold and today labels all its cardboard boxes of nails and such in Spanish. The annual Central Avenue Jazz Festival celebrates L.A.'s seminal black culture on the street that spawned it, yet there is no getting around the irony that the area is now 75 percent Latino. As successful as it has been, the festival feels for all the world like a movie set.

"Blacks grumble that Mexicans are taking over—well, in absolute terms, they *are*," says Fernando Guerra, director of the Center for the Study of Los Angeles at Loyola Marymount University. "Black people, in many ways, are in retreat. The political empowerment Latinos are going through now is similar to the black euphoria of the '60s."

While documenting the growing Latino presence in South L.A., social photographer Camilo Jose Vergara came upon a Black Power mural at Avalon Boulevard and 36th Street and was struck by how the sun-faded images of Afros and raised fists called to mind the ruined frescoes of Pompeii. The South Los Angeles landscape is full of such shadows, suggestions that a once-powerful civilization has been forced by some natural disaster to leave and seek higher ground. In '93, well before the *Watts Times* made its move, the sixty-five-year-old *Los Angeles Sentinel* relocated from its original quarters on Central to the demographically friendlier environs of Crenshaw Boulevard. But even Crenshaw, as I gently suggested to Najee Ali, is not impervious. The Baldwin Hills Crenshaw Plaza, the center of black economic activity in urban L.A., especially as it becomes increasingly identified with Magic

Johnson's myriad business ventures, is gaining more and more Latino foot traffic. The mall, as both a place of destination and eventual point of exclusion for black folk, is taking on new meaning. I have long complained that it doesn't have what I want, that its hard-won overhaul in 1988 left the community with merely a shell of newness and progress. Last weekend the mall observed its tenth anniversary, but we're still looking for what we want, what we lost; in those recesses another population is quietly finding what it needs.

Porches used to be the most important public space black people in L.A. had. A great many of them were Southern transplants, and a porch-sitting culture was something that transposed easily from the South to a city known for its geographic expansiveness, where even the poorest citizen could claim a front lawn, a driveway, a dividing hedge, a backyard. People conducted whole conversations across streets without ever stepping off their porches. A well-used porch was the greatest sign of civility; on my block, the few families that kept their porches empty and the front lights off were dismissed, then mythologized, as kooks or recluses. I visited relatives nearly every Sunday and spent the better part of those afternoons on the porch, sequestered with my cousins; my uncle ran a barbershop on Jefferson Boulevard in the Crenshaw District that functioned as a porch for virtually everyone—businessmen, politicos, family, chess players, retirees, and, oh yes, people who actually wanted to get their hair cut. The dispersal of the Southern contingent, and the rising meanness of the streets, hastened the demise of porches as extensions of home. Like windows and screen doors, they ceased to be points of connection to the immediate world and became merely points of vulnerability to shut and reinforce with iron bars. It's a swift and radical change that would have seemed ludicrous and deeply paranoid as recently as twenty years ago. Joe Hicks, director of the city's Human Relations Commission, explains it thus: "Before the '80s, L.A. was essentially a white city with a historical black population of Southern immigrants. Latinos were entrenched in East L.A. Then there was a war in Central America, the Mexican economy got bad, crack came on the scene, black gangsterism shot up, black people started migrating out—all of this just sort of landed overnight."

The cumulative effect of these trends, aggravated by the death of black activism, has been a growing anxiety among black people that their window of opportunity may be closing, that the long era of a black-dominated social and civil rights agenda may be coming to an end. "The two communities are divergent in that immigrant groups are starting to gain footholds, while blacks feel stymied, or like they're going backward," says Raphael Sonenshein, a professor of political science at Cal State Fullerton. "Latinos are starting to see a glimmer of light. Blacks are seeing it go out."

So we are still reeling and dealing, or trying to. I know a guy out there braving the elements of change whom Najee Ali would be happy to know, one Fred Thomas, who lives in the hinterlands of the West Adams district—not in the grand gentrified mansions with the maid's quarters, but in the area well south of Adams Boulevard that is a liberal mix of houses and apartment buildings. Thomas and his family did a stint once in the San Fernando Valley, but they came back. He and his wife were active in growing the nascent South Los Angeles Little League a few years back; Thomas has long been involved with organizing the annual Louisiana to Los Angeles Festival, known as LALA, which celebrates specifically Creole and generally Southern influences that shaped the black community here. Thomas has watched things go from good to bad to worse and figures that what can best be done now is neighborhood micro-management: absent an articulated black social agenda, tackle the big, seemingly intractable problems of gangs, drugs, and shifting demographics through a series of small but doable things, like baseball outings and park festivals. The only trouble is that, these days, the small things are monumental too, in part because there aren't enough interested parties to see them through. "We have no more immigration," Thomas says of the black population in Central L.A. "No fresh blood. We've spent ourselves out. We've given up a toehold on the property. We look around and see fewer and fewer entities created for us, and more and more created for Latinos."

Thomas states the ambivalence toward Latino growth that many black folks feel: it is a population certainly entitled to its progress—indeed, it is nothing we can stop and, recalling our own immigrant beginnings, most often something we admire—but it also cannot help but stand in relief to our own decline, and heighten attending anxieties. Arturo Ybarra is a Watts resident and activist who has been trying to get people there to make peace with that ambivalence, to go forward in spite of it. Watts went from majority black to majority Latino well before neighboring South Los Angeles. Ybarra founded an annual black/Latino Cinco de Mayo festival, runs a Latino support organization and also heads up a grassroots effort to organize black and Latino parents around public-education issues in Watts. He's had, as you might imagine, the least success with the last endeavor; it has proven particularly difficult to sustain black parent involvement. But Ybarra, a man with a cheerful disposition and the immutable patience of a cleric, is not going away or giving up. "Blacks are going to need us," he says. "They are in a crisis. Latinos have few options, but blacks have even fewer. There's no sense in fighting. Though certain things imply racial hate, it's not necessarily that blacks are aggressing against Latinos because they're Latino. The bottom line is a lack of opportunities, jobs for everyone—that's the most exacerbating factor. No one wants to look at that, because it's much easier to play the race thing."

Yet Ybarra understands that the "race thing" is not immaterial; otherwise he would not have bothered to form a group that builds first on the strength of Latino solidarity. Nor is the "race thing" a case of modern-day xenophobia among colored folks, as the media often makes it out to be before magnanimously dismissing it altogether. Ethnic identity, before being cumbered with politics and focus groups and the latest Disney flick, is a destiny in itself. It is a destiny blacks in the city once had—perhaps they never reached it, but the critical thing is that for a while, anyway, they had something to want. The ranks that are left agree plenty on what they *don't* want—graffiti, gangs, more of those pesky low-income housing units that breed trouble—but even all added up these things are not enough of a cause. We have much free-floating desire, but nothing to want. I hope my own desire puts down roots before I wake up one morning to find that it's led me out of my south-end-of-Wilshire-district apartment to some point too comfortably west of Crenshaw. Or is that Palos Verdes Boulevard? Ah well. Del Amo mall at last—at least—will be within walking distance.

MOTHERS AND FATHERS

My family is my first and most enduring story. My parents are both from the South, New Orleans, and I claim that heritage even more eagerly than I claim my first-generation L.A. status. My mother and father came here and did things they almost certainly wouldn't or couldn't have done back home, where opportunity and space was restricted. L.A. was imperfect, but it had more room than the place they left. The freedom I inherited was actually bigger and more subtle than what they had in mind: the freedom to do, but also to *not* do. To make choices based on my needs and nobody else's. How did I do? What, or who, have I advanced?

THE LAST CAMPAIGN

November 1998

I'm not proud to admit this, but I've never been much inclined to try to overcome my fears. I've always regarded fear less as a trial and more as another essential compound in the periodic table of spiritual elements. Rather than stare down the demons, I tend to make room for them and then go on about my business. Roller coasters inspire terror, so I don't go to amusement parks. A dog bit me in the face when I was eleven, so I've given dogs a wide berth ever since. When a waterbug finds its way from a sewer drain into my apartment, I promptly leave and call a neighbor to come attend to it. I can't bring myself to look at the thing again, let alone step in close enough to whack it with a broom or give it a good spritz of Raid. True, fear can exact a certain price of inconvenience, but in my mind that seems a small price to pay, compared with alternate courses of action—for instance, picking up the bug by the antennae and flicking it out the window.

I am proud to admit that recently I have pushed through some measure of the fear, through the inconvenience and all, because my father needed me to. My father was a member of a local school board for ten years, and when reelection time rolled around early this year, he enlisted me and my other siblings to help him campaign. Campaigning involves a good deal of walking precincts and phone banking—political euphemisms for knocking on strange doors and cold-calling strange, potentially hostile people. I have a dread of approaching people I don't know; maybe it's fear of rejection, of appearing stupid, of reactivating a childhood stutter that, in my weakest moments, threatened to rear its ugly head, like a virus or a volcano, even after I'd outgrown it. But my father, though he could be gruff to the point of intolerance, was self-contained and asked for very little, particularly from his children; and these bids to stay in office were expressions of his lifelong commitment to furthering community good. I could hardly say no.

My fear of confrontation was odd in light of the fact that I'd always loved to perform and had gone so far as to earn a master's degree in acting; then again, it was not so odd given that I craved only the applause and was really too thin-skinned, uncompetitive, and horrified at the prospect of repeated rejection and lack of interest to ever consider acting as a career. Yet as a pitch-woman for my father's last campaign I invoked every bit of actor I could. Ten years had passed since his first election battle; I still harbored dread, but it was tempered somewhat by experience and by the fact that my father was really struggling to hold his seat this time out. Often a lone voice of reason on a hotly contentious school board, my father had grown unpopular lately for opposing the hire of a superintendent whose employment history was eminently questionable but who had many friends on the board eager to bring him in. To shore up their voting bloc, these board members figured they had to oust my father, and so they began circulating all manner of lies about him in election mailers—he was against progress, against children, etc. Nothing could have been further from the truth. Unlike his nakedly ambitious colleagues, my father had never during his ten years sought higher office precisely because he had never been interested in anything but education reform. I was incensed, and moral indignation proved to be just the fuel I needed. The assault on my father's character, on my regard of him as a man of inviolate integrity even in his worst moments, was a bigger enemy than fear.

I walked neighborhoods like a missionary, wielding our modest fliers like copies of the Constitution. I exhorted people to vote for ongoing truth and justice, even when I got nothing more than baleful looks or wary appraisals through peepholes, mail slots, and porch windows—or when I got more than I bargained for, with middle-aged men looking no higher than my bust line as I delivered my spiel. I gave them fliers anyway and figured I didn't care what made them fondly remember the Aubry name and cast a vote for it—far more crucial elections, after all, had been won with less. Most people were polite in an officious or in a Southern-upbringing kind of way; many brightened at the realization that I was Larry Aubry's daughter, that this campaign was a family endeavor. Some had no idea there was a school-board election at all, and didn't care, until I called my father from across the street, where he was walking, and had him brief such folks. Leaving fliers for those who weren't home or weren't answering felt like progress—at least they would know we'd been there, agitating. Any contact at all felt like triumph.

Phone calling was a different, darker experience. I needed the bracing wind at my back, that communing with a live audience, that shot at a face-to-face conversion. The phone allowed for none of that. The phone was where I had to battle my fears the hardest, contain my willingness to retreat the most. Working the phone was performing stripped of all its improvisational, elocutionary glamour and reduced to the cold, hard kernel of selling. I had to sell my father's good name in sixty seconds or less during that window between breakfast and Saturday errands or between weekday dinner and bedtime, like a long-distance service. It seemed unsavory, not to mention contradictory; for all my moral indignation and political and filial faith, I felt like a fraud. And granted phone anonymity and the power of hanging up, people were far more likely to be rude, even vitriolic. With each call I increasingly hoped for an answering machine, so that I could at least get out all my words brightly, with no stutter and no interruptions or sighs of impatience or background noise of wailing children and God knows what else. But I had to maintain calm, even more so than during the walks, because my father was often sitting right across from me at another desk doing the same thing. I could see this was hard for him, too—he was the furthest thing from a performer and was not good at sounding bright right off the bat, even for his own cause—and that touched me unexpectedly. For his sake, I had to make it look easy.

Our small reelection headquarters sat on a major thoroughfare in a town that had seen better days, down the street from a long-shuttered movie palace papered with beauty-salon ads. We had no amenities save a water cooler and an old television set with a wire antenna and no cable. After a couple hours of calling, my father seemed relieved to go down the block for pizza to feed the troops—me, a brother and sister, a volunteer or two. I was bolstered enough by my father's tacit gratitude to take some phone lists home with me to do some calling during the week, after work. Though my resolve slipped several notches in the privacy of home, it nonetheless flared up in its own defense on several occasions. One night I got a real cynic on the line who announced that not only was he *not* going to vote for my father, he wasn't going to vote for any of these shiftless Negro politicians who had been busy selling out community interests for the last thirty years or so. I was stung. "Sir," I said, as firmly and as brightly as I could, "*My* father isn't like that."

"Oh, really?" he said sarcastically. "How do I know that? They *all* claim to be different." I launched into an impassioned recitation of my father's resume, his honors, the details of his history as an education and human-relations consultant. Then I threw all lingering fear of rejection and political good sense to the wind and told the man that my father would absolutely agree with the idea that black politicians had done a generally lousy job and that he'd said on several occasions that the whole school board should be fired because, as a group, they were failing to do their job. What my father believed in most, I concluded, what he would fight for most diligently, was accountability. The man was only slightly mollified. I realized then that no matter how bravely I or my father opened our hearts and told the unvarnished truth, if a candidate hadn't done something tangible—presided over the grand opening of a park, fixed a pothole, even gotten embroiled in scandal—the electorate was not likely to give a damn. Unfortunately for my father, he had done thankless, largely unquantifiable work all his life—striving to get people to coalesce around issues, mediating street-level conflicts that rarely made it to the papers. As much as I admired his work, as a child I secretly wished he had been a plumber or a bus driver, something I could easily explain to my friends. It was no easier now to explain what my father did to adults who often had no more patience for complexities than children. I could only hope that the man would be impressed by the fact that I was willing to argue his points, and that I exploded a lot of hidebound fears in the process; those things together probably weren't as persuasive as my bust line—now there was something tangible—but it was better than nothing. Even, I had to admit, better than an answering machine.

We lost the election. Gathered in our office, surrounded by pizza boxes and sub sandwiches and soda that was meant to be the victory repast, we instead made regular calls to the city clerk's office that sank us deeper into gloom. My father was the most spirited in the face of defeat—he had seen a lot of it in his life. When it was clear there was no chance of winning, he sat atop one of the old desks and acknowledged his thanks for our efforts and said of course he would keep on fighting the good fight, but in a different capacity now. He put his glasses back on and asked if there was anything any of his children wanted to say. I froze—he had never invited this before, publicly or otherwise. I felt him glancing at me out of the corner of his eye, with some amount of longing. I was still. The moment passed from silence to a "well, thank you all again, very much," and we all started eating the last of what we had the heart left to eat.

I wanted to say something; I didn't. Ever since I have regretted not stepping up to the moment and delivering a last, and probably most meaningful, impromptu speech of the campaign years. My built-up courage collapsed in the face of possible rejection, in the face of my father's need to finally hear what *we* had to say. All this time I had faced the masses for my father, yet he was an audience of one I was still uncertain of winning over. As much fear of strangers as I'd overcome on sidewalks and porches and phones, in the end I wasn't quite able to overcome a more deep-seated fear of the familiar. I am waging now, as I have always waged, a private campaign to unseat that fear for good.

MOTHER ROUX

1999

Growing up, I always considered myself to be my mother's child. I liked what that meant: my mother was kind but entirely unsentimental, self-possessed but unassuming, practical above all things. She got married in a plain tea-length dress and short gloves and then gave the whole outfit away because she said she didn't need it anymore; she and my father never took a honeymoon, even when they could afford one years after their wedding, because she didn't attach great importance to such events. I admired my mother's efficiency, her equipoise and lack of wasted motion—these were the models I used to streamline my own imagination, to build my own aspirations of becoming a writer.

I turned out to be like my mother, but also a departure from her. I wanted reasonableness but also excess, flourishes, inconsistencies, stories; as I got older I wanted to dredge up and let fly what she had unceremoniously put away long ago. I was most curious about New Orleans, her and my father's hometown, a place that defined me to myself even though I was born and raised in Los Angeles. When she left New Orleans in 1956 to marry my father and settle here, she didn't go back home for a long, long time, which I hardly understood. New Orleans was magic to me, a place I'd never been to but had heard endlessly regaled in stories told over my head as a child, an acutely Southern but wholly singular city that I had come to revere as the molten spiritual core of our family—shouldn't somebody go back now and then to tend to the heritage, pull up the weeds growing around it? My mother didn't think so. The city lived for her in a diminished capacity, perhaps packed up and given away with the dress and gloves. "Ah, New Orleans," she'd say brusquely. "I don't want to go back there. It's a big ghetto."

New Orleans might well have been a ghetto—like other black children, I knew the rudiments of Southern history practically from birth—but evidence of my mother's greater New Orleans faith filled our dinner every week and teased my curiosity: hot sausage and red beans, *panne* meat, jambalaya, stuffed mirlitons, French bread and butter to go with everything. When my grandmother was visiting, she made apple pie and biscuits from scratch, or pitched in with my mother to make the pièce de résistance of New Orleans cooking, file gumbo. At a time when L.A. was institutionalizing the popularity of brave new foods like wheat germ and soy bacon, New Orleans was implacably fed to us; it described much our workaday world and all of our special occasions, and it lingered in our psyche as indelibly as the acrid smoke from the frying sausage lingered in the blackened hood of the stove, letting anyone who stood beneath it and smelled the convergence of spice, char, and nascent roux know what our real origins were.

Here was the excess, the story I sought, yet my mother did not teach me how to cook. At dinnertime I always pulled Kool-Aid and place-setting duties; the closest I ever came to food preparation was sitting out on the back porch peeling shrimp for gumbo or shucking ears of corn with a paper sack between my knees. At first I though my mother regarded me as incompetent, or herself as too competent to be bothered with training novices—too much possibility of wasted motion. But there was more to it than that. As proprietary as she was about cooking, she was also laissez-faire about it, an attitude that spoke to her own L.A. yearnings to divest the old and investigate the new. She would set the dishes but let us make of them what we wanted, and if we chose to murk up the gumbo by adding more file powder, or if we chose not to eat gumbo at all and make a peanut-butter sandwich for dinner instead—well, that was our business. She wanted us to have space enough for our own lives, for own dishes—what else was this city for? Why else had she come?

Cultivating choices was something my mother revered, in her quiet way. I remember her telling me when I was young that I had better not think about marriage until after thirty, "because after you're married," she said with a kind of finality, "there are certain things you just can't *do*." Shortly after the birth of my little sister, when I was six, I followed her into the bathroom one day to inquire whether or not it hurt to have babies; she hesitated a second before saying evenly that yes, it did, and I sensed even then that she meant something more than physical pain. Despite her loyalty to family, I felt early on that she probably would have loved being a professional woman or business owner just as much. The part of me that was like my mother empathized deeply with her unrealized wishes, the part that was outgoing but self-protective, pleasant but often emotionally oblique—what they call in New Orleans *comme il faut*. I loved my mother for taking me to the library every week, reading to me out loud, encouraging my writing mostly in letting me be. I wanted her to follow where I was going, but I came to realize that she was content by then to stand where she was and see me off. She had made her choices; now she was going to watch me make mine. As far as cooking was concerned, I understood that my mother wanted her own space, that she wanted to be given as wide a berth as she gave the rest of us. It was not hostility but a great need for privacy that drove her, a need to have full run of the world she had settled on for herself; I could look and admire, ask questions and one day be invited in, but I couldn't intrude—exactly the rules I established in my own life as a writer. So it was with the best intentions and with the desire for mutual respect, I believe, that my mother chose not to teach me how to cook.

I accepted that, though the funny thing is I still considered Creole cooking mine in the way that that I considered New Orleans, that place I never saw until I was twenty-two, mine. When people asked me where I was from, I answered, Los Angeles, and briefly reveled in my native city's hip quotient—denim bikinis, *Soul Train*—but hastily added, "but my family's all from New Orleans." People's faces relaxed into understanding; that explained my light skin and straight-curl hair, the strange lilt in my voice and rapid words that often jammed into a stutter and put me in speech therapy by second grade. Too wound up to be Californian, not urban enough to be Spanish Harlem, I fancied myself to be exactly the mélange that was New Orleans: wide open and amiably mysterious and, even if you couldn't figure out which thing it was, generally delightful to the taste.

People might assume, because of my New Orleans bloodline, that I have an inbred culinary talent. Not much is further from the truth; not only do I not make red beans or gumbo, I can rarely make pancakes made from add-water mix come out right. But I don't mind the lack because it has, ironically, provided my mother and me with a reliable source of closeness—while she didn't teach me how to cook, she's always been a willing source of information, should I choose to ask. When I have the smallest food question, I call my mother to plumb her expertise. She enjoys this kind of deference and in these moments can overcome her emotional reticence and feel most confident in her affections for me. There are even a few instances when I am able to air a little accumulated knowledge of my own. I say, "Well, I just used lemon peel instead of the lemon juice, it's the same, you know," and my mother concurs or says, "Peel, sure, and you know it only takes about six lemons to make a glass of juice," as if I already knew that. And for a moment or two we are equals, confidants, two women exchanging timeworn shop talk that enables one of us to call the other in the morning for no particular reason.

More and more, I appreciate that kind of family intimacy. The Creole network that was firmly in place in postwar L.A., that helped define the massive Southern migration here and gave Creolism a uniquely local character, has slowly vanished over the years. In Crenshaw and South Central, there used to my Uncle Leon's barbershop, Henry Marine's, Sid's Louisiana Café, the Feast of St. Joseph Day at St. John of God Catholic Church, and other events at parish halls in that vicinity. All of my relatives once lived in a five-mile radius of each other, which is as close-knit as L.A. communities get; I visited some aunt or uncle almost every Sunday and sat in the backyard on the front porch consuming whatever they had on the stove. Food and family were at every stop, impossible to escape, as crucial to my earliest sense of L.A. as sand and surf.

That experience has changed texturally over time, gotten thinner. My family exploded at the center and moved out to hot, far-flung suburbs with far-away-sounding names like Diamond Bar, Hacienda Heights, and Moreno Valley. The only Creole must-stop from old times is Pete's Louisiana Hot Sausage, on Jefferson just west of Crenshaw. Jefferson used to be a Creole thoroughfare, the street where my Uncle Leon held such political and community sway from his barbershop pulpit that folks called him the mayor. But people no longer use storefronts or porches or sidewalks as sites to gather. Visiting relatives, or anyone in central L.A., is a qualitatively different proposition — you don't want to hang out in the front yard and, well, there's really no one left for us to visit anymore anyway. My mother spends Sunday afternoons now in the aisles of behemoth grocery stores and tells me I really should consider moving away from my mid-city apartment, it's gotten too dangerous; she's been saying this ever since my landlady tried, and failed, to fit my old glass-paned front door with a security screen that allows me to see people without them seeing me. The expansiveness I grew up with has been supplanted by fear, and the whole notion of cultural preservation seems not nearly as important or immediate as self-preservation, the rule of urban law. The closest I get to the family Sundays is holiday pilgrimages to my mother's stove, where I position my face over an enormous stockpot that steams gumbo mist into the blackened stove hood, a hood that holds a full generation of L.A.-permuted Creole dreams. These are fissured dreams, run through with cracks that could be highways—the highest form of L.A. freedom, the things that bind this city together and keep it apart—or simply cracks of age and disrepair.

I do consider, and record, stories. I ask old people questions when I see them, and I ask my mother such questions every day (she's not yet old, and never will be), but offhandedly, as if an account of my great-uncle Lester's exploits in World War II is something that just occurred to me, like a measurement for sugar or baking powder. I must have my mother believe that I'm looking the other way when it comes to New Orleans, because only then will she give it to me, and even then she interrupts herself sometimes with a wary half question, half warning: You aren't going to write about this, are you? To which I answer, in my head, that these stories are very much part of the space she granted me to build as I wish. This is my choice.

I know my mother recognizes this choice more than she can admit. She is more relaxed now, less strict about keeping functions apart. Yet she knows the power she still wields as keeper of the gas flame. When I fell into a crippling depression last year, from the depths of which I decided to stop answering the doorbell and returning phone calls, my mother sent my younger sister by with a plastic bowl full of gumbo she had made for Labor Day. This was a day off, she had cooked—where the hell was I?

I didn't answer the door straightaway—all right, my sister had to force her way in with keys borrowed from my landlady. I didn't talk to her, couldn't talk; I had my mother's tight lips that day, and she left after a while, exasperated. But the bowl she brought for me worked its magic. In my slippery-slope misery I went into the kitchen, poured the gumbo over the rice my mother had packed along with it, found my way to the television and watched something I can't remember at all. Though I had no more inclination to talk, some weight rolled slightly off the center of my being as I spooned up the gumbo in silence, savoring the broth-tenderized chicken and sausage and shrimp like an unutterable prayer, letting the oily roux coat the roof of my mouth like a salve. In the leanest of times, New Orleans was again being fed to me, in its own time. Though alone, I had family enough. I had mother enough.

MOTHER, UNCONCEIVED

2003

Before this story is written, I must first say that the story is not over. I don't have children, but I could merely because it's possible. I'm thirty-nine. At press time I still have ovaries and a womb and they still wait, as they have been waiting since I was thirteen or so, at least that's the way I imagined it. They have incredible patience, and wonderful equanimity—they could wait forever, for nothing, and not mind at all. I could never utilize the creation potential, rebuilt every month with Sisyphean uniformity and persistence, and not suffer any consequences for my laziness/irresolution/ rare good sense. I'm still trying to figure out which it is. I may sit and puzzle it out forever and let the time and the last of the blood slip away to menopause and then, only then, will I breathe a sigh of relief and feel in my marrow that I've done the right thing. Then I will confirm what I've felt all along, what I felt as a small hard seed at thirteen and later as full-flowered righteousness. Right? Maybe. I'm almost certain. Is almost good enough, sure enough? Is there reasonable doubt to this thing? If so, I'm unconvictable, a free woman made free by the murk of desire and doubt, and if not—well, I'm a free woman still. And so the problem.

It cannot be this easy. Culture has long had it that black women are empathy made flesh (also attitude made flesh, but that's another essay entirely), nurturers by nature, or at least by default, cooks nearly from birth. We are founts of blind encouragement, bricklayers of discipline, the most inimitable babysitters and line-leaders you ever saw without even trying. We have steely resolve in our sleep. We have been firewalls for trouble of all kinds—mistreatment of black men, popular unease with black people period—and if we aren't mothers, we have had extensive experience in raising younger siblings and looking after various play sisters and brothers. Not me. I was fourth in a family of five and had no one to look after for a long time; another sister was born when I was six. By then, people recognized my tendency to isolation and deep thought, noted my lack of smiles, and no one brought babies around for me to model motherhood on. I didn't cook, or pretend to; my mother loved me but kept me out of the kitchen. I read, imagined, watched other people. When my sister was born, I was briefly surprised, but too young and too used to a house full of bodies to feel resentful. I did look after Heather somewhat, took her out in her stroller in the afternoon, but in the end we became friends, confidantes with the same odd tastes in music and other pastimes. I felt sororal, not maternal, toward her; in fact, it was she who most often provided me with emotional support during the fitful but sustained depression that has only significantly lifted in the last few years. Heather had the pragmatism and circumspection I seemed to lack entirely, and that I thought all mothers must have. Where she plotted and executed a career in law—getting scholarships, passing the California bar on the first try—I was always getting blown off course, wanting to write but puttering around half-heartedly as an actor and substitute teacher. Of course she got married before me and had a baby two years ago, an event I was deeply afraid would change our dynamic forever. I was very guilty about this fear, which I thought selfish and all the evidence I needed that I was unsuited to motherhood; women were at least supposed to regard each other's pregnancies as good news, circle the wagons of procreational instinct. Black women are thought of as especially guided by such instincts, the least likely to wonder aloud whether they want babies at all, even if a pregnancy is unintended. We have grown skilled at accepting our lot, and pregnancy is no different; for us, it is not choice but charge. And people like seeing us with kids because it completes a picture that is skewed without them, almost unsettling—a woman will always battle the notion that minus kids she is less than, but a black woman battles that plus the notion she is failing socially, culturally, historically. Black women have little individual *she* to work with, despite decades of feminist dogma that has become a very accepted part of American sociological discourse. Those of us with doubts about baby are still very much on the outside.

But the conundrum is that, as I said at the outset, I *do* have choice. It is covert, but it is exercised. I have had more abortions than I care to reveal. My black female friends, mostly careerists, were accepting but vaguely admonishing, and assured me that one day I would go through with a pregnancy (in a couple of instances, they insisted on it, and while I thought it was none of their business I didn't disagree because it felt like they were speaking to something higher, greater, than either of us and our wants; so I said nothing).

I am not at all happy about those abortions; choice does not mean happiness, merely options. Yet it feels disquietingly easy, like a black woman steering clear of troubles is committing a criminal act. I get faint stabs of that unease when I indulge in other luxuries of choice that seem far more innocuous, like impulse shopping or going to movies when I want or sitting alone. I think, I have little right to live this way. Even the fact that I work as a de facto black advocacy journalist does little to assuage the feeling that I'm treading the forbidden path of least resistance. I'm cheating a god I don't even believe in, quite.

And yet. I admire mothers, beginning with my own, who inhabited her role comfortably, but freely admitted she would have done something differ-ent had she not had the five of us. I admire my younger sister, who became a mother but hardly lost herself, or us, in the process: we still do dinner at least once a week, often with my nephew in tow. I love Julian, as I do all six of my nieces and nephews, but loving them has not so far translated into wanting kids of my own. I prefer being the mentor, the reinforcement rather than the enforcer, the figure who can assert opinions but doesn't have to sit in judg-ment. Admittedly, I enjoy the inevitable moments of vicarious motherhood: giving Julian a bottle or a bath, sternly telling him no, offering my teenage niece advice on what to wear because she's asked me for it. But my sisters, the mothers, are constantly living two lives, or three—in my own mother's case, five. I can barely live one to maximum effect. In some ways that's a poor ex-cuse, a twenty-first-century argument for the luxury of solitude and personal space that American culture eagerly cultivates, but that black history and its large-scale struggles have never been able to afford. Despite the unprec-edented black affluence in the country, perhaps I have no right to assume such freedom. Yet such freedom defines all Americans, and if I don't claim them I am further diminished as such, and progress is compromised. Reconciling the cult of individualism with the needs of the collective is the next-millennium version of what Du Bois defined a hundred years ago as the plague of double-consciousness—being black and being American at once. We have not quite pulled ourselves together and still largely shuttle between the two, but in ways the Du Bois could not have imagined. Straddling the notion of motherhood and its self-evident rewards and the American nirvana of self-fulfillment is but one of those ways.

But social theories aside, I reiterate: I don't know. I am not convinced, but I hold out anxiety that I am not convinced for the wrong reasons, like I want a child only because I can. Or because when it's all over and my ovaries and such fall silent, I might feel incomplete, not psychically so much as experientially; part of me is afraid that not having a baby might wind up feeling like the small but nagging regret I harbor for not going out to see the pope the one time he came to town in the mid-1980s. That's not a good reason to not have a child, but it's an American one. As our consumerist ethos has shifted from the acquisition of goods to the acquisition of experience (i.e., you don't have buy Nikes so much anymore as you pay for the feeling of being Michael Jordan for day), the whole proposition of acquiring babies, if you will, takes on a new, unsettling dimension. Maybe this is where I have rare good sense, and my lifelong wariness of doing of what everybody else is doing will stand me in good stead.

My husband is leaving the whole enterprise in my incapable hands; he is not interested in having kids, never has been, but he says if I absolutely must he will probably go along. Since I tend to think everything out of existence or action—my American right, my cultural fallibility—I can see where this is headed. We've only been married a year, and I'm contemplating all the things we haven't done together, all the things I haven't written, but not all the children we could have. I have answered my own question, I know. I answered it long ago. But *thinking* that answer may be the wrong one, that I may have abused more than respected my new-age freedom, gives me odd comfort. It leaves me in the ancient battles that I will likely wage with words, not with any issuance from my womb. I will have to do the job myself.

Education has become a very sterile word, one that conjures up buildings, bureaucracy, test scores, and the like. But for black people, education is much more than the sum of those parts: it's an article of faith, a life-giving force, a creative goal, still the most reassuring thing standing between us and the oblivion that always threatens. Nor does education simply mean "school." It also means mentoring, reaching back, reconciling reality with history. It means showing up and not giving up. Over the years, I have watched black people swiftly losing the battle that education was supposed to have won for us long ago. Today, we fight for education more than it fights for us, and the fight goes issue by issue, sometimes student by student. It is slow and torturous, but essential. These next pieces are about the failures and small victories, within school and without.

HELD BACK

THE STATE OF BLACK EDUCATION

January 2000

First, a warning: the story you're about to read is not news. It's not even a new development in an old story, an update in the strict sense of the word. Many people believe, not too privately, that this story doesn't really have what the news business calls a hook, a prominent element of conflict or urgency that would at least qualify it to hover in the wings waiting for a shot at publication or airtime after the more timely stuff—war, celebrity divorces, ethnic festivals—get theirs. This story isn't at the back of the line—it's not even *in* line, and hasn't been in years. It has its sympathizers in the editorial echelons of newsrooms, but no real ground-level advocates. Yet it's the biggest single reason why "disproportionately represented" has become black people's middle name, why too many of them wind up in prison or poverty or the minimum-wage loop, generally on the wrong side of any statistics that measure social well-being. Despite the very dire consequences of ignoring this story, it stopped being a story long ago and simply became Fate, which no reporter or news anchor wants to touch; if there's no reason for a follow-up announcing that somebody high up got nervous and started doing something differently, the story won't get written in the first place. This story doesn't inspire nervousness. Contempt, disgust, resignation, an urge to flee and seek higher ground, yes—but nervousness, a feeling of something close about to fall hard on your shoulders, no. This story is grave but distant, like death, or the eight-point earthquake that won't, of course, happen in *our* lifetime.

The story is the miserable state of black education. Actually, the story is why it's *still* so miserable after years of desegregation battles, civil rights activism, and mounting evidence that without a sturdy education, one can kiss one's fortunes in the new millennium goodbye. Before anyone starts vigorously pointing to the groundbreaking prosperity of the black middle class in the last couple of decades, let me say: I know. I'm among the brave new petit bourgeois myself. But the fact is that far more of us are being left behind—permanently—than are being moved ahead, and those moving ahead are chiefly advantaged by—you guessed it—education. With all due respect to the Rev. Creflo Dollar and his Trinity Broadcasting ilk, black improvement is largely a blessing of degrees, not God. Which leaves us with the conundrum of knowing exactly how to solve the problem (we've always known—black people more than any other group have clung to the notion of education as the great equalizer), yet not giving the solution the stature it deserves because it seems, well, passé. Or something even less appealing, and less admissible. "Our fault as a [black] community is that we've allowed this to happen," says Theodore Alexander, a longtime assistant superintendent in the Los Angeles Unified School District (LAUSD). "Sure, we have a middle class that's made advances, but when you look at the number of kids who aren't going anywhere . . . We've sacrificed those kids for the betterment of a few." The outrage of the past, in other words, turned out to be for sale. The price of complacency has been steep, and we're still paying it. "The problem is, what was once considered a problem is now pretty much regarded as a circumstance," says George McKenna III, a veteran educator who is now deputy superintendent in the beleaguered, roughly half-black Compton school district. "A circumstance is just the way things are. It's accepted by everybody—white, black, brown. And that's the end of it."

But the stuff of outrage remains. Here's a start: in L.A. Unified, black students as a group are at the bottom of the heap in terms of standardized test scores; they've been there for as long as anybody I talked to can remember. (Random examples from the latest stats: white first-graders scored in the 65th percentile in math, blacks in the 35th—four points below the district average; white ninth graders scored in the 47th percentile in reading, blacks in the 22nd.) Black students, particularly black males, are increasingly overrepresented in special-education classes (though only 16 percent of the general student population, they make up 20 percent of the special-ed population), in part because they tend to be identified early as having behavioral or emotional problems, which are invariably linked to academic problems—and once you're on the special-ed track, you tend not to get off. Historically black schools that have become substantially Latino in the last decade but with the highest concentrations of black students in the district—Crenshaw, Dorsey, Washington, Locke, Fremont, Jordan—have the highest numbers of uncredentialed and absentee teachers (28 percent of all uncredentialed teachers work in District 1, an inner-city district that includes several of these schools). Schools in relatively affluent areas that have imported black populations—such as Westchester, Hamilton and many San Fernando Valley high school campuses—have similar problems of black underachievement. (Example: at Westchester, black tenth graders scored in the 24th percentile in reading, whites in the 52nd.) Location doesn't seem to be much of a factor.

Some would argue that the real factor here is not ethnic but socioeconomic. The problems of black children are now chiefly the problems of poverty and ineffective school bureaucracies. Latinos tend to occupy the same socioeconomic strata as blacks and also underachieve in droves. But Latinos have specific issues of immigration, culture, and language, issues that are institutionally acknowledged by programs such as bilingual education—which, by the way, has yet to be dismantled. Black students' needs have never been acknowledged as such, partly because "black problems" are viewed as pathological and stigmatizing, partly because multicultural America, determined to cast off racism like an outgrown sweater, is becoming ever more reluctant to identify any issues as specifically black. So the response to foundering black education has been more emotional than practical—experts and pundits regularly intimate that blacks need to shore up family values, they lack determination, they're just not capable after all. This is not to say that poverty isn't a big part of the problem, or that problems of African-Americans don't overlap with those of Latinos or other groups that populate the inner city. But to stop at that is to dismiss a particular (peculiar, as some of our Southern forefathers called it) history that gave rise to particular problems that, as much as we are in denial about their existence, are still very much alive. A paragraph from the National Urban League's 1995 almanac, *State of Black America*, summed it up this way: "Low educational achievement among African-Americans has resulted not only from poverty and prejudice, but from the structured expectation in our schools that black children will fail."

Assistant Superintendent Ted Alexander says that at the root of the black-education rot is the assumption that has quietly emerged over the last generation that the need for integration is dead. This is odd, considering that the same people who believe that also believe—quite willingly—that many schools, especially inner-city schools with heavy black and brown populations, remain essentially segregated. This wouldn't be such a bad thing if schools had roughly equal access to resources and some assurance of academic equity, but they don't. The push for school integration was of course a push for this kind of equity—not just for the right of black students to sit in the same classrooms with white—but the truth is that once the right to move about freely was secured, attention to such paltry details as viable equity, or even whether students were really moving freely about at all, quickly waned. Not that there wasn't some follow-up; we had court-ordered busing back in the '70s, the federal response to the fact that the 1954 Supreme Court decision to ban segregated schools was a good start, though not enough. But mandatory busing, which involved busing white students to black areas as well as the other way around, wound up being as unpopular and raising as much ire as the Vietnam War, particularly in suburb-cocooned L.A. It was scrapped, and what remained in its place to do the desegregation job for the last twenty years is what's run out of Alexander's Office of Student Integration Services—chiefly "Permit With Transportation" busing, magnet schools and assorted student-improvement programs focused on the urban core, which includes many schools that not very long ago were primarily black.

Magnets and busing are the biggest components of integration services, involving more than twelve thousand black students. Yet there is no comprehensive system in place that tracks how well these programs are working, whether or not black students—the original impetus for all this—are benefiting educationally or otherwise. What we do know is that last year, a group of black Hamilton High School parents got so inflamed over the ongoing academic failures of black students that they went looking for somebody to blame and wound up pitching the whole campus into a swamp of racial tensions and bitter divisions from which it is still struggling to recover. As poisonous and terribly misguided as that campaign was, the drive to establish some kind of accountability—*right now*—for the institutional malign neglect of black students was understandable, even necessary. Parents were also railing at the fact that black students in Hamilton's humanities and music magnet schools fare so much better academically than their main-school counterparts. (Example: in tenth-grade language tests, black students in the humanities magnet scored in the 61st percentile; those in the main school scored in the 29th.) If one very charitably assumed the parents were not against magnets, as they claimed, then one would have to agree with their argument for some systematic effort to bring the rest of the school up to magnet code. If the lab experiment worked, the argument goes, why not try replicating it en masse, at least elements of it? Why limit the already limited fruits of integration to a few? The reasons why not are myriad, but Judy Burton, assistant superintendent of the district's Office of School Reform, offers this: "The lowest-achieving kids are black and brown. You can't ever discount that fact when it comes to wondering why there isn't more public interest in closing the achievement gap." In other words, race matters.

Alexander exhibits a clear ambivalence about black education that is typical of the local black educators I talked to: in one breath he exalts the successes of his office, and in another, bigger breath he condemns the system at large for dropping the ball. That system, by the way, includes black communities that have relaxed their vigilance over the years right along with everyone else. That riles Alexander most of all. "In '54, that lawyer team [of the NAACP Legal Defense Fund] built a case around the fact that schools were clearly unequal," he says. "But we're at the point now where we need to look at educational outcome, not opportunity. That means putting resources into achieving the outcome you want. We're not doing that." *We* has many meanings here, all applicable: the school system, Alexander himself, the black middle class that has divested itself of the fortunes of the lower, politicians of all stripes. The biggest problem of black education is that an issue that once seemed relatively straightforward has become so cantilevered, requiring so many levels of involvement to address, that a working solution seems more remote now than it did in 1954. And as California politics globalize, Alexander notes, the black struggle inversely grows smaller; the primary struggle now is not education or civil rights or anything comparable, but merely the right for black people politically to remain black. "When I started the Ten Schools Program, I enlisted the help of the United Negro College Fund, and now they're thinking of changing their name to something else," says Alexander, looking peeved. "There's this falsehood out there that we can't wear our blackness anymore, even when it makes sense. [The educational mentoring organization] 100 Black Men wants to broaden its scope to be more inclusive of other ethnic groups, for political reasons. I said that I didn't want any part of it."

The Ten Schools Program, another component of Student Integration Services, began in the late '80s as a frontal attack on the failure of black schools to ground students in the basics early on. It involves a dozen of the historically lowest-achieving elementary schools (two were added to the original ten in recent years) in an area stretching from Southwest L.A. to Watts, and focuses on language development. Equally important is teacher role modeling—for example, male teachers at Ten Schools are required to wear ties in the classroom; women are required to wear hose. "This is about school gestalt, about total school environment," explains Alexander, who fondly remembers such things from his own largely segregated education in post–Central Avenue, pre–Watts Riots Los Angeles. The latest standardized test scores from Ten Schools are both heartening and not: as a group, they outperform other schools in their respective "clusters," which means they score slightly above the 25th percentile (the district average is the 30th percentile). Three of the twelve schools scored at the district average or above; one of those, Bright Elementary, is above the 40th percentile. That means that three schools out of the dozens in the South-Central landscape are average by district standards, which are not very high.

Ten Schools is an elaboration of an earlier program called Triad, run at three low-performing black schools that form a feeder chain: 95th Street School, Bret Harte Prep Junior High (now Middle School), and Washington Preparatory High School. The idea was to forge a single academic community and sense of purpose among students, parents, and school staff at the three campuses. "We had parents giving orientations to other parents, uniform homework procedures, students signing contracts," recalls Charles Palmer, an educational consultant who was principal at Bret Harte during the Triad period. "It was very hands-on. We had progress reports every week—we couldn't afford to wait six weeks to see if our kids were failing. It was very much a village-raising-a-child concept. It was clear that we were all on the same page." Overall, there were modest gains in state test scores for the three schools between 1983 and 1988, particularly at Bret Harte. But Triad, conceived as a model for troubled schools, never became what Palmer and others hoped; when the regional administrators who had originally championed Triad left, it petered out. "The district didn't support the effort," Palmer sighs. "There was no follow-up, no implementation." As with a few other concentrated efforts to improve black education, Triad never made the jump from being driven by personalities to being driven by policy. Institutionalizing anything other than failure in certain neighborhoods has proved to be little more than a notion.

Burton, a veteran of the Ten Schools Program, says that it did grow into a community, forming a tiny ersatz school district with common, well-defined goals. During her five-year tenure as principal at Martin Luther King Jr. Elementary, she says, teachers at various schools routinely visited each other and gave each other critical feedback. High expectations were set in kindergarten. Teaching staff included fifteen mentor teachers and many very good veterans; staff turnover was low. "The only way to increase test scores is to improve day-to-day instruction, and that's what we did," says Burton, noting that 93rd Street School, in spite of being located in South-Central's heart of darkness, experienced similar success (its latest composite test score puts it at the 30th percentile, the district average). But Burton suggests that the district has been unwilling to extend its support beyond the handful of schools for one over-riding reason: money. What with extra school days, professional training and quarterly assessments, the $8 million Ten Schools Program is prohibitively ex-pensive. It hardly needs to be said that such reluctance is costing everybody— kids, parents, society—far more than money. "I think the lowest-achieving schools need specific help and specific efforts," says Burton. "It's kind of ob-vious. Unfortunately, the public sees it as a money or prestige issue. Or," she adds, "a race issue." Kind of hard to tell the difference these days.

Not even the combustible personality of George McKenna could kindle the fires of reform, not for long. Between 1978 and 1988, McKenna garnered national attention as the hard-nosed rookie principal of Washington Prep who in the span of a few years made atmospheric changes at a ground-zero campus. McKenna was in fact the original impetus for both Triad and the Ten Schools Program. He doesn't express much faith in either, or in the for-tunes of Washington ("Too many conversations never become agendas"). Yet he fiercely believes in the notion of academic autonomy at black and minor-ity schools. "At Washington, we were trying to prove that you didn't have to get on a bus to achieve in school," he says with typical brusqueness. "I came from segregation and excellence, and I know that it can work. We had no white children at Washington. Equity is colorblind, and so is excellence." But there were deep racial rifts at Washington during McKenna's reign: he purged the school of much of its majority-white teaching staff, not because of any presumed racial insensitivity, he says, "but because they were not ef-fective. Effectiveness is measured by student achievement. Too many teachers present material but don't teach." In his ten ballyhooed years at Washington, McKenna admits, standardized test scores did not rise sharply—a ten-percentile-point increase, at best. But many other quality-of-campus-life is-sues improved dramatically: student attendance soared, as did college ad-missions and the number of students taking the SAT; incidents of violence dropped steeply. In short, the social and cultural problems that concentrically ringed the core problem of academics were dealt with first; education was something that had to be approached from the outside in. "Test scores didn't significantly reflect all the good that was happening," says McKenna. "And it took about three years of us working at it to see any change. Nothing really changed at Washington until about '82."

McKenna would certainly call himself a proponent of integration, but he wrestles with the term as it's been historically understood. From a purely philosophical standpoint, integration as a salve for black education raises uneasy questions of validation and self-esteem. Politically, it is much more a practical matter, and always has been. "The issue is not so much that the presence of white kids ensures a quality education, but the resources that integration efforts bring to bear on real problems of achievement," says one seasoned urban-education consultant. "The fact is, the system is responsible for educating the children." Holding the system to the legal allowances of integration has traditionally been the method blacks have used to track accountability. "But *real* accountability," says the consultant, "is us applying the kind of political pressure that we have yet to see." And as blacks assimilate and get further away from identifying their culture as one of difference, that pressure will be tougher and tougher to come by. "We've internalized over the years that 'black difference' is bad, so educators don't want to bring it up," says Owen Knox, a consultant and member of a national nonprofit called Educating Black Children. "With ebonics, everyone leapt to the conclusion that black students' speech was a reflection of how poorly they thought, or how dumb they were, when in fact speech is merely a system of symbols representing ideas. The schools all say, 'You must adapt to me,' rather than looking at how they might adapt to students and their needs. It's assumed all needs are the same. They aren't."

Remember ebonics? That was the last black-education issue to penetrate public awareness, and it didn't exactly make a good impression. At the bottom of all the ridicule over black children being "taught" street English as self-affirmation—a popular misreading of the issue—was the very real problem of black students in Oakland's school system failing to acquire adequate language skills. Oakland may have bungled the solution, but at least school officials there recognized a problem that no one else wanted to because doing so highlighted a dreaded "black difference." Everybody with an opinion on the matter declared that black kids can certainly learn like everyone else, then they went home. Forget about black people applying political pressure to substantively address a learning issue; they were too busy trying to put the whole embarrassing episode behind them. (LAUSD, by the way, has a Language Development Program in place to address just such problems of language transition, though according to the nonprofit Achievement Council, Latino males in the program whose primary language is not English score higher than black males whose primary language is.)

Not quite everyone shies away from ethnic-specific orientations. Middle College High School, a small alternative school on the campus of L.A. Southwest College, is all black and Latino; its curriculum includes "The Psychology of Racism," and a required "American Social History Project" taught by a black college professor that covers the historical and other contributions of blacks, Latinos, and women. The latest test scores at Middle College are at least as high as district averages, and in several categories higher. (Random examples: ninth-grade math scores are in the 40th percentile, compared to the district average of 38th. Reading scores for the same grade are at the 28th percentile, while the district average is 22nd.) Seniors go on to college at a rate astonishing for a non-magnet, minority public high school—at last count 93 percent, says principal Natalie Battersbee—and while the typical Middle College student certainly has potential, many are not career high achievers, and others have in fact had academic and behavioral problems at other, bigger schools. Middle College's magic is, first and foremost, a population of 350, not the 3,000 typical of most inner-city schools. Battersbee, who is black, says she knows every student personally. So well, in fact, that she recently advised her top two seniors, who got accepted by UCLA, to go elsewhere. "The admissions people at UCLA asked me why, and I said, 'Because you don't care about a student with a black face,'" says Battersbee, alluding to the anti-affirmative-action sentiment and alarming black attrition rate at the Westwood campus. "I do everything I can to get kids into schools like Fisk and other black colleges where they're nurtured, where they can flourish and grow." Part of the mammoth Los Angeles school district but not quite of it, Middle College can afford its proclivities. But it does seem to prove what McKenna calls an absolute truth of public education: reform, or chaos, or status quo, begins with the principal.

Would that reform started with school boards—not L.A.'s hapless gang of five, which oversees a student population of some 710,000, but Compton's and Inglewood's, with far more manageable populations of 37,000 and 17,000 or so, respectively. Both cities are historically black, but have undergone swift demographic transitions; Latinos now make up roughly half of each. Both have predominantly black local governments and school boards—and, alas, both are slouching toward Armageddon. The Compton school district's free fall is into its sixth year, and Inglewood, despite its greater affluence and more solid middle class, seems poised to follow. While the failure of black leadership to effectively address education is distressing in both cases, Inglewood's failure is particularly so—it has the very dubious distinction of being Southern California's only sizable middle-class burg with a poverty-class school district. Parents with means tend to send their kids out of the district or to private schools. Standardized test scores are dismal. (Despite some encouraging numbers in the early grades, especially at a few beating-the-odds campuses like Bennett Kew and Kelso elementary schools, achievement drops precipitously in the upper grades. Example: in ninth-grade reading, Inglewood's district average percentile rank is 19; for tenth grade, it's 14; for eleventh grade, 20.) A group of Inglewood High students and the ACLU are suing the district and the state education department for not providing them with enough Advanced Placement courses to give them a fighting chance for admission to top colleges. The school board, as a group, has publicly expressed far more interest in running for higher offices than in any of these issues. "It's a twofold problem—black folks can't agree on anything, and there are too many agendas on every count," says a veteran black educator who passionately requested anonymity. "Black school districts usually are a mess. Individual powwows take priority, because everyone in charge is concerned with appearing powerful. There's no holistic sense at all. And important issues get pushed to the background." McKenna agrees that political types of all colors resolutely pay no attention to the failings of students of color. "Compton was the first district in the state to be placed in academic receivership, but it was the fiscal problems that finally got people's attention," he says. "Academically, we had been languishing for years. But our education deficiencies didn't raise anybody's temperature."

McKenna and his brethren—Owen Knox and Charles Palmer and pretty much everyone else who would attach themselves to black-education issues—are of the old-guard, black-advocacy generation that doesn't see a like-minded generation following it into the future. That doesn't exactly exonerate the elders; in the '70s, it was they who, in the movement's postmortem gloom, first began turning away from causes and turning more to material comforts. Organizations allegedly set up to oversee education interests—the Council of Black Administrators, the Black Education Commission—proved to be more creatures of the L.A. school district, more about sharper image and professional networking than about effective watchdogging. (The same could be said, by the way, of many old-line black groups, from the NAACP on down.) The great mobility and diffusion of the black populace in L.A. in the last generation or so has also contributed to the problem of continuity. "It's getting harder to advocate for a population that's decreasing in proportion," says the urban-education consultant. "I mean, it's harder to get people to pay attention to 5 percent of the problem, when it used to be 30 percent." And such diminishment seems more palatable in Los Angeles than anywhere else, because the city has so few activist traditions to uphold. "L.A. tends to be very cut off from education issues," she says. "No one here is really looking for black-education models that work. For change to happen, there has to be public will. Parents and voters aren't willing to vote in legislators and school-board members who will set a standard and keep it there. There are issues that burn in other places in the country—there's a battle over standardized testing raging in Massachusetts, and in Texas they passed a law that says teachers must inform students of their credential status." That, of course, was one provision of an education-accountability bill that Governor Gray Davis recently failed to support. "Here in California, people have no idea," says the consultant. "But there are a whole series of questions in this state that we're all dealing with—class issues, post–Prop. 209 issues. All of this is so desensitizing when people who are trying to make something happen keep trying and trying and don't get anywhere." Also, she points out, "a certain level of advocacy across the board has simply moved on. The white parents who used to be up in arms over public education have moved their kids out of harm's way and into charter and private schools." Blacks have experienced more than a trickle-down effect of this kind of civic ennui—it hasn't rained, it's poured.

Reform efforts face an uphill battle and a dubious history. Triad fell by the wayside; Educating Black Children submitted a comprehensive blueprint for improving black-student performance to LAUSD, which the district officially accepted two years ago but has yet to implement in any meaningful way. The Hamilton High School parent group has joined forces with similarly concerned groups across town, including the yeomanly Parents and Students Organized based in Watts, to form Equity Network; whether another, saner brand of education activism will prevail remains to be seen. Owen Knox is helping to grow Watts Learning Center, a tiny South L.A. elementary charter school—just kindergarten and first grade so far—that is predominantly black and has less than half the population of Middle College High. The focus on making students and parents equal stakeholders, of custom-tailoring teaching to student needs, is very much Triad's, Ten Schools', Middle College's—"building a community of learners," says Knox. All students enter second grade knowing how to read efficiently. "What we're demonstrating is that with greater participation, we have greater success. The school becomes part of the community, not a distant entity that's a wholly different environment from home."

Black education reform is also going to have to happen alongside the Latino-ization of Los Angeles Unified, which proceeds apace. "It's going to take extremely sophisticated leadership to navigate this, to sidestep an explosion," says George McKenna, understandably not sounding very optimistic. "If we as blacks don't keep focused on a black agenda, how can we expect anybody else to?" Whether having a black woman as board president—namely Genethia Hayes—will make a marked difference in the fortunes of black children is any psychic's guess. Fellow board member David Tokofsky says the district is at least now more willing to disaggregate data at troubled schools, which will allow it to more thoroughly assess instruction and track moneys spent—in other words, to actually practice accountability. Parsing information is certainly a good thing, but it's only a precursor to remedy and action; in the meantime, problems that are already generations old continue to fester. "What we're lacking overall are the social architects, engineers, and politicians who want to build those bridges over troubled racial waters," says Tokofsky. "Frankly, I don't think anyone's sat down and thought about black education since 1966." At millennium's edge, prevailing black philosophy has made an odd portent out of that '70s theatrical confection *The Wiz*, which touted black liberation through a fairy-tale belief in self-creation, and admonished: don't nobody bring me no bad news. Genethia Hayes remarked at a recent gathering of concerned black citizens that the reason black students are getting such short shrift is due to the very fact that nobody's watching, or nobody wants to. The new century will shortly determine whether those words prophesy a different and difficult course, or if our newest school board member will be reduced to singing the same old song.

MAN AND SUPERWOMAN

December 2001

One of the great peeves of my adult life has been an underdeveloped understanding of the phrase *giving back*. Black people place a particular, non-negotiable emphasis on giving back—though how much we actually do it is highly debatable—and the older I got and the more certain I grew of its importance, the less clear it became. How to give back? When? Who best to give back to, and how much to give? As the millennium closed out with so many leaks sprung in the dike of social progress, any spot you might try to plug up with good intentions hardly seemed worth the effort. Sending checks to charity was too passive, giving change to the occasional homeless person—who was black too often for comfort—too easy. Yet none of this dampened my yen to do.

Part of what drove my altruism, paradoxically, was the prospect of being a heroine, if only for a day—a comic-strip savior of the Wonder Woman variety. I had a latent, never-quite-realized ambition to act and, as years passed, an increasing jones for a live audience; as a writer I could argue that I performed on the page, but I knew that in writing, unlike acting, the real performance—the soul-baring, naked-emotion stuff—was done in isolation. I wanted my performance witnessed publicly by people who were likely to be impressed. I needed applause, questions, fixed looks—not letters to the editor. So I decided to teach, something I had done in the past rather halfheartedly, but something that did allow for performance.

Through a program called PEN in the Classroom, I secured a position conducting a ten-week writing workshop at Jefferson High School deep in South Central. I picked Jefferson in part because it had the greatest need, but also because of its peculiar but emblematic history: once revered for the education it afforded black students in segregated times, now, decades into post-segregation, it had become a symbol of what had gone terribly wrong in inner-city schools. In Jeff's faded but distinct Art Deco foyer were framed photographs of famous grads like Ralph Bunche, Dexter Gordon, Dorothy Dandridge. The place was full of ghosts and retained an eloquence so weary it could barely stand—an apt setting for whatever performances I might have in me.

On the first day of the workshop, I played the cheery, confident professional, a low-rent Wonder Woman swooping down from enchanted Hollywood to spread a little magic to a neighborhood greatly in need of some. The kids were standard-issue ninth graders, roughly half black and half Latino. They were polite in a threadbare sort of way, meaning they kept snickers and running sotto voce commentary to a minimum. They had grown up with wide screens and WWF wrestling and music videos with million-dollar budgets; they had seen do-gooders in their time, and didn't need performances from the likes of me. They understood I was there to lead them in writing, though they didn't quite see the point. Though when I mentioned how much a typical reporter's starting salary was at the *L.A. Times*—$60,000 sounded about right—there were audible gasps. However many zeros they were used to seeing in the salaries of big athletes and entertainers, they were clearly unaccustomed to any such evidence of income at home.

And I noticed that poverty, despite putting everybody in the same proverbial boat, had wrought distinctly different effects. The black kids sulked in their seats, slumped, and fidgeted, talked out of turn, and though they were full of opinions and a certain pubescent energy, it had a bitter edge. It was energy that radiated a cynicism rooted not in experience but in non-experience—in what they felt was *not* going to happen, like success and college—a cynicism of dead ends, of having seen and felt the setups before, of a justifiable belief that nothing would change. The Latino kids were quieter, more contemplative, and more hopeful about their state, evidenced in the bios they wrote for the first day of class: Latinos described their neighborhood as subpar, and explained that not enough people were working. But they also felt South-Central had been unfairly stereotyped and that, unbeknown to the general public, things were looking up; the black kids said the neighborhood was subpar and left it at that. The contrast confirmed what I had long suspected—the immigrant narrative, through no intentions of its own, was supplanting the closed book that the black narrative had become. Black people had run out of frontiers of all kinds quite some time ago, and I realized it was going to be tough making a case for imagination with much of my class. For them, it was not possible to visualize or essayize their way out of hopelessness, listlessness, or a lack of direction. The best they could do was effect catharses on paper, unburden themselves in a way they probably hadn't before.

Everybody wrote excessively about boyfriends, girlfriends, first loves, and broken hearts (a pleasant surprise for me—maybe some of them couldn't dream, but they could still fall in love). They all wrote about missing parents—dead, divorced, never on the scene, or still living in Mexico—and ad hoc families, about violent or absentee fathers and about being taken care of by cousins and siblings and grandparents. They all enumerated points of faith in God, even as they doubted his game plan. They all spelled rather atrociously. The Latino kids seemed to be more accepting of their fate than the black ones, because they believed that a better fate was on the way. One girl, April, wanted very much to believe that too, but couldn't quite, and instead wrote angrily, for pages, about all the trouble she'd seen and felt obliged to carry around with her like so many books. April was dusky, slender, with elaborate braids and white sneakers and a foot that tapped the floor nervously, unthinkingly, as she sat. One day after class she followed me to the parking lot and demanded to know where I was going next.

"To work," I said.

"Work? Where's that?"

"Oh, Hollywood," I said, waving. "Over that way, off the freeway. Not very far from here." "Dang!" exclaimed April, with a curious mix of wistfulness and annoyance. "That is *far*."

Indeed it was. I felt a little surge of satisfaction in her grudging admiration—a Wonder Woman moment—then a bigger sting of conscience about coming here once a week, for one hour, rallying the troops and leaving. *Everybody* had left—that's why things were so rotten around Jeff now—although if everybody who had left in the last couple of generations came back and put in an hour once a week, things would likely not change much either. I felt at points much like I imagined April felt, gratitude and contempt for the colossal opportunity and colossal failings of history and its inadequate, insufferable creed of giving back. I bought April a birthday cake on her fifteenth birthday because she said she'd never had one. She saw me coming up the steps with the cake and the paper plates and plastic silverware and let out a whoop before I reached the landing: "You remembered!" She crowed and clapped, triumphant, much to the amusement of the other students. This was the first time I felt sure I was giving back, and it had nothing to do with writing.

The following week, emboldened, I read aloud "The Love Song of J. Alfred Prufrock." T. S. Eliot's poem had transfixed me in college; it had made majoring in English an urgent, even noble endeavor. The kids shook their heads at the more esoteric imagery, but they perfectly understood Eliot's mourning of lost civility and a new alienation that would define, and deform, the rest of the twentieth century. They appeared to understand the concept of the antihero well enough to never have questioned its existence; for them it was not a literary conceit but a daily reality. "I am an anti-hero," one black student wrote during an exercise, "because I try and get A's but I never do. But I keep trying because I know God is there."

I signed up for a second PEN workshop not so much because I was satisfied that I had given something back, but because I had found new fellowship in a very unlikely place. These kids, black and Latino, felt like friends. The experience had forced me to admit that, for all of my political and philosophical support for the betterment of the Inner City, I had written off these students many times, usually after a spasm of anger over new graffiti on my block or watching, much to my distaste, a mag-wheeled truck reverberate with rap music. I had written off the black students first. Theoretically there is no harm in merely thinking evil thoughts, but if the thoughts are racial they leech into the soul, and even if they don't inspire evil acts, they might keep you from acting at all, which in the end is the greater evil. In prompting me to act, these students were keeping me in touch with my better nature, or at least in view of it, which was more than I expected and certainly worth the weekly drive.

When I walked into the classroom this time, my heart sank: the room was full, and the students were more prepared and attentive than the first group. They were also all Latino. I felt the tug of resentment over that lost frontier, the withered chances; I felt hoodwinked. I was needed elsewhere and here I was, unable to leave, as boxed in as those black kids. With a very grown-up effort I put all that aside and started my spiel: Anybody here know what journalism is?

Over the ten weeks I was there, I developed the same affinity for this group as I had for the first; one black student eventually showed up, but that's not what made the difference. The difference was a girl who approached me shyly at the end of that first disappointing class and, with a reticence she was clearly fighting to overcome, confessed a lifelong desire to be a journalist, like me. Her name was Marta. She needed me as much as April had; she acknowledged it as readily as April could not. I quickly began looking forward to Marta, to William, to Kurt, and everybody else. Directing their imaginations sustained me as much as it did in the first class, with its increasingly rare complement of black students. I only felt pangs at times, ironically, because this group performed so well, not because they spelled any better but because they articulated dreams and wishes when I asked them to and demonstrated such willingness to try to make a leap when I requested it. They had a sense of duty to do right by dreams where their black counterparts, by and large, felt dreams had been wronged into a kind of irrelevance. The best I could assume was that any faith or optimism I encouraged would have a trickle-down effect, that everybody at Jeff would benefit from the improved outlooks of a few. History in these parts, of course, dictated otherwise.

I learned later that April had been kicked out of Jeff, as she had been kicked out of other schools. She had literally run out of places to go.

THE GLAMOROUS LIFE

October 2010

Annette Starr Hudson was one of an increasing number of stories that by 1999 I didn't want to do. Not because I didn't think they were worthy, but because they wouldn't matter. They wouldn't lead to change. By the late '90s it was evident that no new order was rising from the ashes of 1992, nothing like it, and I was getting exhausted by older people who had now lived through two major civil disturbances eager to tell me how coherent and up-and-up everything used to be, and how the riots twenty-seven years apart were a sure sign that the greatness and the sense of zooming possibility that had drawn everybody to L.A. in the beginning could never come again. The apocalypse was complete, and now everybody was rushing to get in their personal histories and postmortems before the world stopped listening altogether. Generational breakdown was a big, bitter theme. People supported the young folk in theory—they were the future, receptors of the past, etc. But beyond theory, sentiment about the young broke sharply in another direction. Much of it went something like this: if the troublemakers acculturated by hip-hop and gangsta rap could somehow disappear and leave the well-meaning among us alone, if we could strain the rogue element out of our neighborhoods like pulp, the rivers of community would run clear and we'd all become immediately visible to each other again. Everything would flow and we could get on with things. And it wouldn't be a bad thing if the parents of the young disappeared too, because Lord knows they didn't have home training, and it was their generation that had started messing things up in earnest after the '6os, with their righteous self-absorption and no idea how to parent, no idea what to pass on but having kids anyway.

These things weren't said exactly, or in one sentence or one sitting. But as the twentieth century started folding up its tents and taking account, resentment and a bit of panic crowded the pitches I heard about the old glory, about the buildings that used to stand and the classy stores that were just as good, relatively, as the white folks had, the programs black folks used to work for that used to help so many. People insisted that if I wrote those things, the world could really know what had taken place in L.A., and maybe then they'd see the light and turn toward it, and we could all turn for home.

I was very doubtful about that, but I was open to stories. I had been partial to stories since I was a little girl and devoured fables and Greek myths and picture books and fairy tales; the stories I wrote now for newspapers about ordinary people loomed as large to me as tales about gods and monsters, because they were characters trying in their modest ways to bend brutal cosmic forces to serve their own vision of goodness, or a vision of something else. I made heroes or antiheroes out of everyone, and every remembrance about the fallen kingdom of black glory was a clean page on which to write another chapter of a great, tragic-leaning narrative I thought of as a black American version of the Mahabharata. It was our history extending infinitely into space—how we came, and were still coming to be. I was a scribe for a bible nobody could imagine was being written, and that was the secret joy of what I did. Reporting was a pedestrian, almost undercover word for bearing witness and making that witnessing mean something much more than twenty column inches on a Sunday, with a photo.

But by 1999, narrative and the whole enterprise of story and witnessing were becoming tedious. I was doing it in a vacuum. People were still interesting, and they were glad for the attention, and I was still glad to give it. But the stories didn't advance the big narrative enough. They didn't advance *me* enough, as a journalist or as a fellow black citizen in a city where advancement was always promised to be around the next corner or beyond the next groundbreaking. I was tired of expecting, of craning my neck. I needed to shift my gaze elsewhere, put down the notebook and not care for a while in order to clear my vision; the black struggles detailed to me with such indignation had all lodged together in my head and stuck there like the gorge in the belly of a snake. It seemed to me that the sheer number of stories I collected about better days condemned black people more than they could possibly enlighten them, making us all look like fools for having too easily relinquished something that was so obviously valuable. I suppose we were fools. But as a writer, it was hard to know where to go with that information, and I didn't want to be burdened with trying to articulate in a noble, neutral way both the truth and the unknown solution. Everybody came to me thinking they were shoring up that solution with their life stories and cautionary tales, but it was all right angles that added up to no shape or edges at all, just a kind of spatial dissonance that I had to stop looking at and listening to lest I go blind and deaf. I had to get out from under the crushing weight and the disorienting weightlessness of the black Mahabharata, put away the clean pages so that I could rediscover them. People continued to call me or to spontaneously offer their story at a reception or some other event, saying with sudden, glint-in-the-eye fervor at the realization I was the press: "Now here's something you should write about, if you really want to make a difference." I would take all suggestions, but I resolved to do nothing, not yet. The narrative would be extended, refined and resolved in a nominal way, like bars of blues music. But that wouldn't happen today, for weeks or even months. History had come this far dragging black-folk imbalance behind it. That imbalance was alarming, but it wasn't going anywhere: history and injustice were shackled together for good. That was clear by '99. Stories could wait.

It was at this point that I agreed to meet Annette Starr Hudson, an old person with a glorious and allegedly instructive past. Was there any other kind? My mission had flagged to the point that I was sulking more than a little bit because my subjects seemed not to reciprocate my interest in them, not really. Maybe I had just started to notice. Of course, it wasn't *their* job to write stories, it was mine, but still—I was somehow missing appreciation or acknowledgment by the elders for my efforts. I felt like a hack, a soldier duped into fighting a barely justified war I had no hope of winning. But on this one I couldn't say no. It wasn't Annette who wanted to meet me, it was her intermediary, my older sister Kelly. She had met Annette in a chance encounter near her office and almost immediately befriended her, taken her to breakfast and the like. She swiftly moved on to evening and weekend outings with Annette, bought her crab cakes, did some errands. In the process of all this my sister found out that Annette had once been a significant black-community person in her day, in the '50s and '60s, and now she was living in a senior apartment complex south of downtown, near the University of Southern California. It was close to the a.m.e. church that had built it, a new brushed-steel-and-industrial-carpet kind of place touted at its opening in early 1992 as an important step forward for the community, for *us*, a coming together of spirit and purpose in a city that at the time a few months away from the fires of April. Kelly told me Annette lived alone, was single with no children. Years ago, when she first came to L.A., she'd lived on the same street as an aunt and uncle of ours, and knew the whole family (L.A. is a much smaller town than people imagine). She had been married, but the husband, or husbands, were long gone.

I nodded at this report, pleasantly surprised by the family connection, but overall I felt little except a kind of impatience—this particular glory tale was nice but familiar. For her part, Kelly was clearly fighting an impulse to feel sorry for Annette, but knew vaguely that that was too reductive a feeling for a woman she had just described as important, so she said instead that I ought to meet her. "Maybe for a story, you know," she said brightly, as if struck by a new idea. "Could really be something there." Again I nodded, because she was probably right, certainly right, but I was irritated by the suggestion, like a bear being poked out of its winter sleep with food that it doesn't need and won't need for some time. Kelly didn't see my irritation, or ignored it. What could be more beneficial to all parties involved than a story? What couldn't it conquer?

I didn't expect her to see. I didn't understand my sister in many ways, and I especially didn't understand how she could so quickly ally herself with somebody she didn't know, even if that person was interesting and in need. Annette wasn't the first person she had befriended this way; Kelly tended to collect circumstantial relationships like coupons or lottery tickets, keep them as things of potential emotional value that could pay off big at some point. Her openness with strangers fascinated and appalled me. I wasn't a gambler, and I was always wary of losing my privacy against my wishes. I admired my sister's capacity for empathy but guarded my own limits; I talked to people as a vocation, not as a hobby, and though I had nothing against seeing them again, I didn't want them to infiltrate my life. My sister's life, on the other hand, was somewhat porous and exposed to the elements, prone like water to taking the form of whatever or whoever she happened to be next to. Not that we have nothing in common. We both smile big and talk fast, which makes people think we're more alike than we are. Growing up, we weren't exactly close, and her overtures to me as an adult often came in the form of suggestions for people I might use in my stories. It was our intimacy, her offering. I didn't decline, mostly because I had nothing to offer on my own, so I almost always said yes to the overtures, at least to the possibilities. But I was weary; I didn't say when I'd meet Annette. Maybe a Sunday. It took me weeks to make good on that.

Annette received me with visible impatience. She lived in a small, square apartment in the complex on Adams Boulevard near Hoover Street, close to the Interstate 10. The building was antiseptically clean and cheery, with shrubbery and security and everything that people in the neighborhood lacked, especially seniors. Everything the church had promised. Annette hated it; it was one of the first things she told me. "Honey, I got to get out of here," she said as I stood in the apartment's tiny foyer. "God! I used to have a real big place, so many nice things. This is nothing." She waved an apologetic hand at the kitchenette and walked, stiff-legged, in the other direction. Annette was petite and cinnamon-colored. One forearm was in a steadying cast, the result of a mild stroke. She wore a tasteful but dramatic kimono-like print robe and a short, gamine haircut (a wiglet now, she confessed later) that was the same color as her skin. The wall in the foyer was lined with plaques, the usual assortment of congratulations and proclamations from politicians and civic leaders and media representatives commemorating Annette for a job well done. Familiar. And something else on the wall: a giant oil portrait of Annette from the shoulders up, a close-up that can only be described as Hollywood. In the painting Annette was young, but had a sober look; her face tilted at coquettish angle, and her eyes, slightly closed, looked dreamy. Her red lips flirted with a smile. Beyond the painting and the foyer was a living room with a couple of coffee tables cluttered with framed photos of Annette in evening gowns, the short hair chicly swept to one side; she was posing with Judy Garland, Duke Ellington, Tom Bradley. Annette had known a lot of famous people, and had considered herself one of them. Maybe she was a community builder with a well-worn story about how things had gone south from the good days, but she was also a star, a fact embedded in her name. That was mostly who she was. She didn't need me to tell the world this story. Nor, in her mind, was the story over.

The freeze in me thawed a bit, and I became genuinely curious. Over the course of the next several hours I learned that Annette was part activist, part Zelig, part Bay Area diva (she once worked as a Lena Horne look-alike for a modeling agency) who had made history by founding the first known charm school for black teenagers in Oakland in the 1950s. Before that, she had been the first black makeup artist in the Bay Area for Merle Norman Cosmetics, the company that pioneered the whole notion of makeovers and the right of all women to embrace glamour for its own sake. Annette transposed that idea to the charm school, which she dubbed Annette's Studio of Transformation. The idea was that young black people learning social graces and shoring up their sense of personal worth could overcome their pariah status in society at large, or, barring that, overcome it in their own heads. Her students learned the art of comportment for themselves and for the sake of a world that assumed they were inherently too crude and undiscriminating a race to ever truly have class. Annette was determined that they break through such thinking. She was light-skinned and knew better than most that racist sentiments fluctuated in direct proportion to skin shade and hair texture; in our conversation she said to me, with the directness of another age, that because of those sentiments she always paid particular attention to the "black ones."

I bristled at that but couldn't condemn it. Annette was right. It struck me as very poignant or very banal that black youth in California studied social graces in a quest for the most rarefied sort of equality—learning as well as white folks which fork to use for a salad, how to ask the opposite sex out on a first date—when black people in the South at the time had to drink water in the park out of broken spigots, find the back door to places like movie houses where there was no use for, or even knowledge about, proper silverware. But manners to Annette were not just manners. They were a metaphor for the most crucial but least quantifiable social advantages—good standing and the public's high regard—that black people did not have and that civil rights demands could not touch. If Annette's studio could not dispense these advantages, it could at least help articulate a desire for them. The studio gave speech lessons, posture instruction and synchronized-movement classes that produced something Annette rapturously called a "movement choir," which she demonstrated by sweeping one arm out and over her head in slow arc, like a ballerina. "Oh honey, it was beautiful," she said wistfully. "We were really something, boy I tell you."

Annette's reputation was such that an Arkansas chapter of the NAACP approached her about counseling the nine black Little Rock students who in 1957 were experiencing more than the normal share of teenage angst, to put it mildly. Maybe because what she was doing seemed less ridiculous in California, which was racially repressed but not quite as burdened with the vicious traditions of the South, Annette never went to Little Rock.

In the '50s, success for black students generally meant marrying well or learning a trade. But in the '60s the definition expanded to include college degrees, activism, and political appointments. Annette took triumph in any form. In her living room she carefully unfolded a newspaper clipping, a yellowed photo of a disabled black boy seated next to a canvas on the floor, painting with his feet—one of her students. "Oh honey," Annette said glowingly, "he was *something* else."

She decided that day we were friends, much like she had done with my sister. "My babies!" she declared when I left, like she'd found a last missing piece of something she'd been searching for but hadn't recognized until I turned up. I didn't resist because there seemed no reason to, not yet. I was almost flattered to be somebody else's discovery—to be a plot point in somebody else's story rather than one I was writing. A nice reversal. But Annette had expectations, and they weren't modest. She started calling me on the phone, more frequently than my friends in high school ever did, to talk or to vent about being old (another thing she hated) or to reproach me about not returning the last call as promptly as I might have. She was a grandmother, a girlfriend, a frantic new lover—where were you, why didn't you get back? She sulked openly and didn't suffer excuses.

To my own surprise, I liked Annette and didn't mind her demands; maybe I needed them. I liked her contradictions, starting with the fact that here was a woman who had taught delicacy, subtlety, and balance—she had actually made students walk with books on their heads—who was blunt and often abrasive. I wasn't sure if this was her nature or if she felt she had no time to waste because she was in her '80s now and the world was getting no better, or at best had gone stagnant. The abrasiveness was anxiety about all the things that needed to be done still for the race, all the justice not yet realized, and how the hell could that happen now? What would it take? We shared the same questions, the same fatigue. Annette's discontent also had an element of vanity that I appreciated: things were still ugly, and she hated ugly more than anything. Hated that she'd lost the mystique of beauty and promise that animated a painting that was no longer a mirror. Hated the presentation in the '90s of young black people in clothes that were either voluminous or too tight, hated talking smack, hated their own embrace of that as ordinary and nothing to challenge. Complacency about ugly was screwing things up more than they were already screwed up, Annette said, and honey, that was saying a lot.

Then there was the rehabilitation of Annette herself. After years of being in one spotlight or another she wanted the attention back, though not really the journalistic kind —that was too workaday. She wanted a boyfriend. In her mind that was reasonable. I had just gotten rid of mine, a mistake who had gone on ten years before drifting away for good, and she eagerly proposed that we go in search of men together. I was amused and then, when I realized she wasn't kidding, curious. What would that look like? I could see her casting about for a new beginning in her life, trying to mark a new stage rather than concede to a final one, and the man quest would help matters. She insisted her expectations in this case were modest. "I just want somebody who isn't broke down, you know," she told me. "Somebody nice, healthy, maybe got a little money. I ain't dead yet!" The money especially would be welcome; Annette had a lifelong penchant for nice things instilled by the bourgeois expectations of the Creole class—though not strictly Creole, she qualified on many counts. And she'd known my family. Though I was hardly Kelly, I tried to cater to her, lift her spirits. Once, when it was raining heavily and she claimed to have no acceptable food in the house, I drove over to deliver shrimp from a nearby Japanese takeout. I thought I was being heroic, maybe even easing the cosmic racial injustice a bit. Annette opened the Styrofoam box and fingered the contents warily, tightened her mouth. "You call that shrimp?" she said sourly. I was taken aback. The gesture only reminded her of what she didn't have, rubbing raw the fact that the work she had been so passionate about had brought her some renown, but no riches.

Annette and I agreed that the 1990s had been a shit time for black folk, despite its material comforts for so many. It was bewildering. Annette said she liked Bill Clinton in one way: he was more sympathetic to black people for sure, a Southerner from Arkansas to boot. But what had he done, really? Why did it feel as though Republicans were running things and Clinton was smiling at us from a distance? Race progress had become a well-oiled show, and our people were suffering or suffocating beneath the curtain that had dropped on us like lead somewhere in the '70s and hadn't lifted more than a few inches since. Everybody danced now in front of the curtain and performed or paid lip service to justice and equality, including all the elected officials who had praised Annette over the years and been so kind and given her framed proclamations and certificates. Annette was pissed about all of it, starting with the decay she saw in her neighborhood, which the apartment complex, thinking it was doing her a favor, fenced off. Annette was an idealist, a diva at times, but she had no use for isolation. She said that young people in the streets looked more abandoned and unconsidered today than they had in the '50s when they were legally kept out of things.

"Diversity!" She spat out the word so hard, the teeth shifted in her mouth. "Everybody says they like diversity and such and such, they want it and all that, but that's a lie! A boldfaced lie! Honey, we've gotten too good at lying about color. And now we don't know what we really think about so many things because we fool ourselves." She knew something about lies and self-delusion. She had been badly mistreated by her first husband, a good-looking man who was also a brute. Her real compass was her uncle Henry Starr, a well-regarded jazz singer who had inspired her early, after her mother's death; she had figured she had talent, too, and that it would be applauded and known. That was the glory she wanted for herself, and later for other Negro children who, unlike her, were much too ready to be consigned to shadows. Children who couldn't conceive of themselves as exceptional, who couldn't see the point of standing up straight and looking the world in the eye and wouldn't have, if Annette hadn't put books on their heads. That was her fight, making them believe not that they were worthy — that was too small — but extraordinary.

Annette hated being old, oh honey. It was a big part of ugly. It was not what she signed up for or what she ever expected. Old age also meant advancing invisibility, which to Annette was a death more incomprehensible than nonexistence. She sighed at the thought with a resignation I rarely saw. Honey, she said after a moment, have some kids. At least one. Promise me that. I nodded noncommittally, smiling. I would do no such thing. I knew that besides seeing me as a girlfriend, Annette was starting to see me as the daughter who might have been — I was prickly, restless, driven to be something larger than myself but easily distracted by trifles like hair color and shopping. I hadn't known Annette long, but she was thinking that I might be the legacy she hoped was out there. Kelly was willing and helpful, a godsend in many ways, but she was not that. I was.

In the spring of '99, I met a man who swiftly evolved into my fiancé. Annette was thrilled by the whole story and called me several times a day for details. I didn't care. We took Annette to lunch down in the Marina, where she and Alan could be properly introduced and Annette could be served the kind of shrimp she would eat. Afterward she said I was damn lucky to have found him. "He has a good heart, honey," she pronounced, a little knowingly, as if she'd had a hand in our meeting. At our wedding on a brilliant day in October, in the first year of the new millennium, she sat in the front row in a wheelchair that she was by this time using almost routinely. She was more confident than ever that she'd find somebody, certain that now that I had a husband with a wide circle of male friends, he could make a match. Why not? He was a high school teacher, and that's what she had been in her life, more or less. In the meantime Annette had another idea. She wanted Alan to let her come to his history class and "speak to the kids" because, she said adamantly, the world was as dire as she'd ever seen it, and she wanted to minister to the bad feeling and dissatisfaction she knew was out there, thick as smoke, among the young people. Ministering is what she had been known for, and what she was determined to be known for again. My husband liked Annette enough to agree to it, though he told me that he frankly expected little from such a visit except the admonitions of an old woman. He would tell his students to be courteous.

I accompanied Annette that day to class, of course. I was happy for her but fearful it would all go awry, fall over, or not go at all. I was relieved to be proven wrong. Annette had no speeches, no grand stories to tell or advice to dispense. She sat on a stool in front of the class, leaned forward heavily on her cane and confessed in an earnest, scratchy voice that she had no idea what was wrong with people these days or what to think about the days ahead—did they? The students were startled to see an adult, an old one at that, not directing them but laying bare vulnerability and an exasperation with the world in a way that was almost adolescent. History didn't matter because all of its successes didn't square with how things were now, and she wanted to know why the hell not. Now was what mattered, and she'd expected more, deserved more. They *all* did. The sophomores were incredulous: instead of exuding nostalgia, Annette was seething with discontent. Not about the past, but about now.

They dropped their polite indifference and started volunteering thoughts on the world's injustices and heartbreaks. One girl, plain and overweight, was so overcome with even having the floor that she broke into tears. "It's okay, honey," Annette called out sympathetically from the front of the room, thumping her cane for emphasis. "Go ahead, let it out. I don't blame you a bit. Exactly how I feel! It's nothing to be ashamed of." When that class was done, my husband invited her to stay for another. The distraught girl got Annette's number and ended up calling her at home later.

Annette was terribly excited; something had cracked open. Here was the new beginning she sought, the entry into a new age. She phoned me repeatedly, bubbling over with new ideas: she wanted to take her act on the road, book regular gigs, launch a mobile School of Transformation for the new century. But as her sense of destiny soared, her health took a dive. She didn't have a single disease, just too many conditions for her body to overcome: diabetes, stroke aftermath, age itself. She still longed for a man. She complained more loudly, gripped my arm tighter as she walked fewer and fewer steps. She stopped walking. Over the course of the next months the cane gave way entirely to a wheelchair, the wheelchair to a bed. Then the bed to a curtained spot at a euphemistically named health center that was really a hospice. She lost the ability to speak; doctors said it was due to diabetic shock. I thought that Annette didn't have the energy, finally, to recuperate and put herself back in play one more time. It was simply too much.

But the fact she had no fight left didn't mean she accepted loss. Not at all. Loss was one more thing to hate. In the army-like hospice bed she lay thin, nearly bald, one hand curled tightly under her chin like the claw of a bird, equally annoyed and terrified of what was coming next. *I don't want to do this*, her eyes said. *This is not it at all!* She wasn't done. I replied with my eyes: *Yes, I know. Sucks.* Not comforting but true, and Annette, for all her espousing of the good life and denouncing of how things were, preferred the truth.

She died at the hospice on Fairfax in 2002, on a day as brilliant as my wedding day and as full of promise. I miss her cracked voice, her diatribes, her battered but unburied plans for the future. I never wrote her story. I wonder what she would have thought of the now, a decade later, with Obama in office and the end of the world more clear and present than either of us anybody could have imagined. Oh honey, she'd say. This is really something else.

THE BOY OF SUMMER

November 2002

Earlier this year, walking among rows of student artwork as a juror in an annual countywide competition, I was stopped in my tracks by a portrait of a pitcher straddling a mound. Baseball was one of my great adolescent loves.

For innings and months and languorous seasons at a time, the Dodgers spoke to everything that made me increasingly delirious but that I could hardly get words around: sun, air, group license to scream, the incrementally exquisite thrill of the wait between a pitch and a ball in play, the liberty to construct a hero out of nothing more than the way he tossed his helmet to the grass or squinted resignedly up into the outfield light. So it was that in a collection that boasted some elaborate wrought iron and ceramic sculpture, I was taken with this modest piece, tissue paper and watercolor in a cardboard frame propped against a wooden school chair. The pitcher, done in bold black strokes with his throwing arm cocked back and his brow set, floated in an unlikely sea of pastels. He was moving yet suspended, plain but as fancifully colored as sherbet, a quirky but lovely irresolution of doing and dreaming in the context of baseball.

I looked on the back of the portrait for contact information, and for a brief explanatory essay about the piece that was required in this competition (as a judge I didn't wholly agree with the requirement—art should and must speak for itself—but in this case I hoped the student had complied). The artist was Deandre Connors, a sophomore at Locke High School. His essay was really more a long caption that said he chose the subject not because he played or even watched baseball, but because he was seven feet tall and was already weary, at sixteen, of the assumption that he was a basketball player, or that he would become one. "So I drew baseball because I'm imagining what else I might do, or be," he wrote. "But I don't like it much. Maybe I'll like it better someday. But I don't think so."

I observed, as I did each year, that there were many other noteworthy pieces in the exhibit but precious few other entries from Locke, or any other inner-city schools. I tagged Deandre's work with a purple Post-It and hoped a few other judges would follow suit, so that it might make it to the next round of competition. It didn't; the game was fierce. On an impulse I went back to the pitcher and copied down Deandre's name and number, and the number of his art teacher at Locke. I would call and offer to buy it and in that way Deandre would know that his effort, and his significant representation of his school and its woefully underrepresented ilk, had not gone unappreciated.

I phoned him at home. At first his mother was guarded—*what* do you want with my son?—then slowly impressed. I talked to Deandre, who was friendly and cheery and didn't seem nearly as surprised to hear from someone like me as his mother was. He said he'd been doing art ever since he was a kid. He agreed to sell me the baseball piece before I even got the request fully out; when I asked if a hundred dollars was alright, he exclaimed, "Sure!" Could I come to Locke and pick it up next week? "Sure!" Could I meet him fifth period, in his art teacher's room? "Yes, sure!" he said once again. "I'll see you then."

But I didn't see him then. I showed up on the appointed Thursday and announced to the folks in the main office that I was there to see one of their very talented students, that I had a very good purpose, and so on. I got indifference and a few baleful stares in return. "You can't see any student here unless your name is on a list," said one woman with frighteningly long nails, pointing an index finger at a piece of paper with some difficulty. "Sorry, ma'am. Those are the rules." I asked to see the art teacher, Mr. Acuña, and after a few more stares somebody summoned him on the phone. Well into sixth period he came to the office, wearing a paint-stained apron and a distracted air. "Sorry about this," he muttered. "You'd think this school would be happy about you being here . . . Come next week and ask to see me. We're having an art show, and you can meet Deandre." I said that would be fine, that it was no inconvenience, that I didn't live very far away and that Deandre likely didn't know or remember the visitor rules. Mr. Acuña looked at me a little queerly and said, "Deandre's in special ed."

He didn't say anything else, and I didn't ask for anything else. But I felt my good deed immediately pucker around the edges—who was I meeting exactly, and what did I have to prepare for? Driving over to Locke High from Inglewood, where I lived, was sobering enough; it was not in fact that far east, as I'd told Mr. Acuña, but Manchester is a thoroughfare of several planets, and at San Pedro, east of the Harbor Freeway, it collapses into both Mars and Pluto—an unlivable molten core right in the center of the civic galaxy, and a frozen sphere millions of miles away from the center of anything. I worried about Deandre, whatever he turned out to be, thriving in such a place. This was his home, the field where he should have advantage over time, the sky that should expand infinitely with his wishes. As I drove west, I imagined how it must look to Deandre, and felt vicariously hemmed in.

The next week at Locke, a student met me at the office to take me to the art show. She led me across a big, razed quad, through a cafeteria, over a worn stage, past the gulf of a backstage that was strewn with odds and ends that looked not like remnants of props or costumes, but generic stuff cleared out of somebody's house months ago, maybe years, and laid at the side of a curb. Finally we came to the last place we could come to. The art show, lacking a room, was set up under an outside tent. Everything was carefully arranged, and mostly everything displayed the same potent simplicity and verve that had attracted me to Deandre's work. He saw me and stood up from where he was sitting behind a table—unfolded himself, really, like a crane rising from a nest. He was indeed seven feet, a height that may seem normal in professional basketball but isn't in real life. He dressed in jeans and a windbreaker. He wore glasses. His hand swallowed up mine entirely when he shook it; one of his hands appeared a bit crooked, unusable, but not too much. He took me to his baseball portrait, which was arranged among other pieces of his, and said proudly that since we talked, another person had offered to buy it. "It's a very good piece," I said as seriously as I could without being patronizing.

I gave him an envelope with a note card of thanks and congratulations on his artistry, and, of course, his money. He graciously didn't open it, but he did admit he'd been looking forward to my coming because he needed to buy clothes for some upcoming events—graduation, a dance. I gave him my business card, told him to keep in touch about his work. He said he would.

I had the piece decently framed, and now it hangs in my living room with the prints of Klimt and van Gogh, and the jazz photos. That it is the only original piece of art in there is deeply and repeatedly satisfying. And last month I drafted Deandre's pitcher as a kind of patron saint of the long-thwarted Angels as my husband and I watched them battle their way daily to their first World Series title. Fans in Anaheim proudly say that now, many more people in the world know the names of their players and where they live. Thanks to the magic of baseball and to a victory of a much more ordinary but no less self-illuminating kind, I can say the same thing about Manchester and San Pedro.

UNSOCIAL STUDIES

THE REAL LESSONS OF HAMILTON HIGH

May 1999

The Hamilton High School story is not what you think it is. It is not what I thought it was. It is melodrama that can only be described in epic terms, so here goes:

This is a Greek tragedy playing out in the furthest reaches of the Western world—at a modest but comely red-brick high school in the hinterlands of West Los Angeles, just off the Santa Monica Freeway. This is a story riddled with ironies, some of which are infuriating but most of which are profoundly saddening, because they illustrate how real issues can be obfuscated by people who wrap themselves in the mantle of reform but who actually advance very small, and often poisonously small-minded, agendas. This is about no leaders. This is about the utter failure of collective reason in an age of fevered individualism. This is about the powder keg of racial frustration that keeps blowing up at odd and seemingly inappropriate moments because, thirty-five years after it relinquished its last legal claims as enforcer of a social and economic apartheid that was birthed in slavery, white America is content to live in a state of perilous ignorance about the persistent inequities of black and white. This is about the Faustian price black America often pays for being heard, about the ill-conceived celebrity of a justifiable rage. This is not about us, and all about Us. This is about a white friend living on the Westside who immediately and fearfully inquired upon hearing the rudiments of this story, "Is there going to be a riot?" This is about a flashpoint of brilliant possibility colliding with banal disbelief.

This is L.A.

I. The Big Issue

In April, I got a call from a coalition of black parents who were eager to meet with me to discuss some distressing incidents of racism at Hamilton High School, which also houses two magnet schools, humanities and music. I didn't know anything about the story beyond what I'd read in the April 17 L.A. Times. Some students and parents had staged a protest on campus against some magnet teachers they felt were racist and were exacerbating a separate and unequal educational situation. At a school that was once upon a time largely white and was now largely minority—chiefly black and Latino—minority students were doing markedly worse academically than their white counterparts. This has become an all-too-common story that has prompted alarmingly little concern. The parents were particularly irate about the fact that the magnets, which had more white students, had more resources and more access, and consistently outperformed the main school on standardized tests—no accident, they said. Money and success follow white children; low expectations and dismal academic performance dog minority children (of course, minority students in the magnets performed markedly better than their main-school counterparts, too, but I put that fact aside for the moment).

This summary sounded reasonable to me, and I was glad that black people were publicly advancing a cause that never got enough headlines or generated enough moral outrage. It was time. I vaguely recalled my younger sister, a Hamilton magnet alumna, tangling with her teachers back in the '80s, complaining that she and her friends were singled out, and getting suspended once—had racism played itself out even then?

Probably. I would bring this story to light.

I met with the parents in the Crenshaw district, in an office building on a tree-shaded block of Leimert Park Village. Wil Wade, chairman of the African American Parent Coalition for Education Equity (AAPCEE), led the discussion around a long conference table with five other parents and two students. He wore a business suit and clasped his hands together on top of the table; he didn't lean back in his chair once. The parents began by saying they had called me because they didn't want the real issue here—the systemic inequities of public education, the concerted miseducation of black and Latino children—to get lost in the furor over the teachers. They pointed out not only that the magnets (40 percent white) were glaringly better than the main school (90 percent minority), but that minority students in the main school were not being tracked in college-prep courses—advanced placement and honors classes seemed to have predetermined white populations. In a post-affirmative-action world, this was unacceptable.

"The issue isn't race, it's equity," explained Wade. "The white parents are afraid that we want to take money away from the magnets, but that's emotional. That's not true. My daughter's in the [music] magnet school. But I'm not interested in only doing for myself, getting mine and being done with it. We need to make sure these issues are addressed for the benefit of all the kids, all the generations coming behind."

So far, so good. This AAPCEE was actually a sister chapter to the first one, which was started at Westchester High by black parents who had similar concerns about a school that shares Hamilton's demographics and white-flight patterns. The parents stressed that the majority of teachers at Hamilton were good and dedicated, but that there were an influential few who were poisoning the well with their racist and cavalier attitudes. These teachers were aiding and abetting institutional racism, and eliminating them was a crucial first step toward the coalition's ultimate goal of bringing some balance to the system. The chief offenders were two humanities magnet teachers, Gregg Beytin and Alan Kaplan.

Beytin, who taught journalism and government, had allegedly thrown a chair and cursed at two black students, who voiced complaints; he was subsequently reassigned to a nearby administrative "cluster office." The Beytin incident is what sparked the April protest, according to the *Times* story. I asked for details. "We don't know exactly what happened," Wade said, almost casually. He deferred to a student, Kwabene Haffar, who said that according to what he knew, Beytin did not throw a chair; he wasn't entirely sure if Beytin's outburst was aimed specifically at the black students. It was here that I felt the first stirrings of doubt—if Beytin acted in this instance like a hothead but not a racist, orchestrating an anti-racism protest around the incident seemed rather manipulative. I was down with the general cause, the big issue, but realized I had no fix on the teacher issue yet.

The discussion moved swiftly on to Alan Kaplan, the teacher for whom the parents reserved most of their animus. In his social science and American history classes, Kaplan addressed racially inflammatory topics. Haffar said he transferred out after only one day because Kaplan posed the question, Why is it no one sympathizes with the slavemasters? The most egregious of his lessons, the one that set AAPCEE in motion against him last June, centered on the school's gospel choir. The parents said they had to do battle with the Student Improvement Committee to secure funding for the choir, which was led by a non-credentialed teacher named Fred Martin. The funding was granted, and the next day Kaplan held a discussion in his classes on the dynamics of interest-group politics, using the gospel choir as a model. This lesson, the parents asserted, was one of many ways in which Kaplan degraded black kids. He also co-opted the affections of his pet students—the "talented tenth," Wade said derisively—and cowed the others, then set the two groups against each other. Kaplan was not only racist, he was facilitating nothing less than intraracial warfare on campus. He had to go.

The coalition had been pressuring the school district for his transfer, and that of several other magnet teachers, since last summer. But the district was not cooperating, and the "good ol' boy network," as Wade put it, was still in place. The parents wouldn't rest until it had been broken up. They had called me because I am black and wrote extensively about black issues, and they had confidence in my ability to do this story justice. I shifted slightly in my seat. I rubbed my eyes. I suggested for the sake of argument that Kaplan and company had many students and parents supportive of them who were black, perhaps as many as were sitting around this table. What could I assume about that?

Wade nodded knowingly. "He brainwashes people," he said. "They're afraid to speak up. There are people who don't want to be on the front line. They may look like us, talk like us. But they're not us."

II. Fear and Loathing

Magnet schools were created in the late '70s as a response to a federal court order to desegregate public schools across the nation. By law, they can be no more than 40 percent white; students must apply for admission and are chosen by a combination lottery and point system. In L.A., as elsewhere, after mandatory busing proved a political and practical disaster, magnets were ushered in as the most viable alternative to forced integration, though they were not without their critics.

The dissension over Alan Kaplan and his role as guiding light of Hamilton's humanities magnet has a long and turbulent history. Since he joined the magnet in 1982, black parents, faculty, and administrators had grumbled sporadically about his confrontational teaching style, his push for college-level work from high school students and, most of all, his insistence on dissecting the roots of racism as a way of fully understanding American history and the American gestalt. Gregg Beytin, who's also been at the magnet for much of its eighteen-year life, had a similar philosophy and teaching methodologies; he and Kaplan were chief architects of the magnet's "whole life" approach and its integrated course work. But it was Kaplan who first raised hackles, in 1987, when he shared a lesson with other Hamilton teachers about the impact of racism on the test scores of minority students; one of the readings for the lesson was an article on black test scores written by Salim Muwakkil, who cited a group of education experts who were exclusively African-American.

Three black teachers in the room promptly began complaining that Kaplan had no right to be teaching anything about racism because he was white, and as far as they knew he might have some nefarious plan to destroy the minds of black children. Beytin eventually came to Kaplan's defense; the other teachers later petitioned the principal for Kaplan's and Beytin's removal, but ultimately failed. Still, both teachers were investigated exhaustively before school officials declared there was no evidence of racism. And the die was cast: Kaplan and Beytin, and by extension the entire humanities magnet, had been branded a hotbed of racist and professionally elitist activity. That Hamilton's magnets were fast acquiring national reputations as public schooling that worked only seemed to stoke the fires of discontent; faculty divisions widened. After eighteen years at Hamilton, Beytin says there are black teachers on campus with whom he has yet to have conversations.

The anti-Kaplan camp found an unofficial leader in Evelyn Mahmud, a black assistant principal who started out as a teacher in the humanities magnet and over the years became increasingly identified with black dissatisfaction. (Mahmud did not return repeated phone calls or respond to faxed questions for this story. Neither would anyone in the coalition agree to be photographed.) According to colleagues and parents, Mahmud was philosophically against magnet schools, which she regarded as havens for white students, and came to regard Kaplan as a standard-bearer of what was wrong with them. She remarked to more than one teacher that she thought Kaplan was racist and that she didn't approve of his dating black women. Eventually she became allied with the parents who would form AAPCEE, and last May sided with them over the issue of renewing funding for the school's gospel choir. The choir was funded annually by the Student Improvement Committee, a democratic body consisting of parents, teachers, and students that divvied up money for everything from security guards to music-magnet aides. A straw poll indicated that the choir might lose some or all of its $13,000. When the parents got wind of the poll, they stood up at the committee meeting and loudly decried anyone who opposed the gospel choir, an entirely black group and a symbol of main school ethnic pride, as racist; if moneys were not approved, they said, they would call out the NAACP. One black student on the committee said she felt so physically threatened by the choir faction that she abstained from voting altogether. Funding for the choir passed by a landslide.

The following day, as Kaplan was teaching his political-action lesson based on the choir-funding vote, Mahmud walked unannounced into his classroom to observe; not forty-five minutes later she walked out. The subsequent complaints she made to principal David Winter about the lesson precipitated the formation of AAPCEE and a full frontal attack on Hamilton's inequities. The coalition sent out a three-page letter detailing its grievances, which consisted mainly of charges against Kaplan and a short paragraph about low minority-student achievement and college-prep tracking. The charges against Kaplan ranged from the general to the gossipy to the frankly loony: he "demeans children"; he "tells students and faculty that he can't teach non-magnet students"; he often "talks about his private life in class and his preference for dating black women"; he "refers to himself with gang names such as 'Mule-Dawg' . . . All African-American and Latino students are *not* in gangs. Is this what he should be teaching in school?" The letter was sent to school district and to elected officials and every black activist group in the city—including the NAACP, the Brotherhood Crusade, and the Urban

League—though not to Kaplan himself. (Interestingly, AAPCEE's contention that Kaplan denigrated the gospel choir by calling it a "social impact group" is self-referencing: on the last funding request form that Mahmud submitted, she wrote that the chief beneficiaries of the choir are "students at risk.") The letter prompted two separate investigations of the charges, which went on for months and were ultimately dismissed as groundless.

Undaunted, the coalition mailed out another letter in November, this time to the entire Hamilton faculty. It praised the mostly responsible teachers, but warned against the few who "seek to use race and religious intolerance to isolate teachers from students and parents of color . . . These misguided teachers give good teachers a bad name." The letter concluded by urging teachers to join AAPCEE's cause of educational and racial equality.

The day after the April protest, before a scheduled gospel choir performance on campus, director Fred Martin alluded to it by exulting in the fact that Beytin was being punished and that the humanities magnet was finally getting its due. Those in the audience later complained to school officials about what they perceived as blatantly partisan and wildly inappropriate remarks; they demanded disciplinary action against Martin, as action had been taken against Beytin, but nothing happened. Meanwhile, AAPCEE continued to agitate for Kaplan's ouster. "It's pure McCarthyism, a witch hunt," said one black source close to the investigations who asked not to be named. "The parents probably have very viable concerns here, but their real agenda is so polluted, [the concerns] get lost. They represent the misdirection of black-power energy that strips the real issues of all credibility."

III. The Learning Curve

Kaplan and Beytin's supporters, not surprisingly, agree. But one irony among many is that they also agree with AAPCEE about the urgent need to address educational inequality at Hamilton and elsewhere—and they credit the embattled teachers with ensuring they learned that. Nor does anyone believe that Beytin should not have been disciplined for losing his temper in class, but they say that labeling the incident racist, and proof that the school is racist, was either sloppy thinking or pure opportunism. As it turns out, Beytin never threw a chair; he blew up at a white Jewish student, and principal David Winter, after discussing the incident with Beytin and others, determined that race was not a factor. Beytin had in fact been instrumental in helping to restructure the main school, establishing distinct courses of study—Communications Arts, Global Studies—as a way of giving it a magnet-like identity and setting a tenor of reform.

"I don't condone his temper, but his temper has absolutely no color line," says Winter Johnson, a senior in Beytin's government class. "I'm very outraged. I don't have a teacher, my magnet is crumbling. I totally disagree with all the allegations of racism. [Kaplan's and Beytin's] attitudes aren't always the best, but they're such great teachers. I've learned so much. They've totally revolutionized the way I think about everything. This whole thing is dumb."

Even those inclined to assign Beytin and Kaplan the greatest culpability stop short of calling them racist. "These guys can be insensitive," says Stu Bernstein, director of the district's Office of Intergroup Relations. "They could do with heavy-duty human-relations training. Race is something that we all live and breathe — that's our legacy. But I honestly don't think they're racist."

A large problem *not* discussed by the coalition is the students' self-segregation: on the quad, magnet kids tend to hang out with magnet, main school with main school. Among black students, such cliquing is more loaded, and no doubt contributes to the parents' general sense of campus inequality, though the blame for this particular inequality can hardly be laid at the feet of teachers. One recent graduate of the humanities magnet recalls her and her friends' overt derision of their main-school counterparts: "We looked down on these students as ghetto, uncultured, and unintelligent," says the alum, who asked not to be named. "The term 'original Hamilton,' which referred to the main school, was code for 'black.'"

After promising to do so, the coalition never put me in touch with dissident black students other than the two present at the Leimert Park meeting. In contrast, at a school management meeting the Monday following the protest, the outpouring of support for Beytin and Kaplan was oceanic; one ex-student testifying to their influence openly wept. Kaplan's supporters in particular are astonishing in their number, ethnic variety, and consistency of comments. When he was being threatened with removal after the gospel-choir incident last year, students circulated a "Save Kaplan" petition that garnered well over a hundred signatures in one class period, and more than a hundred letters of support arrived from parents, students, and alumni. To a person, they cited his uncompromising academic standards and intellectual rigor. He could be overly impatient, they said, withering at times and overbearing, yet it was all in the interest of getting students to challenge their lazy assumptions about the world and to think for themselves.

"He's so strict, you have no choice but to learn," says Nefertiti Takla, an eighteen-year-old humanities magnet senior. "He catches your attention by talking about the real world — racial problems, social problems. He does it all. Once in a lesson, he totally destroyed stereotypes of people, especially those of African-Americans. A lot of people take him the wrong way, if you're oversensitive or immature. If you call him a racist, you have to point to the fact that he's Jewish and he makes fun of Jews."

Kaplan got letters in Spanish, from whole families, from black and Latino students in the magnet and the main school, who claimed they had learned more about black and minority history from him than from anywhere or anyone else. They said that Kaplan is great because he doesn't just teach history or social science, he teaches the interconnectedness of everything. He examines concepts, attitudes, ideas that tether history to psychology and literature and pop culture; parents say that they began looking forward to their kids bringing lessons home so they could learn something too. Sample lines from the letters tell a formidable story: "From this painfully honest man, I have learned to search for the reasons policies are the way they are" . . . "As one of his students, I have been exposed to new ways of seeing society and its composition, without a biased mentality. Mr. Kaplan teaches in a away incomparable to any other by allowing the student to uncover thematic similarity through historic information" . . . "While I was on an interview for the Massachusetts Institute of Technology, I told the interviewer that Mr. Kaplan is the best teacher I ever had. I am a black student, a male student who knows from my experiences that Mr. Kaplan is not in the least bit racist" . . . "As an African-American male, my desire to succeed and dispel the distorted societal view of African-Americans is now considerably stronger because of Mr. Kaplan's commendable lesson plan and teaching ability." If this guy is brainwashing people, it would behoove us all to find out how he's doing it.

Many black parents and students say AAPCEE is doing some serious mau-mauing, beating everyone over the head with accusations of white oppression and creating such a charged atmosphere that no one who takes issue with them—black or white—will do so publicly. That includes such mammoth "white" entities as the teachers union and the entire school district; the only school-board member to address the Hamilton situation thus far is not Valerie Fields, who represents the Westside, but Barbara Boudreaux, who doesn't. At a recent board meeting, Boudreaux, a self-styled champion of black causes, loudly sympathized with the coalition and declared that the district must look into the possibility that black children "might be experiencing retribution from those teachers currently under investigation." Clearly, Boudreaux knew nothing save what AAPCEE had told her. With the exception of student-body president Dominique West, an African-American, the students who showed up at the board meeting to speak in support of Kaplan and Beytin were not allowed to take the podium.

The groundswell of quiet opposition to the coalition is getting less quiet, and more organized. An Internet dialogue among Hamilton alumni produced a Web site where people can log comments and join a contact list of Hamilton supporters. Lenn Kano, a twenty-six-year-old magnet alum who informed me of the site and has been tracking the situation since last year, says Beytin and Kaplan were so formative in his own life, he has no choice but to play the intellectual activist now—questioning the status quo, discerning real motives, exposing hypocrisy. "[District folks] figure if they just keep quiet, let a few heads roll, this whole thing will go away and that's worth it," says Kano, who is Japanese-American. "I hope the central issue in all this doesn't get lost, which is that there is ongoing segregation in terms of the magnet and main school. The funny thing is, Mr. Kaplan understands more about the problem than anybody in the administration."

There is a counter parent group spearheaded by Alice Wallace, who is black. Wallace has twin daughters in the magnets and says she and others are flat-out tired of being psychologically bullied by a small group that claims to represent the sentiments of most black parents at Hamilton. They are tired of the inference that because they don't wholly embrace AAPCEE, they are sellouts, whitewashes or, worst of all, infected with the disaffection of the black bourgeoisie. Wallace says what's so distressing about AAPCEE is that it rightfully claims representation on the one hand—speaking to systemic problems of blacks and Latinos—and completely exploits it on the other. Still, Wallace knows all the ramifications of publicly breaking ranks with a black group—over the issue of white teachers, no less.

"I had to do some soul-searching before I jumped in," she says. "But black parents were saying to me, 'These people [AAPCEE] are crazy!' I figured it was time for this stuff to stop. When my daughters had Kaplan, they would come home from school actually excited by what they were learning. They don't say that about too many teachers. He's cutting-edge, provocative—as a parent, I hear the things he says and sometimes think, 'Well, I might have said it differently'—but you have to respect him." Wallace says she has confronted assistant principal Evelyn Mahmud about what she sees purely as a vendetta, asked her why Fred Martin has not been disciplined for his stumping at the gospel concert. She also questions why the coalition is expending all of its energy on Kaplan and the magnets if its real fight is with institutional problems and the main school. "For them, Kaplan is the battle," says Wallace. She has settled on a name for the counter parent group, which has roughly a hundred parents and students on its roster: Reasonable Adults and Children for Education. RACE, for short. "We have to act fast," says Wallace. "The school year's almost over."

IV. The Slavemasters

Gregg Beytin says that after all the racism battles in and out of the classroom for the better part of twelve years, it's come down to this bizarre Waterloo. "I'm actually kind of glad that it broke like this, because tensions had been brewing for so long," he says. "If I cut and run now, it would be admitting defeat." Beytin is an excitable guy, glib and prone at moments to hyperbole and sweeping political allegory ("This is a little bit like fundamentalists against the Enlightenment"). Ursine and slightly rumpled, he has a clear passion for his work that is being sorely tested by all this. He wants to be back in the classroom. He says that if Alan Kaplan leaves, he will likely leave too, as will at least a dozen other teachers who are poised to put in for transfers pending the final district decision about Beytin's place at Hamilton. If he is axed, Beytin believes, the humanities magnet will fall, and status-quo education—handouts, crossword puzzles, safe, antiseptic discussions about antiseptic readings—will prevail. Beytin says that such a void of challenges is racism at its most insidious, but that is exactly what the coalition seems to want. "I'm trying to stay afloat, trying to save my school, but this will be with me the rest of my life," he says. "Being called a racist is very, very serious, and we've been soldiers in this war a long time. If they want better education for minority kids, I'm in complete agreement. If they want to say, 'That person did it,' then I say no. What infuriates me is that we are not part of the problem, but we could be part of the solution very easily. We do a better job of raising minority achievement than anyone."

Kaplan is the last one to talk here. Initially he didn't want to talk at all; he'd had his fill of allegations and misrepresentation and his words being taken out of context, plus he figured that Beytin had talked enough for the both of them. But it was odd, being the eye of this whole storm yet never once being a voice in the *Times* stories. So he talked.

He's more low-key than Beytin, more deliberate but no less intense. Once he overcomes a certain wariness, he is actually eager to talk and to throw ideas up for debate; it seems to be his second nature. He paces at points, slowly, and tugs at his goatee a lot. His voice is a little ragged—from teaching for eighteen years, from the last year of stress, from both. He grew up in the

Valley but sounds a lot like Brooklyn. "I'm not perfect," he says, shrugging. "I've made mistakes. The kids get all of me, which means they get my bad moments. Having high expectations may even be construed as racist, but social promotion—passing kids from one grade to another without demanding much of them—is more racist."

Kaplan is mad as hell, partly because his career is on the line but mostly because students might be shortchanged in the future. "Those who don't hold you accountable don't care about you," he fairly snaps. "Yes, I'm speaking to mainly black and Latino students when I say, 'It's shameful that you read four years below grade level,' but I don't single out black kids—I talk about everybody. I talk about Westside white girls who use language like 'You know, like . . .' We are elite as a magnet, but that doesn't mean we're better human beings, of course."

He recalls with some bewilderment an incident that occurred last year. Kwabene Hattar, the AAPCEE acolyte and his student nemesis, had put up posters announcing lunchtime meetings of his new black student group; the posters denounced racist teachers at Hamilton, thinly veiled allusions to Kaplan and others. Principal Winter objected to the posters, saying they were inflammatory, but Kaplan taught a lesson on the issue and concluded that Haffar had a First Amendment right to display them. Not long afterward, during an evening open house, Haffar's mother stormed into Kaplan's classroom, where he had a poster displayed. She tore it from the wall and upbraided Kaplan for stealing her son's "property" before storming out. This sort of blind resistance wounds him the most.

Reflecting on the troubles of the last year, he admits, "I contemplate leaving every day. But I owe it to the people who defend me to stay. I love my job. I don't think the [AAPCEE] parents are cynical opportunists, but I think their analyses are flawed. We're on the same path until it comes to what should be done about the problems."

Kaplan has never spoken to the coalition, which refuses to meet with him and will not agree to mediation. (Wade's explanation is a heatedly rhetorical, "Do you negotiate with a Bull Connor? Do you negotiate with an Orval Faubus?") He doesn't have much hope it will ever happen. He does hope that Hamilton will survive. "Hamilton's got it all," he says. "Race, class, underperforming black kids, reform movements, integration, white flight. We're ground zero. It happens here, or it doesn't. We're a model for the city, the nation."

V. Coda

This story did not prove to be as illuminating as I'd hoped. All the paths—expansive and narrow, splintered and righteous, clearly marked or elided by intent—did not merge into one path, or two. I wound up with more *What is this story about?* than I started out with. I lost sleep. I struggled with my own loyalties and preconceptions and sense of absolute fairness. I wondered more than once if there *is* such a thing, and decided that, like its parent notion of democracy, fairness is something we must make real for ourselves when the occasion demands it. I wondered if the coalition would make good on its promise to move on to other schools where low black and Latino achievement is entrenched—Jefferson, Locke, Jordan, Fremont, Manual Arts—and where there are no white-populated magnets to put these failings in front of television cameras and on editorial pages for a couple of weeks. I wondered if they would hold black and minority teachers and administrators as accountable for racial inequity and psychological damage as they have held these white teachers. I wondered if they would picket and circulate letters and refuse to mediate and make lists of demands. I wondered if they would invoke "our children" so vociferously and with such high purpose.

Alice Wallace doesn't think so. "The real story here," she says matter-of-factly, "is very uninteresting."

POST SCRIPT

THE COLOR OF LOVE

February 2001

Two years ago, if anyone had asked, I would have said that I would probably never marry. I had nothing against the institution, but by my middle thirties I had come to believe that the marriage I'd always imagined might never happen. I didn't find this tragic; I found it liberating. Not getting married meant absolution from a number of entanglements I could do without—a deadwood relationship, compromised living space, the halfhearted internal debate about whether to have babies. While I embraced the idea of marriage, I embraced solitude in equal measure. I found a certain elation in the prospect of a future in which I could allow my emotions and shoe-buying impulses to run free. At age thirty-seven, my desire for freedom seemed to have neatly trumped my yearning for anything, or anyone, else. And that was fine with me.

In this rare state of contentment, I met Alan Kaplan, who was forty-three and in a state of extreme discontent. We met at his house on a Sunday afternoon, though he didn't want to meet me at all, let alone on a weekend. He was a white public high school teacher who had become the epicenter of a racially charged controversy at his campus. Because I am a journalist with a particular interest in matters of racial justice, I had been enlisted by an irate group of black parents at the school, and subsequently by my paper, to do a story about it.

According to the parents pushing the story, Kaplan was guilty of racial impertinence. (These parents hoped that, as a black woman, I would be sympathetic to their viewpoint.) They said he was intellectually arrogant in a white-privilege sort of way, eager to overwhelm his black students' frail sense of self-esteem by, among other things, extending the discussion of slavery to issues of latter-day segregation in his classroom. Kaplan insisted that the system failed black and white students alike, and asked his students to confront the racial achievement gap in his classroom and to question why teachers have different sets of expectations for black and white students. The parents felt that identifying latter-day segregation was not his business or his purview. According to them, Kaplan's insistence that he was only trying to do the right thing was merely a cover for the fact that he was improperly fixated on race—he had issued himself a street-gang name, K-Dawg, and even dated black women. "You *know* the type," the leader of the parent group said meaningfully, and a bit wearily.

I did. This also was not the first I'd heard of Kaplan or his exploits: my younger sister, Heather, had been his student in the '80s and had complained regularly about his intransigence. Many of her complaints, I vaguely recalled, had to do with race. Heather's an attorney now, and when I asked her whether she thought Kaplan had been racist, she argued vehemently with herself for about ten minutes before giving something of an answer.

"He was harder on black students than on other students," she said. "He definitely had issues about race, and he wasn't always diplomatic about expressing them. And he'd get mad with me because he felt I was squandering my potential, not living up to myself. I don't think *that* was racist per se."

I thought of all this as I rang Kaplan's doorbell one Sunday in April. Yet I was more than willing to get his side of the story. I was also intrigued: what sort of white man would keep pushing the racial envelope in this day and age? He was either exceedingly honest or exceedingly boorish, or both. In spite of everything, I had liked his voice on the phone when we talked to arrange this visit—rough-edged, with the nearly unconscious authority of a veteran teacher, but younger than I had expected. He didn't bother to hide his uncertainty.

"I must tell you, I'm *very* reticent about seeing you," he said, already sounding regretful. I gave him my usual pledge of open-mindedness and then said we had to meet right away, as I was on deadline. Sunday, at his place? I heard a startled silence and prayed I hadn't pushed too far—without him, there wasn't much of a story. "All right," he said. "Do you take cream in your coffee?"

It turned out to be the powdered stuff, which I don't really take but took because he gave it to me. I sat on the floor of his tiny living room because he had no coffee table, and I preferred the floor as a writing surface. Kaplan was dressed in jeans and an old T-shirt. He had the resigned look of a man headed for the gallows. He was nothing like the odd, obsessive recluse I'd imagined, the sort who would erect a wall of racial self-righteousness around himself and loudly proclaim himself to be K-Dawg. Instead, he had tousled brown hair, a graying goatee, and sad eyes that nonetheless burned bright and curious: he wanted to see exactly how his death would unfold.

I stayed at Kaplan's house for nearly five hours. Talking to him was terribly easy. He had a native charm that was rooted not in assurance but in attentiveness and honesty, even as he detailed the ugliest moments in his ongoing battles with nervous parents and administrators who objected to his teaching style and his determination to impart the hard lessons of race in American history. (As for the moniker K-Dawg, he said one student had given it to him as a kind of joke, because despite being very familiar with racial issues, Kaplan was as un-hip—and un-hip-hop—as they come.)

He sat on the floor opposite me and offered more powdered cream and I said yes. Nearly three hours into our interview, he asked if I was hungry. Did I want dinner? It was my turn to hesitate, and his turn to look abashed, afraid that he had overstepped his boundaries. "Dinner?" I asked, pretending to mull it over. "That'd be good." He gave me a place setting, salad, and lasagna that he'd heated up in a microwave. He didn't eat because he didn't have any more, I learned later. I also learned that 364 days out of the year, Kaplan, a quintessential bachelor, never had anything to eat in the house. His refrigerator typically contained nothing more than a couple of jugs of ice water and a pack of batteries; and he used the stove so infrequently that he'd had it turned off several months before my visit.

We sat at his dining table, and the climate between us shifted as the sun shifted and day lengthened into early night. He leaned forward on the table with his hands clasped tightly together, as if in prayer or anticipation. I noted that he smelled faintly woodsy, that he wore a diving watch and no other jewelry, that the fluorescent light above the table revealed his eyes to be perhaps more green than brown. He cocked his head and furrowed his brow in mock gravity and asked me about myself: How did I get started as a writer? How was my sister doing? Did I work out? "Nice arms," he said as decidedly as he had said anything all day. He didn't look abashed now. I thanked him, feeling inexplicably delighted, because I didn't work out at all and knew somehow that he knew that.

As a reporter, I was somewhat used to this kind of intimate rapport. He was trying to save his skin, and I must say I have always been prone to falling in love with my subjects—for an hour, or a day or two at most—taking the prolonged conversations and forced intimacy to heart before writing a story that either favored them or did not, and then filing it all away in my professional memory. I welcomed such encounters because they stood in—briefly—for genuine love and connection. I could believe what I wanted about my subjects in my mind's eye, without ever crossing a line or committing my prejudice to paper. My professional encounters serviced my romantic ideals, illuminating them briefly, sometimes even brilliantly, before I moved on. In such a context, I could allow that Alan Kaplan was sweet, affecting, a perfect gentleman, a wonderful listener, good-looking even. If he was a villain, I could still give him the due afforded by my writer's license and the vast but inconsequential space between interview and story. At 10 p.m., he walked me out to my car and stood at the curb, waving until I was out of sight. I felt less like I'd had an interview and more like I'd been on a date.

I'm still trying to sort out what happened next, though admittedly, I'm not trying very hard. The skeletal sequence of events goes something like this: Kaplan and I talked some more; I interviewed more people, wrote a story in the span of about five days and published it. The story sympathized with the racial inequities in public education, but disagreed with the black parents' indictment of Kaplan. I never heard from them again.

Kaplan and I never stopped hearing from each other. He showed up at my door, unannounced, with flowers—a thank you for the story, he said. I got more flowers. We began meeting regularly on weeknights at a coffeehouse to unofficially confirm that we had to keep meeting. We talked on the phone one night from midnight to six without saying anything of consequence, hanging up bleary-eyed but completely bewitched by the fact that we had staggered through the strangest and most intimate hours of the night together. His eyes began looking less sorrowful and more hopeful. He talked about his frustrations with racial dishonesty and he told me scores of other things about himself as well—his romantic failings and underdeveloped ambitions, his passion for jazz, guitars, and baseball.

This time, I didn't write anything down. I didn't want to. We were so obviously in love that neither one of us bothered to say so. We did wonder aloud about the propriety of a reporter falling for a source, but we couldn't do anything about it except keep a low profile for a while. On our first official date beyond the coffeehouse, we thought we'd go to a movie, but instead we wound up driving around Los Angeles to avoid being seen together. We sat in his big old Lincoln on a road high up in the Sepulveda Pass, among the hills that divide L.A. from itself, and talked for hours more.

There was never any question that I would marry Alan. I did, in October, roughly a year and a half after we first met. My sister is still flabbergasted that I married the teacher who loomed the largest in her adolescence—she sometimes slips and calls him "Kaplan." There is and always will be the race issue—the raised eyebrows on both sides of the color line, the people who question our ethnic loyalty and politics. This is no surprise, especially considering the ethnic rancor that brought us together in the first place. We understand the questions others may have about our relationship, and we often raise them ourselves. The concerns we each had about race before we met remain firmly in place, perhaps even more firmly than before. We do not want to be poster children for interracial marriage or the latest diversity campaign. Love for us is a triumph not of integration but of imagination, the wild-card coupling of a pair of resolutely lonely hearts who chose to navigate the same rough, but potentially magical course.

MARRIED PEOPLE LIVE LONGER THAN SINGLE PEOPLE

2009

I find out my husband Alan has cancer the day before I'm supposed to fly to South Africa. I have never been there and haven't been off the continent for a while. This is not an official diagnosis, though it will become one. It's a very educated guess by the ear, nose, and throat doctor, Dr. Smith, a black woman with a Caribbean accent, elaborate braids, and a bright, confident manner. The confidence flashes a sharp edge at moments, like a knife under a noonday sun, and I think that Dr. Smith is a woman who needs everything in place. She likes order and precision. She probably goes to church and has no ambivalence about making life and death pronouncements. I envy her more than a little.

Dr. Smith is tracing the cloudy gray mass on a screen in front of us with her index finger, the results of Alan's CT scan. "It's about six centimeters," she says. She sounds almost happy, like she's describing a fetus. "I can't say for sure, but if I had to give you my three best guesses, they would be cancer, cancer, and cancer." What would be your fourth guess? I want to ask. I don't. Alan looks pale in the hyper-fluorescent glow of the screen that in the darkened office looks like a crystal ball. He'd found a lump in his neck two weeks before and thought it was a swollen gland; I'd felt it and thought it was too hard for a gland and must be something else, though not something serious—a hardened gland. Wasn't there such a thing? Dr. Smith continues in the same energetic tone. "The prognosis for this, if it is carcinoma in the third stage, is about five years. That's not counting radiation and chemo. Married people survive longer than single people." She smiles. "You must think positive and stay strong."

I want to raise my hand and say immediately that I must be recused. I am not known for being positive thinker, even in good circumstances, that I've been clinically depressed in the past over meaningless bullshit—a broken necklace clasp, an uncooperative computer. Alan is going to have to apply elsewhere for a wife and/or positive thinker, at least for a while. Instead, I fold my arms and nod like I'm a doctor myself. Uh-huh. I say I'm supposed to go to Africa in the morning, wonderingly, like I think this non-diagnosis and the date of my trip is a funny coincidence. I say it like I'm at a party and the conversation has momentarily turned a little somber—nothing a mixed drink and a good dance single can't remedy. Dr. Smith's smile tightens.

"But you're not going, no," she says. "*I* wouldn't go. This is not settled. It's just starting. He will need more tests. I'm sure your travel companions will understand." She smiles again. We wait to hear, Don't worry, we don't know for sure, don't think anything yet. Dr. Smith is a believer. She isn't going to waver from what she thinks—what she knows—is truth.

I don't go. I make my apologies to the health foundation sponsoring the trip. Of course its people understand; it's a health foundation, after all. Its whole purpose is to expose media to the ravages of disease in various parts of the world; I don't need to do that now.

I have bought a new set of luggage for the trip that I quickly store in the garage. I'm secretly a little relieved to be grounded: twenty-two hours on a plane sounded exhausting, possibly dangerous. I'm not pathologically afraid of flying, but during those long stretches in the air, when you mark off the cities and states and finally countries, and then you are flying only over water and horizon in the vast space between continents that are connected only by bare archipelagos of clouds, you get rattled. You feel small and frozen, like you're hardly moving at all and it may take a million years to get where you're going. You look around the plane for reassurance, but the faces reading magazines or turned aside on starched pillows staring out of porthole windows at increasing nothingness look smaller than you do. You've got to be the big one in your own mind, the one who matters enough to keep the forces of a crash or some other fantastic event at bay. You alone will make things all right. That's what I think of when I fly.

Dr. Smith orders a biopsy and sends us to Dr. Osborne, a surgical oncologist. He takes out tumors in the head and neck. We're still not sure there is a tumor, or what kind of tumor it is, so Dr. Osborne is a bit of a figment, a precaution. I decide precaution is good, like having low-calorie snacks to maintain a sensible weight. He is here simply to ensure success that already exists; I almost relax. Dr. Osborne is young, not quite forty, I think, though his bio says he's been a surgeon for nine years. I do the math in my head, but it doesn't add up—he's always too young. He's also black, like Dr. Smith, which impresses me. I frankly thought he was not the doctor when he came in, but somebody less, somebody to prepare us for the doctor; I'm not self-loathing, but like all black people I suffer from racial and social conditioning, have studied its roots, and am always working to correct it. Sometimes it has its way anyhow. Dr. Osborne is low-key and handsome, with the air of a celebrity or somebody very used to being stared at. ("A gunslinger," Alan says later. "Very cool. I like this guy.") Dr. Osborne has ordered another test, a PET scan that will screen Alan's entire body for any abnormal cell activity. He is also doing another biopsy. This is all insurance for the deal that's already closed: Alan is all right. The doctors have good intentions and are giving this lump their best instincts, but they are wrong. I don't hold it against them. I can go to Africa next year. In fact, I would prefer everybody err on the side of caution, and they have. The mistakes they're making are entirely forgivable. Doctors, I want to say, it's okay that you sounded the alarms and canceled regularly scheduled activities, you were just looking out for us. If more people were as conscientious as you, the world would be better off. Not a problem that the alarms deafened me to ordinary life inside of two minutes, and raised to shouts all the voices in Alan's head that mumble about eventualities and the almost ecstatic inevitability of things dying or coming apart. No no no, you warned us for a good cause. You were looking out for us. We suffered briefly for a very good reason.

Dr. Osborne is going about his office arranging a further exploration of Alan's throat and sinuses with admirable cool (or is it intensity?) I watch him, content. Suddenly my heart bursts. He is doing for best—for me! For us! I'm deeply moved by the progress and efficiency of it all, carried out by these black doctors at a top-notch hospital in West L.A. It's a wonderful country. I momentarily regret a lack of patriotism I've learned not to feel for the last thirty years. I don't regret the lack—I really had no choice—but I wonder what it might have been like to have felt this way all along, the expectation that things will work, and they will work in my favor. I like this feeling. I must do more of it.

While Dr. O probes Alan's nasal apparatus, Dr. Smith finishes her biopsy. We get her call, a voicemail, on a cell phone in the middle of a movie on a Friday night: the results are negative. I swell with relief and a sense of validation that make me feel bigger but weightless, like a character on the screen. Of course! I settle back into my chair. I resolve to begin saying the pledge of allegiance at public events again, once in a while. Or I'll stand and say the words in my head. That should be enough.

Enough is not enough. Things are not over. Dr. O consults with Dr. Smith about a second biopsy. Dr. Smith is sticking with her initial suspicion of the mass; she explained in our first visit (our shock at her quick proclamation of "cancer, cancer, and cancer" didn't slow down the dire predictions a bit) that a needle biopsy can be a crap shoot because you draw out fluid that may or may not show malignant cells, even if their presence is likely. "I'm not surprised," she says briskly, almost contemptuously, in her voicemail message that initially sounded so exonerating. "We expected that." Dr. Smith doesn't like to be wrong. I am still sure she is. But I'm still happy to indulge her professionalism because it's so much better than not giving a shit. Tiresome as this diagnosing is turning out to be, I'm almost proud that Alan and the nature of the thing in his neck is being fussed over, like a prize. Neither one of us has ever had been the object of so much medical speculation, and it's rather nice, like being important guests at a hotel: we want for nothing.

Alan goes for biopsy number two. He's game. Like me, he's not convinced anything is wrong, not because he's an optimist, but because he thinks most prognostications (other than his own) are wrong. Call it optimism by default: until he has hard evidence, it's just people talking. Alan's right. At this point it's merely words. But we appreciate the doctors' efforts; we're both magnanimous skeptics. The walk from Cedars Sinai back to the parking lot is bathed in brilliant sunshine, flanked by restaurants, shadowed by a busy shopping mall across the street that Alan good-naturedly hates for its chic clientele and that I like for the same reason. We could have been coming from that mall and the walk would have been exactly the same, the satisfied walk from place to car and car to place that everybody has in Los Angeles several times a day, in one form or another, without thinking. This is the way it is for us still; this is one of those walks. It means nothing, yet it is our connective tissue, our cartilage, the hard frame beneath the elaborate but sometimes perilous surface of silks bought at half-price and dinners out, and whatever else matters on a Friday when life opens up again to the abandon of Friday night, and then Saturday and then the denouement of Sunday. Life is good.

Dr. Osborne calls me at home, on a Wednesday. He wants to talk to Alan. "Let me get you his cell number," I say helpfully. He pauses, reads the number back to me and says evenly, in that cool way of his, "OK, very good. Thanks," and hangs up. I hold the phone simmering with a mix of embarrassment and dread. Why couldn't he have told me something? Am I not next of kin? Don't I have the proper authority? Why didn't I just ask him straight out? I feel stupid, like I offered my hand in greeting or raised it in a sign of peace and it was ignored. I go from being an important hotel guest to being a nobody, a cipher, a housecleaner who only happened to answer the phone. I hate it. I've been played. The faith in the ordinary that I've had all week turns into crayon scribbles on a dirty wall, psychobabble told to a deaf man. It means less than nothing.

I want to make sense of the bait and switch. Is it my color? Disrespect from a black doctor? The thought is unbearable, but possible. It's happened before, more times than I want to admit. In black circles there is always so much chaos bubbling beneath the social order, it's hard to know one thing from the other—indifference from dishonesty, truth from imagination, art from life. The phone rings again. Dr. O? It's Alan. "The biopsy is positive," he says, almost shouting. In the background I hear the shriek of chairs being yanked away from desks, the clatter of movement, whooping bursts of laughter. "It's malignant. Sorry for the noise, honey, it's passing period. And I tutor at lunch. We'll talk later." I can't do later. It suddenly ceases to exist. At a loss that I need to fill up with something, I call my mother, who immediately says we should get a second opinion. "The doctor is crazy," she says confidently. Many people in my mother's family have died in hospitals; few who go in have come out healed or whole. As a result, my mother ranks doctors somewhere below insurance agents and phone solicitors. "She told you the test was negative, now she's telling you it's positive. Must be lying about something." I call Alan's mother. She, in contrast, accepts the verdict. "Malignant," she repeats. "I thought so. I had a feeling. We'll just have to go from here." Bernice is grave but doesn't mind the gravity. It's the way things are. She's from New York, aspired once to be a Broadway dancer, but is a realist by temperament. My mother is practical too, but came by her practicality in a very different way. Raised in the Jim Crow South before moving to L.A. to get married, she learned to resist reality from an early age: the way things *are* in New Orleans was a bottomless, uneasy idea. She preferred to keep to her neighborhood and its pleasantries that buffered her from the pain of race that lay just outside it. But our mothers have become friends, which astounds Alan. That's one of the many things he'd anticipated would fail or come apart or not happen in the first place. So far he's wrong.

Alan says the biopsy is right. He's dropped his skepticism: Dr. O isn't a crank, he's the director of a head and neck cancer institute who called him in the middle of his class to announce results on paper, a scientific outcome (the carcinoma is not in the third stage, by the way, but the fourth). It is evidence. I can see Alan relaxing, a little grimly, into a whole cancer arc that has already taken shape, including the walk to the car that yesterday felt like the most unremarkable of acts but that is now a first step into a journey to God knows where. But Alan likes knowing. He likes measuring what he's up against, what he has to pay, how extensive the damage; he likes knowing where the end is. I'm astonished and have yet to move past that to the end of anything. It makes sense: the doctors have no idea where this cancer started. They're sure the mass is a malignancy, but the site where it spread from has vanished. The immune system can do interesting things, Dr. O says, including shutting down the original tumor. Happens about 10 percent of the time. He figures that because the malignancy appeared in Alan's neck, in a lymph node, the likely site of origin is in the vicinity—throat, tongue, soft palate, sinus. I shudder at the options. I've never heard of sinus cancer. Dr. O implies that not knowing the location of the primary tumor is both good and not quite bad, but annoying—good because of course the tumor is gone, annoying because he doesn't know which area to target for treatment. That means they'll have to target everything.

I don't know this yet, or I'm not listening hard enough. It will take me time to sort out all the information that unspools from the mouths of doctors and gets bigger and longer until it covers the floor completely, like ticker tape, and I have to pick up one end and work back, or forward, to the other. The doctors are very patient and often repeat the information twice and then always ask, Are there any questions? I tend to say no, even though I have lots of small questions that I seem unable to articulate; it's like being constipated.

I suppose I don't want the doctors to think that I have any questions—I'm a journalist for fifteen years and am supposed to be a fast study. I don't want to be made a fool of again, stick my hand out and get blank looks or no takers. The cancer (because that's what it is now) is confounding enough. Alan is no help with questions, nodding almost preemptively though the doctor sessions. Questions don't matter to him at this point: he's taken the assignment and now, in his mind, we simply have to plow through it. He assumes the plowing will be tough and nasty, and isn't interested in details. But I'm interested. I live by details, worship them, fear them. I get paid for them. I've not told Alan this, but I spent years reading the details of cancer stories with a rapt horror, like I was reading true crime novels: I thought, Those poor people! There but for the grace of God, etc. But the reading wasn't all cheap thrills. I was distressed for hours by these stories, sometimes days. But I was keenly aware that I was the real hero because I was alive, because I walked through the bullets that missed me by chance but felled the cancer people by the same chance. I was stunned and relieved to be that special, the unsung kind of special that comes with being ordinary, unambitious, but, incredibly, disease-free. It was a hell of a combination. I was grateful and thoroughly paralyzed by the gratitude. What could I possibly do to make up for the fact that a boy a third my age got terrible headaches at seven, slowly went blind, and succumbed to a brain tumor at ten? The only thing that made sense to do was not to have the tumor myself. To keep walking clean through the bullets knowing there was nothing I could do make it clean. To think of myself as a hero after the battle had been won by someone or something else.

It is late summer, a month and a half after the diagnosis. Alan is having surgery to remove the tumor. We (my parents, his mother Bernice, sister, brother-in-law, their children, and a couple of friends experienced in crisis management) sit in the Cedars lobby in front of its brilliant plate-glass windows, waiting. Distinct from us and other knots of people getting coffee and swapping encouraging scenarios about whoever they're waiting for is a woman at the end of the corridor, sitting alone. About noon Dr. O emerges from the operating room, and we leap up—Alan already?—but he moves past us like we're not there at all. He stops at the woman at the end of the corridor, who struggles out of the chair and onto her feet as if struggling out from under the unpleasant end of a dream. The doctor waits like he has all the time in the world and not another surgery to perform in forty-five minutes. He crosses his arms and starts talking; she looks up into his face (she's short, almost gnome-like) with a kind of wonder, like she's looking at a painting on a museum wall: for a brief moment I want to laugh. As Dr. O talks, the woman's face falls, slowly—first an eyebrow, then another, then her mouth pulls together like rough stitching and sags under the weight of her brows and the bad news. She sways slightly on her feet. Dr. O keeps on, grave but composed. He doesn't take his eyes off her, which is good, because his eyes seem to be the only thing keeping her upright. Finally he straightens, and she nods and sinks into her chair, unloosed, the sun at her back. He seems to not notice, not out of unkindness but necessity. He strides back our way down the corridor and stops this time. "You're next," he says.

But I'm not worried, not after the woman, who I'm convinced has absorbed any shocks that might have been in store for me. I'm sorry for her, but relieved. We resume waiting. About three o'clock there are a couple of celebrity sightings—Goldie Hawn, clutching a pillow, followed by Kurt Russell a few minutes later. They're headed to the maternity ward, just across from surgery. She's petite and sculpted, smiling in a practiced way and very blond; he's rough-shaven, with longish hair. They're both wearing dark glasses. A low murmur ripples through the lobby, but little else—this is Cedars, after all, frequently the hospital to the stars. This isn't Grauman's Chinese or the walk of fame: nobody in the lobby wants to look like a tourist. But the sudden appearance of some longtime Hollywood royalty has the undeniable air of magic, and we go back to our magazines and quasi-naps with confidence that this—the stars, the newborn baby they're deigning to visit like wise men—is a good omen. Things will turn out all right for us.

Dr. O reemerges from the OR around 4. We surround him silently, bracing ourselves for the chance a bullet hit its mark and that our optimism is completely unfounded. Yet Dr. O is happy, to the extent he can be happy. Alan's tumor turned out to be more or less encapsulated, like a marble, cornered by lots of good warrior cells, and came out pretty clean. Seventeen surrounding lymph nodes were uncontaminated. No evidence of a primary tumor. In the recovery room, Alan is groggy but normal. His neck is swathed in a bandage and fitted with a drainage tube, his dark hair is grubby against the pillow and his eyes are half-closed. He looks almost sexy. Tired in a languorous way, like he spent a day on the beach. I pat his chest. He turns and looks at me with some difficulty. I move closer. "Toby," he whispers. The name of one of our dogs. I laugh easily this time. This is good, or bad luck isn't the absolute catastrophe I imagined. There are degrees of it, like there are degrees of everything. I decide we're living on the good end of bad: the bullets have grazed us, but not cut us down. It happens all the time, every day, people living with bad luck that they take into their previously unsullied homes like they take in a boarder. And instead of ruining the place, the boarder eventually becomes part of the household, like furniture there's no room for but that you keep anyway. It might even have a use.

In another auspicious development, Alan is moved into a deluxe recovery room, a Cedars VIP suite, because it's the only kind available for the night. It's got a bathroom with a shower, throw rugs, a couple of sofas and a coffee table with magazines. The spacious windows look out onto the neon of the beckoning mall. Alan's sister pulls off her shoes and announces she is taking over for the night; I can see she wants to talk to him, confess the grievances of her own life that she's been withholding because of her brother's cancer. There's no need for that now because the cancer has been dealt with, the bubble of tension around what might be going on in Alan's body broken and gone. I say goodbye and go home and to feed and walk the dogs. It's a little later than their usual dinner time, by about three hours. That's all the disturbance for now.

In late October, we go out to dinner to celebrate our seventh anniversary. It's the day before Alan is scheduled to start radiation and chemo. (He got the diagnosis the day before his birthday; though things are looking good, I fight the temptation to see a latent cosmic pattern unfolding against us now, militating slyly against our good bad luck). He is now in the hands of Dr. Drazin, a treatment oncologist. Dr. D is almost entirely opposite of Dr. O—relaxed and genial where Dr. O is deliberate and controlled. He wears a yarmulke and a plaid shirt but no white coat or anything that labels him as a doctor. He chews absently on the end of a pencil as he talks to us about his plan of attack, about the survival and recurrence rates of this kind of cancer, or the kind he thinks it is. "We want to knock this baby out of you," he tells Alan. "So we're going aggressive—chemo every week, radiation five days a week. Hey!" He spreads his hands and smiles. "I don't want to see you back here, ever." Somewhat reluctantly, he reiterates Dr. Smith's earlier assessment of the survival rate being about five years. "But you can't take that literally," he adds, rolling his eyes. He pulls out a big book from a high shelf, riffles through the pages and mutters disapproval like he's looking at carpet samples. "Ah! Here we are. These rates change all the time, year to year. They're based on age, based on the kind of medicine and treatment you get, based on your overall health, all that stuff. Stats have changed just over the last couple of years, when this thing was published."

I feel better. Five years sounded imprisoning, a small measure of time that, as I get older, increasingly feels like three years or two. The Iraq war has been going on for four years already, but its terrible declaration felt like yesterday. Five years are a couple of outstanding movies, a vacation, a reorganized closet. They're fine, serviceable. I'm glad to have them. But it's not much to be grateful for: I want *more* to be grateful for. Dr. D understands. He hates those five years too; they're the cheapest grade of carpet in the book that require no effort to sell, but that give no satisfaction to either the seller or the buyer. Dr. Drazin has every intention of giving us just what we want. "Let's do this!" he exclaims. He shakes our hands vigorously, and we're out of his office and back into the implacable sun and the long shadow of the mall. We make the same walk to the car that we made in August. But we walk in a different era, and everything looks and feels appropriate but removed, possible but not actual, props in a new act that may prove useless for the time being. The world has stayed put while we have shifted a couple of degrees north of it. Alan doesn't rail at the mall, and I don't plead with him to let me stop in; for both of us, in a very real way, it isn't there.

Alan is in treatment. Before he started, Dr. D offered him, in the most casual way, the option of being fitted with a feeding tube for the next two months. The G-tube is meant to bypass the throat in case the radiation Alan will be getting on his neck makes swallowing more or less impossible. The doctors don't really worry about cancer patients getting too little food, but they don't want them getting too little water: radiation cooks you through like a microwave, and constant drinking is a must. "But I had a guy who just finished up this treatment, and he didn't need a tube," Dr. D said, shrugging. "You never know." Alan went with the guy's odds; he hates the idea of being an invalid or looking like one. No G-tube. I'm glad—tubes and pouches reminded me suddenly of my Uncle Lester, who had his entire colon removed because of cancer and spent the remaining twenty-five years of his life wearing a bag and steering clear of anything resembling a social life. But I briefly worry. Throwing a perfectly good precaution like a G-tube to the wind might be viewed as a lack of humility by the gods of our good bad luck; the guy who made it through his treatment without a hitch isn't necessarily the lone woman at the end of the corridor whose misfortunes leavened our fortune because we occupied the same time, space, and circumstance. This guy who made it is a story, an idea. He isn't real. Still, the surgery and recovery went well, and we are brash enough to believe in the seven weeks afterward that the universe is rebounding and we have choices. I let go of the small worry. No G-tube.

Things are fine in the beginning. From the day of the first infusion of chemo, I hold my breath. I fear the chemo most, remembering from my true-crime cancer readings the endless nausea, hair loss, and hollow, spectral looks of patients as they desperately tried to survive the cure. Nothing so dramatic happens, almost nothing at all. Alan's battery of anti-nausea meds (mostly anti-psychotic drugs, which surprises and amuses me) seem to keep any effects of chemo at bay. His hair doesn't change. He tells me he almost enjoys spending hours hooked up to an IV with nothing to do except read or nap or something he feels too pressed by work to do at home. He's still teaching school. His students have made him good-luck and going-away cards that are detailed and touching; a few students shed tears when he announced his cancer over the summer and again at the beginning of the fall. They fully expected him to go away for the length of his treatment and reappear some time later, which is what he thought too. But it's not working that way. He stays the first week and then the second. The students are glad, if a bit wary. They're glad Kaplan doesn't drop dead before their eyes and create unnecessary trauma for them; they love him, but need him to be well.

He is well, sort of. Then the third and fourth weeks develop a haze, like smoke from a far-off fire that gradually drifts into your neighborhood and stings your eyes as badly as it's stinging the eyes of the real victims living fifty miles away. We're both the smoke and the fire. The daily radiation is taking its toll, or to put it more precisely, taking the skin off Alan's neck. It's turning red and raw, like's he's undergoing a chemical peel. His mouth and tongue blossom with sores. His salivary glands shrivel; eating is fast becoming a bitch. Too soon he finds it difficult to swallow, or do anything at all with his mouth. He talks less. Eating and drinking are equally onerous, and though I've stocked the refrigerator with six-packs of Ensure and chocolate Boost, they go slowly. Halfway through the treatment the only thing Alan can ingest on a regular basis is Jell-O. I've never made the stuff in my life, and now I make it constantly, in all flavors and colors. I can't make enough. When Alan comes home from school (he still goes), he goes straight to the kitchen for the Jell-O, sucks down about a quarter of a giant bowl, and collapses into bed. The dogs are puzzled by Alan's absence, by the lack of joyous greetings at the door and baby talk, But they smelled trouble early on and don't make any demands. When he goes to bed, they clamber up behind him and lie vigilant at the footboard. I do all the walking and feeding and game-playing, and while they're not entirely satisfied, they accept it for now. They assume things will change back at some point.

At about week four I realize that this is not the cancer tragedy I had in mind, that perhaps I wanted. Our good bad luck is holding, but it's very dull. The comings and goings—school, hospital, home, drug store, grocery store, home—are tedious but not worth complaining about. Alan is less and less well as the weeks go on, but he's operational and doing okay by some universally understood measure of cancer patients undergoing treatment. Dr. Drazin has seen worse and is nonchalant, though he chews his pencil and frowns during one appointment because Alan's not drinking as he should. Fall moves along with the same speed and efficiency it does every year once the month drops below August. I don't do much of anything except watch Alan, pick up prescriptions, make Jell-O, urge him to drink, tend to the animals. Everybody wants to help. A neighbor comes by with rice pudding (which he can't eat, not just because of his mouth and throat, but because he hates anything with milk in it). Another neighbor brings an inspirational video made by a self-healed Christian prophet who once claimed she once had a tumor on her abdomen that was so big, she carried it around like a sack of groceries. Other people bring protein powders and plant mixtures and other things they swear are better than conventional medicine, especially chemo and radiation, which intentionally poison the body, after all, and by definition aren't good for you. Alan isn't interested. He only wants to get through with the energy that's getting harder to come by. This is the endurance phase that he expected but couldn't imagine. In a good moment he tries to eat a bit of chicken or mashed potato, but recoils almost instantly at the pain. I'm more annoyed than devastated, as I would be at a leaky faucet that turned into a gush after the plumber went home—why the hell can't something work around here?

We settle into a plateau of crappy cancer-treatment weather. Not much temperature change, rather like the city itself. Alan goes to work. When he's home, he hacks and coughs and sometimes gags, the panicked sound you might make if your throat was stuffed full of raw cotton. I detest this sound because it has taken over, it has enveloped him and now he lives deep in the belly of the radiation whale. Despite what Dr. Smith said, it's clear to me that Alan doesn't need a wife at all. He is married to that cough/gag that he anticipates and learns to take care of; he escorts it another room if it gets out of hand. The climax is a long, terrifying retch that produces vomit, mucus, or nothing. It's a moment of repeated intimacy between Alan and the imperious cancer cure that I can only stand by and watch, or hear from outside a bathroom door—what are they doing in there? When comes out he's dabbing the lingering cough/gag tenderly with a Kleenex. He ignores me entirely. I am jealous and fretful. I say, "Are you all right, honey?" in the dull voice of a be-trayed woman who's discovered the betrayal and must live with it. Most times I'm left alone to watch television or wash dishes—lots and lots of forks and spoons, which is odd, considering Alan doesn't eat. When he's not nursing the cough/gag he eats Jell-O and applesauce with plastic spoons because utensils make everything taste like metal. The dirty forks and spoons are mine; I'm eating at moments now, not in complete meals. I'm aware that I'm not prop-erly sympathetic. I'm living like a roommate, a single person sharing a space with another single person that we're renting not by the month or the week, but by the minute—I take only a minute in the bathroom or bedroom before he hulks in and needs me out, because he needs to sleep or pee or cough/gag uninterrupted and alone. Of course, I say, and go away seething.

People try to make legend out of all this. They say Alan is brave, and I'm at least as brave for being so forbearing. According to some, we're doing the impossible in holding up at all. "You must be totally stressed," sighs the wife of one of Alan's teacher friends. "You got to make sure to take time for your yourself. Give yourself credit, treat yourself well." For what? The plain truth is I'm not suffering, Alan is. I have nothing to endure except the numbing ex-perience of watching it happen. To me there's a good deal of self-centeredness in the notion that I have some cross to bear here. My idea of crosses is much bigger than this. They start with life in the South and urban ghettoes like New Orleans and leaving a place that didn't love you, living in a place that didn't give you a choice. Crosses are carried by the homeless and the over-looked and the untended and the forgotten. When people encourage me to treat myself kindly, I feel a flash of hostility at their presumptuousness. The fact of the matter is, Alan is the one oppressed these days, and I do what I can to ease his oppression, which isn't much. When he lays down for the night at eight o'clock, it's my job to sit and fill the silence that never used to come so early; I take out a book or watch television or take the dogs out. This is the lesson of the South that I absorbed through my tight-lipped mother, that you must not run panicked through the hail of bullets that are more or less constant, but walk through them at a leisurely pace. I get it. The gods of the good bad luck must see that our life still stands upright, that its frame is bat-tered but is unmoved, and I can hold it up by myself if I need to. But I must be around to hold it. To leave Alan and go for a massage or a night out, with him in a dark house and in a vacuum of sleep that is no longer just sleep, is unthinkable. If there is any sacrifice I'm making, it's the decision to stay put.

Six weeks pass, then eight. Alan loses weight and his clothes shrink into his body like plastic wrap. He swallows minimally. He grows hoarse, then loses his voice altogether. Still, he goes to school. I have no idea how he's teaching classes. People are helping him out, he says. Students are being co-operative, other teachers are taking up the slack; one takes over his last period every day so he can go to radiation. I figure he must be scaring the students straight, bad as he's looking. In addition to about thirty pounds, he loses hair at the nape of his neck—the radiation obliterates everything in its path—but the loss inexplicably creeps upward until the whole back of his head is white-bald. The rest of his hair grows on, unconcerned, and the overall effect is that of a very pale man carelessly wearing a brown toupee. It's comical, but I worry. I e-mail Dr. Drazin—should Alan stop working? No, he replies. Let him go. He'll know when it's time to stop. I'm not sure. Alan told me in the beginning that he wanted to go to work because he wanted to save his sick days for when he was really sick. That was funny at the time; it isn't now. When was Alan thinking of using those days? For something worse than cancer? It occurs to me that he does want something to be worse, so that he can say later with no irony that the cancer treatment wasn't so bad. He's already preparing the memory.

In late December, Alan finishes treatment. He feels terrible, wrung out. On Christmas Eve, after a brief excursion at the dog park, he gets out of the car and falls down on the driveway. He says he only lost his footing, but later on, after I press him, he confesses that he fainted. After spending several frantic minutes trying to locate doctors and get some authorization on a near-holiday, I hurry him to Cedars. It turns out he's dehydrated and has to be given an IV for a few hours. I sit in the room with him and we watch Christmas specials on TV, or I watch and he dozes. The chemo ward is quiet, tranquil; people have treatment every day of the year, I know, but they all managed to avoid coming today. It's brilliant outside, sunny and crisp, beckoning. I know the mall is open, and I contemplate suddenly going across the street and wandering among the sales and color and crowds that have lost their seriousness about gift-buying at this point and are merely out to take in the day. Take in the last hours before Christmas with a wonder that it's here already—really, what happened to August?—and reflect on the fact that after the great pause of tomorrow, when the mall will be as still and empty as it's bustling now, the year will resume, only to fold up its corners and close down in less than a week. Finished. I want to feel the sweetness of that kind of loss, perennial and reassuring, separate from the loss I'm feeling now. But that isn't possible. I have to sit out this loss before me, wait to see what its final shape is and what the parameters are; I can't waiver. I have nothing to buy, anyway. I likely never did. I only craved the experience of the place, the closeness, the shared quarters, and sense of a journey wholly inconsequential but eagerly undertaken for that very reason. What have I been eager about lately? Nothing comes to mind. I have been too submerged in consequence. I've hardly floated but I haven't drowned, either. This is my excitement for now.

In the dull of winter—dull for L.A.—Alan recovers, slowly. He goes on ten-minute outings with the dogs, then twenty. He murmurs to them. The dry mouth that clicked audibly when he talked and made eating a chore begins to subside. Everything still tastes of metal. The sores that had gotten almost medieval start to heal, though any spice stronger than table salt is still a knife in his palate; he coughs, but the gag dwindles, then disappears. At school, everyone is relieved that he seems to have weathered the worst and is now only improving. He takes an interest in his appearance again and shaves off the lopsided hair, which alarms me—I don't like shaved heads, but more importantly, I don't want to disturb the hair that is; the gods of our moderate luck may not like it. There's still time for things to turn. Alan's straight hair grows back curly, which surprises him unpleasantly but makes me think the gods were watching, annoyed at the act but not vengeful. Alan doesn't gain back weight, but he's growing conscious enough to like the fact that he's lost the stomach paunch and meaty shoulders that he had pre-treatment. Now he's narrow, almost delicate, his body in line with the smallish hands and feet that he always hated. He's always wanted bigger hands, for the sake of a stubborn sense of machismo but also to better play the guitars he collects and trades and lovingly stores in a spare bedroom. He isn't really playing again, but when he does, when he plucks and strums in the evening hours after work and before dinner (we're having dinner again, of sorts), I trust he's not thinking of the inadequacy of his hands. Meantime, his new hair is looking thicker and darker than before; his hairline is less receded and he has virtually no gray. I resist attaching any meaning to what looks like a good omen for sure. It's just the way it grew this time, I tell myself. Next time—I stop there. Anticipating next time is as far as I want to go.

Just before spring, Alan has his first follow-up PET scan. Dr. Drazin calls the same day to say that it's negative. The scan is clean. He acts like it's no big deal, like it's what he expected to tell us all along because this is what we'd asked him to do. This is where we were all going to end up, the gray canvas showing nothing that preceded this entire episode. But the world is different. The cancer is undetectable, not necessarily gone, and because we'll never know how it arrived, we're going to have to end up here, at nothing, again and again. It's an entirely uneventful but wonderful place to be. However far we fly, this is our destination from now on.

PUBLICATION CREDITS

Full or partial versions of the following pieces first appeared in the *LA Weekly* and are reprinted here by permission: "The Butt," "Black Like I Thought I Was," "Fire and Ice," "Blue Like Me," "Losing New Orleans" (originally titled "Washed Away"), "Thoroughly Modern Mammy," "Behind the American-History Curtain," "The Accidental Populist," "The Empress's New Clothes," "Homeboys in Outer Space and Other Transgressions," "White Man with Attitude," "Welcome to Inglewood!," "The King of Compton," "Lost Soul," "Held Back," "Man and Superwoman," "The Boy of Summer," and "Unsocial Studies."

"Blackness Itself" (originally "These People") and "The Eastside Boys" first appeared in the *Los Angeles Times*.

"The Last Campaign" was first published by UnderWire.com.

"Falling for Tiger Woods" and "The Color of Love" were first published by Salon.com.

"Mother Roux" first appeared in the Salon collection edited by Kate Moses and Camille Peri, *Mothers Who Think* (Villard, 1999).

"Mother, Unconceived" first appeared in *Rise Up Singing: Black Women Writers on Motherhood,* edited by Cecilie Berry (Doubleday, 2004).

"They're Going Crazy Out There" first appeared in *Geography of Rage: 1992,* edited by Jervey Tervalon (Really Great Books, 2002).

A partial version of "Barack Obama: Miles Traveled, Miles to Go" first appeared in *The Oxford American*.